To Glenda
from Del
Christmas
2012

CONVERSATIONS WITH KRESKIN

CONVERSATIONS
WITH KRESKIN

The Amazing Kreskin &
Michael McCarty

A Special Foreword By:

Roger Ailes
Chairman and CEO, Fox News
Chairman, Fox Television Stations

Artwork by Patrick Flanagan © 2011

Published in the United States by Team Kreskin Publishing.
©2012 Team Kreskin Productions, LLC
West Caldwell, NJ & Simsbury, CT
In association with Gicleé Creative Productions, LLC, Simsbury, CT
First Printing Hardcover Edition: October 2012
ISBN: 978-0-9859882-0-3 (hardcover)
ISBN: 978-0-9859882-1-0 (epub)
ISBN: 978-0-9859882-2-7 (epdf)

Book Jacket Cover Art & Illustrated 8-Page Full-Color "How Kreskin
Became Amazing!" Artwork Insert By:
Joe St.Pierre
Comic & Graphic Novel Artist, Pop Art Properties Company
www.PopArtProperties.com

The Amazing Kreskin's Dedication

In DEDICATING THIS BOOK, YOU, MY DEAR READERS, SHOULD KNOW THAT THE recipient of this dedication had no idea at all that I had him in mind. Indeed, this decision was made before he was even approached to contribute to the book. My decision was made on August 15, 2010, when he attended a dinner, along with 90 other people who played pivotal roles in my life and with whom I wanted to share the joy of almost miraculously completely beating a serious medical illness. I used him in a mental test involving playing cards. I hadn't seen him for a while, and as we shook hands I decided at that moment to dedicate this book to him.

To Roger Ailes,
whose support and belief in me
from the early days of my career
has had a special impact in the
continuing voyage of my life's work.
—KRESKIN

Michael McCarty's Dedication

THIS BOOK IS DEDICATED TO THE AMAZING KRESKIN, BECAUSE HE IS JUST SO truly "amazing."

Thanks also goes to family, friends, fans, and bookstores, including Bear Manor Media, Mom, Cathy, David and Robbie Leonard, Steve and Linda and Brenna and Amanda, Dave and Julie Thompson, Kevin, Michele, Linda, Anna, and Scott Madsen, Ray Congrove, Daniel Shields, The Hultings, Camilla Bowman, Ron Stewart, the other Michael McCarty, David Menefee, Mark McLaughlin, Sue Leabhart, Joyce Grubbs, Mel Piff, Leslie Langtry, David Letterman, Filmfax, Cristopher DeRose, Pam Kaufman, The Source Bookstore, Joan Mauch, the Midwest Writing Center, Bert Shinbori & Jacobson Staffing, Dr. David Ade, the memory of Kitty The Bunny, David Dunwoody, the Horror Writers Association, Sandy DeLuca, Bruce S. Larsen, Christopher Kowalsky, The Neumiller Family, Jack Suchy, Marcus F. Griffin, Latte, and my wife Cindy, who has shared the journey of life with me and made it shine.

Table of Contents

A Special Foreword

"Kreskin: My Very Unique Friend"
By Roger Ailes
Chairman and CEO, Fox News
Chairman, Fox Television Stations

P EOPLE OFTEN MISSPEAK AND USE THE PHRASE *VERY UNIQUE* TO DESCRIBE a person or situation. Of course, it's incorrect because *unique* means being the only one, being without equal, distinctively characteristic. That describes Kreskin—unique. I first met him in the mid-1960s. I was booking talent for *The Mike Douglas Show*, a daytime talk variety show that became the most popular program of its kind in the country and at one time had a larger audience than *The Johnny Carson Show*. Mike Douglas was an Irish singer and performer who everybody liked, and his show went on for 20 years. I was executive producer during the years that the show grew the most, up to 182 markets in the United States. I was also searching for unusual talent, people who could captivate the audience and get them buzzing.

I was tipped off that there was a performer at a high school auditorium in Easton, Pennsylvania. His name was Kreskin. He had an unusual enough name and intriguing enough description that I drove in the snow to that auditorium to watch Kreskin's performance. He did hypnotism, he did card effects, he did other things, and he was spectacular. At the end of the evening, he said that his paycheck had been hidden somewhere in the auditorium. If he found it, he got to keep it. If he didn't find it, he would forfeit it. And of course, everybody held their breath. Kreskin eventually found the paycheck.

We invited Kreskin down to meet with *The Mike Douglas Show* staff. The first time we met we just talked to see what he might be able to do for the show, and he said that he would be able to predict the headlines in the newspaper a few weeks in advance. He would write it down and then we would give it to a deputy sheriff to hold in a safe. He would come back on the show in 3 weeks, we would hold up *The Philadelphia Inquirer,* and then we would open his envelope.

With only very minor changes, what we took out of the envelope absolutely matched the headlines of *The Philadelphia Inquirer*. I have no idea how he did it, and the audience did not have any idea how he did it either. Mike Douglas always believed Kreskin could read his mind and often would say, "if that guy's coming in here let me know because sometimes I'm thinking about things I don't necessarily want people to know." But Mike loved Kreskin, as did many other people, and Kreskin went on to a great career. I believe he went on to have 118 appearances with Mike Douglas alone and hundreds more with Joey Bishop, Merv Griffin, Johnny Carson, David Letterman, Jay Leno, Joan Rivers, Dinah Shore, Regis Philbin, Tom Snyder, Phil Donahue, Jimmy Fallon, Jimmy Kimmel, Howard Stern, and several others.

Of course, everyone wants to be the first to have found Kreskin because of his uniqueness. Now, 45 years later, he is still performing, still holding audiences spellbound. Nobody knows how he does what he does, everybody loves him, and he is still unique. Nobody has ever tried to match or beat Kreskin, and I doubt that anybody ever will.

He did a television show for 5½ years that was produced by a Canadian television company, where he had 22 minutes and 3 segments per show, and that show was a big hit throughout the world. He managed to come up with phenomenal segments that surprised everyone week after week. His final segment each week was to do something with a celebrity, and that would be the classic climax of the TV show. It always worked, he never failed, and the audience always left buzzing. Kreskin once, as a friend, came to a party at my house because at that time my 7-year-old son had some of his classmates over for a pool party. Kreskin graciously came and within 20 minutes was performing for the children and their parents because he loves an audience and the audience always loves him.

When Kreskin was in his early childhood, he spent at least 2 hours a day handling playing cards, so he could cut a deck of cards at any number you would call out. I have never seen anybody work with cards as well as Kreskin, and I've seen many people try card effects. He's the best. I watched him on *Merv Griffin* and *Johnny Carson* many times, and it was clear they were desperately trying to figure out Kreskin. With Kreskin, there's no way to figure him out. You just have to enjoy him. He has provided priceless moments to American audiences since the 1960s. He also cleared up and exposed many fakes and frauds, including the so-called spirit communication between Houdini and his wife. He's exceptionally well-read and knowledgeable in the area of mind control and ESP.

Recently he invited some friends to a country club in New Jersey where he said he would make a special announcement. Although I've done many things in my life, my wife is impressed that I'm a close friend of Kreskin's. So she came with me to the special announcement. Kreskin announced that he had been diagnosed with cancer, prostate cancer, and that he had been performing while going through treatment. It was a deadly cancer that could have ended his career. However, the announcement on that day, August 15, 2011, was that he was now completely cancer-free and healthy. And of course everyone cheered.

Audiences are as interested in Kreskin today as they were a half-century ago. Between television, media, and concerts, he's done thousands of appearances around the world. In one year, he did over 300 appearances.

He was such a star that we asked him to co-host *The Mike Douglas Show* for a week, and it was a very special week. Kreskin is a household name today, and if anybody even thinks something that somebody else is thinking they'll announce, "I'm like Kreskin." Children love him and parents love him. An unusual, wonderful, kind, and unique performer, Kreskin, alone and above the rest, and he is, and will always be, my very unique friend!

Kreskin's Preface

IN PREPARING FOR THIS BOOK, I WAS PLEASED THAT MICHAEL MCCARTY raised questions that we knew my fans often ask since I'm receiving constant inquiries from around the world. In responding to what I know you, my readers, are intrigued and curious about, I almost feel that the title of this book could be *What's on Your Mind?* I have also expanded beyond this and felt it was time that I reveal many of the behind-the-scenes intrigues that have taken place offstage throughout my career.

My life has been an adventure, taking me all over the world and into unusual settings. In spite of the dramatic predictions I have made over the years, I certainly could not have foretold that in the 1980s I would be in a courtroom defending my pronouncements about hypnosis. Yes, being tried by a jury no less! I'm not sure I ever thought I would be a subject of a motion picture done by Tom Hanks. In spite of what some may think, I can honestly say that the category of this book is that of nonfiction. I want to share with my readers how my abilities as a thought reader have encompassed areas of today's society far beyond pure entertainment, touching upon the political arena, crime, and clinical psychotherapy as well.

Hopefully, my enthusiasm is pouring out of these pages onto the cover of the book. The cover was done by one of the world's greatest comic artists, Joe St.Pierre, and wait until you come upon the beautiful

8-page full-color insert "How Kreskin Became Amazing!" Even having written 19 books, I must tell you, my dear readers, that what you are holding in your hands now is one of the most exciting and special expositions of my entire lifelong career. Wow, what a kick this book has given me!

Michael McCarty's Preface

I FIRST MET THE AMAZING KRESKIN WHEN I WORKED AT THE FUNNY BONE Comedy Club in Davenport, Iowa. I had helped him find a location for a séance he was going to do for the media. He wanted a famous Quad-City haunted house. So I arranged for his séance to take place at the Phi Kappa Chi fraternity house at Palmer College, which was a well-known local haunt.

Kreskin was impressed with my arrangements and agreed to let me do an interview with him. Before the interview, I had lost a filling in a tooth. I'd taken some painkillers and proceeded with the interview.

The world-famous mentalist was getting ready for his show later that evening. He was facing away from me, putting on his tuxedo jacket. He then asked, "How are you feeling?"

I said, "Okay."

"How about that tooth? It must be bothering you."

That took me for a loop.

"The one in the right-hand corner of your mouth. I feel a lot of pain," he continued.

For the rest of the interview, I stared at Kreskin's shoes. If he read my mind, he'd just see his own shoes!

Kreskin was in my first book, the *Giants of the Genre* (Wildside Press, 2003). The day *Giants of the Genre* arrived at my home was the same day that The Amazing Kreskin was performing in my hometown at Circa 21. Before intermission, Kreskin talked about *Giants of the*

Genre. He introduced me from the stage and had me stand up to take a bow. Kreskin clapped, and everyone in the audience clapped. I felt like I had just won an Oscar. I do interviews. This is my job. No need for applause.

Kreskin has been such a great friend for over 20 years and instrumental in my writing career as well. I interviewed him for a number of newspapers and magazines over the years including *Filmfax, Gallery, UFO, Alternate Realties, River Cities' Reader, The Moline Dispatch,* and others I am sure I have forgotten over time.

I also interviewed him in my book *More Giants of the Genre* (Wildside Press, 2005). Kreskin wrote the introduction to my book *Modern Mythmakers* (McFarland and Company, 2008) and the afterword for *Esoteria-Land* (Bear Manor Media, 2009). He also wrote a blurb for my book *Masters of Imagination* (McFarland and Company, 2010).

And if that isn't enough, Kreskin appeared as a major character in two of my vampire novels. No, he didn't play a vampire. He was himself, surrounded by vampire characters in my book *Liquid Diet: A Vampire Satire* (Black Death Books, 2009) and my ebook *Midnight Snack* (Whiskey Creek Press, 2011).

Fast forward 18 years to January 21, 2010. The Amazing Kreskin was doing a show at the Isle of Capri Convention Center and I was going to go see him. It had been ages since I had seen one of his shows. I brought my mother and a good friend of mine, Ray Congrove, who was a talented photographer. After the show, Ray, Kreskin, his road manager Kevin, and I met up and had a late night snack at Village Inn.

I was reluctant to bring up to Kreskin that we'd been talking about doing *Conversations with Kreskin* for almost 5 years. When Kreskin was free, I was working on one of my books, and then when I was free, Kreskin was working on various projects.

It was getting late, almost midnight, and I had to get up by five in the morning to go to work. Kreskin surprised me by bringing up the topic. "Hey Mike, when do you want to start *Conversations with Kreskin?*" That proved to me that he could read minds.

I wrote this book, and that is truly amazing. My one goal with this book was that readers should feel like they are in the same room with Kreskin and me, listening to what we said over coffee or tea, a pleasant conversation for all.

1 | He's One Amazing Guy!

HE'S BEEN CALLED A PSYCHIC, A MEDIUM, EVEN A SAINT. BUT THE FACT IS, The Amazing Kreskin is like most people, except that he has developed an extraordinarily heightened sense of mental perception.

From the age of 5, he was fascinated with magic and would perform for neighborhood children. At the age of 11, he developed an uncanny determination beyond his years when he received permission to study the entire psychology section of his hometown New Jersey library. Soon Kreskin began to perform professionally, billing himself as "The World's Youngest Hypnotist."

For some six decades, Kreskin has been exploring the unusual powers of the human mind, but with a rare combination of wit and showmanship. His very name has become a part of pop culture. On stage or television, Kreskin seeks to reveal the thoughts of audience members, plant suggestions in fully aware subjects, and dazzle with feats of extraordinary mental projections.

He has appeared on more than 500 television programs. He even had his own TV show, *The Amazing World of Kreskin*, which ran for 5 years during the 1970s. In the late 1980s, he starred in *Kreskin's Quest*, a series of internationally syndicated specials.

MICHAEL McCARTY: You claim to be a mentalist, a mind reader, but not a psychic.

THE AMAZING KRESKIN: I have no supernatural powers. I can't foretell the future. I don't know why more psychics don't spend more time at the race tracks (laughs).

I can read thoughts if people concentrate. I can describe incidents in their lives. I am not a healer. I can't make objects move by the power of my mind. I am basically a thought reader. But I have no special psychic powers.

McCARTY: You have the largest private library in the world on the subject of the paranormal. You also collect Sherlock Holmes and Dracula books.

KRESKIN: My library, which is a separate building on my grounds, now numbers over 9,000 books. Since I read three or four books an evening, if I am traveling for a sustained period it is not unusual for me to take a separate suitcase filled with books.

When you read the writings of Edgar Allan Poe, Bram Stoker, and Charles Dickens, you will find they reflect a fascination with paranormal phenomena. To think that two centuries ago, Dickens practiced mesmerism—which, of course, was the prelude to what we call hypnotism—and "treated" a friend for stressful problems because the general medical techniques of the day proved ineffective.

McCARTY: I find it interesting that you collect books about Count Dracula and Sherlock Holmes, probably the two more interesting literary characters ever created.

KRESKIN: The two characters that were made into movies the most, Sherlock Holmes and Dracula, are my all-time favorite fictional characters. There have been over 200 Dracula movies, and well over 150 Sherlock Holmes films. Some people have described me as the "Sherlock Holmes of the mind." I found that very flattering. At least they didn't compare me to Dracula! (Laughs.)

Every year *TV Guide* presents a quiz. In many years it would ask the question: "What movies have been seen more than any others on television?" The answer is, of course, the *Sherlock Holmes* renditions done by Basil Rathbone and Nigel Bruce.

The other question *TV Guide* would often ask: "What fictional characters, aside from Disney's, have been made into the most movies in cinema history?" The answer is again my two favorite characters: Dracula and Sherlock Holmes. I prize the studies that have been made of Dracula, especially by Raymond T. McNally and Radu Florescu, who wrote a brilliant piece entitled *In Search of Dracula*, which traces his origins. The research goes back to a real character in the Transylvania area named Vlad the Impaler. (Vlad Dracula, *Dracul*, is derived from the Romanian word that was variously interpreted as "devil" or "dragon.") He would take some of the subjects of his kingdom and simply impale them on spears while he himself dined. Sometimes he even drank their blood. Incidentally, one of the most intriguing renditions of the novel *Dracula* was done in 1985. It not only had the original *Dracula* text, but also photographs of acted-out or posed scenes from the book, which are interspersed in the novel. We have to understand that Dracula possessed telepathic, hypnotic powers. The ability of the vampire to control others through his or her will is one of the basic traits we associate with such characters.

McCARTY: In your other books and work you have collected for your library, what kinds of things have you discovered about the paranormal?

KRESKIN: In the works of Edgar Allan Poe, you have many references to mesmeric phenomena. His classic short story "The Case of M. Valdemar" is truly a morbid horror piece in which a mesmerist is brought in to comfort a man on his death bed. After placing the man in a mesmeric "trance," it was found that he lived considerably longer than was expected. At the climax of the story the gentleman begged to be released from the trance. Finally released, he slowly decayed into a putrid mess. He evidently had been dead for some of the period during the trance.

Telepathic phenomena are found constantly throughout classic horror and science fiction stories that have proved prophetic of today's new developments. From the bygone era of witch doctors, healers, and magicians, to the philosophies and beliefs in mystical phenomena, my library is far from a narrow perspective.

I have found it fascinating to witness the hypnotic phenomenon and its influence as it has developed in areas of modern spiritual and psychological thought. From its origins in mesmerism and hypnosis, it evolved into a spiritual movement that acknowledged that mediums in trances were able to "communicate with the dead."

Today, we have a movement of individuals claiming to "communicate with the dead." They do not refer to themselves as spiritualists, but rather as channelers. Tables do not move nor does ectoplasm emanate from their mouth. Gone are the mysterious lights dancing around the room and the strange sounds and whispers in séance rooms that prevailed in previous centuries, up to and including the 1930s and 1940s. Today, a channeler may suggest that he or she is in conversation with your deceased ones.

McCARTY: Let's talk more about Edgar Allan Poe. Several of his stories are still very scary almost 200 years later.

KRESKIN: When we read some of the old literature, including the great horror stories such as those written by Edgar Allan Poe, there is often mention of people being buried alive. That theme appeared in several of Poe's stories, including "Berenice," "The Fall of the House of Usher," and "The Cask of Amontillado." This theme wasn't exclusively for humans; Poe even had animals being buried alive, such as in "The Black Cat." The stories had tremendous impact on much of society in those days, because there was a great fear of being buried alive.

McCARTY: The Victorians had such a fear of this; they even had an organization called the Society for the Prevention of Being Buried Alive.

KRESKIN: The methods of diagnosing death were very primitive in those days, and in many cases, aside from feeling a pulse, a mirror was held up to a person's face to see if there was any breathing. The highly sophisticated techniques today to study narcolepsy and so on just simply did not exist. Consequently, the idea of the living dead or people rising from the grave was not as remote as we may think today. Indeed, there were scores of cases in which, for whatever reason, bodies were exhumed from a grave days or months later and the lid of the wooden coffin was found to be gashed and scraped because the buried person came back to consciousness and tried to claw his or her way out of the coffin.

In the years that followed, it was not unusual for the wealthy to see to it that when they passed away the family would have a telephone put in their coffin, which if used would ring inside the family kitchen of the deceased individual, so great was the fear that they would gain consciousness and breathing in this horrendously confining limited area. I often wonder how many times the phone may have rung and family members who were to be the recipients of a large bequest in a will just did not bother to answer the phone!

Since there were periods in history when belief in vampirism was widespread, it was decided that one of the ways of fighting the awakening of the vampire was to bury him facedown. In this way, if he came to life and tried to crawl out of the grave, the barrier would be the earth, which he would never get through.

When I was a kid, I remember hearing on the radio a story of an incident in India where a body was being prepared for the Ganges, with scores of relatives and friends escorting the funeral march. Pandemonium broke out because before the family reached the Ganges the body sat up and walked.

McCARTY: Very cool. Let's go back to being buried alive and the story of an event that really took place.

KRESKIN: Indeed what I'm about to recount was planned for me to demonstrate or tell on the ABC TV series *That's Incredible!* on which I had a couple of appearances. This particular segment dealt with horror and the true story of Washington Irving Bishop. At the end I would demonstrate what Bishop had done in front of a theatrical club in New York when he apparently died. ABC decided at that time and for evening watching and with young people as part of the audience that it was too macabre to show. Within a couple of years, I decided to tell the story on my half-hour television series. It was one of the most dramatic half hours of the series.

Washington Irving Bishop was in his own day a kind of mentalist. He certainly had a great deal of heightened sensitivity and intuitiveness and was successful in his performances. He attended an actors' social gathering in New York at the Lamb's Club in 1889 and was part of that group of famous and near-famous actors, actresses, and show people. Someone asked him if he would get up and demonstrate his mental abilities, and he proceeded to do so. During a demonstration, while he was attempting to use his keen sensitivity and mind, he collapsed on stage. Fortunately, there were two physicians in the audience who came up to attend to him. The affair had a tragic ending. For all intents and purposes, Bishop appeared to be dead.

I should add a parenthetical detail. Bishop carried on himself a note stating that he suffered from what in those days was a malady called catalepsy. When writers, including Poe, wrote about the strange affliction, a person seemed to lose all signs of life and in a sense was in kind of a suspended animation, but the person was alive, just not diagnosed as such. There would be no film on the mirror that they held up to a person's face, and so on. Bishop's note said that if he ever collapsed and appeared be without life, they were simply to protect his body, rest it somewhere where he would be safe, and cover him with a blanket to keep him warm. He would then regain consciousness in a couple of hours. Many people in show business knew that Bishop suffered from catalepsy but did not come forward.

Bishop's mother, who was a highly emotional, hysterical-type personality, was finally told that he had passed away, or had apparently passed away. Knowing the situation, she rushed to New York City. In those days embalming was very rare. She hurried to the funeral parlor, saw him lying there, and proceeded to wipe his brow and stroke his head. As she did this, the top of his head fell off.

Just so there's no misunderstanding about what I just said, her hand literally helped remove the top of his head. I have a photograph, a morbid photograph, of her looking upon her son. The stitching where his head was sewn back on was so primitive in those days that it almost looks grotesque. She went into hysterics.

What had happened was that two doctors who were fascinated and inquisitive about Bishop's mental abilities decided on their own, without consulting a family member, to perform an autopsy on his brain to see if they could figure out what gave him such mental abilities and then proceeded to have the top of his head sewn back on. This nightmare and horror story became a grotesque news piece, and the public read what seemed like a morbid piece of horror fiction.

Oh yes, the doctors were taken to the courts and were tried, and for various reasons released with no charges ever held against them. Today we look upon this as an obscenity. To pursue such an action without the permission of the closest kin almost seems beyond reason. They never expected to be exposed. It was the mother's nightmarish exposure of his skull that brought this to such a climax.

For years after that, controversy reigned. Was he alive when they did this dastardly act or had he died? There's no question in my mind that most of those in show business who knew of his affliction were convinced that he was alive after that final performance and killed by the doctors.

McCARTY: Do you enjoy Halloween?

KRESKIN: Next to Christmas, Halloween is my favorite time of the year. It allows us to embrace and take a sample of what we had in our childhood. It is an exciting period of flight of the imagination.

Every kid has been told about or had to grapple with being afraid of the Boogey Man. The Boogey Man really reflects the mysteries of life, the unknown, the darkness, the shading. Halloween is a chance to revert back to our childhood. In each of our lives there lurked a scary house or some fear of what was around a certain corner. We have all lain in our beds at night while it was pitch dark and imagined what was in the shadows.

In a sense, I think that with all the truly frightening fears we have in society—the rampage of crime, the terror caused by the drug movement and certain of our cities being out of control—Halloween is a safe way to be frightened.

McCARTY: Is it really possible for a subject to be made to commit crimes against their will?

KRESKIN: Absolutely not. This is a position I have held for over 30 years. Even though I was sometimes referred to as a hypnotist early in my career, I came to the conclusion that people were not under any hypnosis or in any special state or trance whatsoever. The subject was fully conscious, alert, and wide awake, but responding to suggestion. The illusion that they were in a trance was based on the idea suggested by the hypnotist, and believed by the subject, that in order to respond to suggestion one had to relax, become drowsy, sleepy, and close one's eyes. This has been a theory and cultural belief for a few hundred years.

McCARTY: The downside of being a celebrity is having stalkers. Have you had such encounters?

KRESKIN: Many of us in the public eye have had the unfortunate situation to be harassed by stalkers. These are individuals who become obsessed with a public figure for various reasons and find that they need to trail, endlessly communicate with, and in their own personal way become obsessed with the figure. In Los Angeles, I understand that the police department has its own unit that deals with that problem.

Through the years, I have experienced an array of such characters. I feel a desire to call them "loonies," because they can certainly interfere with the personal calm that everyone deserves in civilized society. Indeed, in one case in the State of Washington the FBI always notified me when a certain person was released from prison or other institution, his time being up. In turn, I had to notify the FBI when I went into certain states because of the travel ruses that this individual used.

Another stalker was a particularly interesting character. I don't know how many times she'd been institutionalized, but one wondered if it would have been better for everyone if they just threw the key away when she was institutionalized. We became aware of her when my road manager at that time, Sam Losagio, and I started to notice her appearing in the front row of a number of shows in Atlantic City where I appeared for several weeks throughout the summer. It was obvious that she was always sitting in the first row for every single performance.

Sam rushed into my dressing room not long after that in the fall to tell me something he couldn't believe—she was again in the front row. Except, mind you, the show was in Florida. The next day I had some appearances in nearby states, and we noticed a taxi driver in each city, the same taxi and driver, and, of course, she was in the front row at all the theaters. In one situation, I had to fly back to New Jersey where I had a performance the very next day. Lo and behold, we saw a taxi outside of the venue, and she proved to have found her way into the theater. The driver confided to my road manager that indeed he was making quite a living. He had driven her overnight across the country so that she could be at this program, and on and on it went.

What was most perplexing was when she appeared at private performances as well as the public ones. One was a private fundraiser for a medical group; the other was for a religious group. She was in the audience at both. Sam questioned the people running the affair in both cases. We found her ruse. She learned of my itinerary by calling various agents that booked me under the guise of being a promoter herself, and they gave her my itinerary. She proceeded to call the people who booked me for private affairs and pretended to be a reporter doing an in-depth study and article on me, and in every case the organization agreed, feeling it was a very positive thing.

What was especially unnerving was an appearance at the Downingtown Inn in Pennsylvania. It was a famous resort hotel, and a showroom had been named after me. I was in my hotel room in the late afternoon and suddenly there was a banging on the adjoining door to my room. The person banged on it so hard that she managed to break it open, confronting me. She saw the anger in my face as I called the authorities to contend with the intrusion. We don't know how she had found out the room I was in and convinced the front desk to give her the adjoining room.

To understand what public figures have to contend with, let's take this further to a day Sam Losagio and I had returned from a tour. We drove to my home in New Jersey, and he proceeded to go to his home in Easton, Pennsylvania. He saw his folks and later called me. It turns out an individual had finagled herself into their home and was questioning and interrogating them. The description was clear—it was the same woman!

Hard as it is to believe, it ended 2 years later with a frustrating, pathetic situation. My late dentist and dear friend Dr. Sy Fish called me one day. He had an office in Hillside, New Jersey, approximately 40 minutes from my home, and, yes, he had a new patient who he had to remove because of her inquisitive and bizarre behavior. Yes, the very same woman....

McCARTY: You have been a big fan of Mandrake the Magician *comics for a long time. Would you care to share an anecdote?*

KRESKIN: I have told this story on a number of occasions of how the real stimulus for my life's work came at age 5 when a member of the family who was in high school gave me a comic book. It was an Action Comics, and it had a hero in it called Mandrake the Magician. It was written by Lee Falk and drawn by Phil Davis. Mandrake was in white tie and tails with a beautiful black cape with red lining. He really wasn't a magician. He had hypnotic abilities and telepathic powers with which he fought crime. Within weeks, the character of Mandrake became a pivotal force in my life. I would playact with friends as Mandrake, and instead of playing cops and robbers, I wasn't a cop, I was Mandrake solving crimes.

The years went by and about 15 years ago a conference was held in Sardi's Restaurant in New York, a show business location for many years. It was held by a group of scholars and researchers in the area of comics. Some were professors at universities and others were writers. They had as their special guest Lee Falk, the creator of *Mandrake the Magician*. I was asked to attend because so many knew that the character Mandrake had been an inspiration for my career. Lee Falk spoke eloquently not only about *Mandrake*, which he had been writing since 1935, but also his classic character *The Phantom*. What a legacy. Sometime later into the proceedings, Lee Falk stopped and said that the person who had come closest to epitomizing the character and the abilities of Mandrake was, you guessed it, The Amazing Kreskin. As he said this, he nodded to me. Needless to say, it was one of the very special moments in my life.

McCARTY: Over the years you have held séances. Can you tell us about one of them?

KRESKIN: Not too many years ago, I held a séance in the quaint little town of Marshall, Michigan, at the Museum of Magic organized by the prominent newspaperman Robert Lund. He is no longer with us, but he and wife Elaine, who survived him, amassed an extraordinary collection of memorabilia in a museum that contained billboards, references, articles, letters, and private pieces from great magicians through history. The Museum of Magic still exists today and maintains its status as one of a kind.

McCARTY: Kreskin, later on in this book, we are going to have a couple of chapters about Harry Houdini and other magicians of the 20th century. Please continue about the séance at the Museum of Magic.

KRESKIN: We decided to hold a séance, the only one ever performed in the museum, in an attempt to communicate with Bess Houdini. Of course, everyone had tried to communicate with Harry Houdini. We had at least 40 people in the main part of the museum, including a television crew from CNN. The séance was aired on *The Larry King Show* the next day for Halloween.

Harry Houdini, who was noted for his promise to attempt to return from the dead, has never to seem to answer the telephone (laughs).

What was truly remarkable is that as we sat quietly I requested Bess to somehow show evidence of her presence. We all saw remnants of Houdini appear. Pictures, a large billboard suspended from the ceiling, and a thick, heavy milk can modeled after the cans that were used to deliver milk years ago. The particular milk can that appeared was comprised of iron and large enough for Houdini to enter, even after being filled with water and sealed with a lid. This was one of the greatest moments, as Houdini would have escaped the confines of this container.

The container was very heavy and had two sturdy handles attached to each side, strong enough to lift the container. Out of nowhere, during the séance, I noticed a padlock that was hanging open from one of the handles that started to swing back and forth in continuous movement for the next 30 minutes or so. Trickery? A magical illusion? Absolutely not! None of us had the intention of this happening!

McCARTY: For the past few years, you have been going to third-grade classes and influencing them almost hypnotically when you read Dr. Seuss books. Why did you decide to do this, to promote literacy? Are kids easier or harder to hypnotize?

KRESKIN: For the past few years, if my schedule permits, I would on Dr. Seuss Day find my way to some grade school with the purpose of reading a Dr. Seuss book. That is one of the first books that was ever read to me by a teacher I had in kindergarten. In those days we sat on the floor as a teacher sat in a chair and read to us a colorful fairy tale or what have you. In this case, Miss Sinclair read a book by Dr. Seuss called *The 500 Hats of Bartholomew Cubbins.* It absolutely enchanted me.

She had, as is my copy, a large-page book that she could turn to the 25 or so of us so we could see the large pictures or drawings. The premise of the book is mystically simple. A young man had come from home walking a distance into the main part of the kingdom. It was the day when the king was coming through on his chariot, with all the king's men, guardsmen, etc. following. Everyone bowed and took off their hat, and Bartholomew did likewise, but something happened. The carriage backed up, and some of the crew ordered Bartholomew to take off his hat. At first he was perplexed, but reached up and found another hat. When he took that off, another appeared, and so began this mystical story. Indeed when he was taken to the kingdom in preparation for losing his head, the guard could not chop off his head with the ax because another hat kept appearing.

The chronicler was counting the hats, and, before you know it, it was up in the hundreds. The later ones were rather picturesque. They were filled with gold and jewelry-like pieces, and the final one was a priceless piece. The story had a romantic mystique of mystery, but also concern for his welfare. The magical denouement at the end endeared him to the king, for when he left the castle to go back home he was carrying a large bag of gold pieces the king had given him. If you put your mind in a child's thinking, the story has poignancy to it, fear of loss of life, perplexity as to what to do, some of the qualities that are part of mature, older fiction. But the first time I read this to a class, I realized that I had in front of me just youngsters. And by the way, my audience was never limited to the third grade. I invited teachers to bring in the rest of the school, and there were times when we had kindergarten through fourth grade.

I also wanted the first row of kids to be close to me. After all, I'm used to influencing people, not only by the way I touch them or glance at them, but a certain aura that I can project. I warned the students that they better pay close attention, not to me, but to what happens around me, and within about 10 to 12 minutes of telling the story I was able to see that I was influencing and enrapturing some of the students so dramatically that they were *seeing* the very same hats that I was seeing, as I indeed was not simply reading, since I've already memorized so many pages, but removing from my head hats that I was throwing on the floor. By the end of the reading, scores of students throughout the room were standing and pointing out the hats. And invariably, teachers that attended have asked me what in the world did I do to cause the students to not only become engrossed in the book, but also to find themselves living scenes from the book. There were no hats, there was no physical evidence in my reading of such, but I had created a hallucination that students saw piles of hats on the floor that I had been apparently pulling off of my head.

I have on one wall in my kitchen a letter in which almost every student signed their name as having experienced what they felt was an incredible kind of hypnotism. Yes, kids are highly receptive to suggestion. I have skills which I've honed over the years, and I'm able to create responses without the façade of a trance in ways that many hypnotists don't really understand. I feel that I need to take advantage of it, and what an opportunity to promote literacy it is. The students will look back upon how deeply involved I was in a book, and they can use that as a model, a memory, to become deeply involved in a book. Not an MTV fleeting moment on a screen, not a quick blurb on a cell phone, but immersing oneself in the pages that one is holding within one's hands. That is such a gift, and there is no way that I could ever find a substitute for the more than 9,000 books that fill my personal library.

McCARTY: I understand you've commented on a number of occasions on Whoopi Goldberg's last book, entitled Is It Just Me? Or Is It Nuts Out There?

KRESKIN: Yes, there are some humorous and some sad messages that the book communicates. The cover has her sitting on the john, and she explains why. Years ago Carol Burnett told me this happened to her as well. What am I saying? In the past when Whoopi and Carol Burnett have used public bathrooms, they've had the experience of someone coming into the ladies room and reaching under the door of the stall with a sheet of paper and a pen asking for an autograph. I swear to God, Carol Burnett has confirmed this to me on many occasions, and Whoopi has had the same crazy dilemma. Oh no, I haven't had that happen to me, and if I'm stifling a chuckle, I'm also stifling relief.

But beyond the people who are doing this and probably not even realizing the setting of such an intrusion, I think we're finding, as Whoopi has, that we're so overwhelmed with media blitzes, quick reads, and brief responses that people are not necessarily giving themselves a moment to reflect on some of their actions. Teachers, grade school and higher, invariably tell me of the incredibly strong language students use today. We really can't blame them, as they hear this on the media, they're overexposed to it, and perhaps the parents may not be as firm in admonishing them if bad taste is used. The bottom line is that we're becoming so filled with stimuli that the time we spend sympathizing with any depth is disappearing, and I believe the reason is that our reflections are becoming dulled by endless stimuli, often in the form of violence.

Years ago it was possible to have seen a double feature in town on Saturday and another double feature on Sunday. That's about it. It was rare for anyone to see more than four movies in one week. Today people of all ages can see scores of movies in a short amount of time. If they are of a strong, violent nature, my concern is that it will inevitably have a dulling effect on people's emotions, and real trauma or misbehavior will simply lose the impact and concern that it should have.

McCARTY: You once played chess with world chess champions Anatoly Karpov and Viktor Korchnoi blindfolded?

KRESKIN: Karpov and Korchnoi were bitter chess rivals vying for the world championship title. It was a classic confrontation: (Viktor) Korchnoi, the Soviet defector, versus (Anatoly) Karpov, the Soviet champion. Much of the media attention became focused on Korchnoi's accusation that the Soviets were using a hypnotist to break his concentration. And, in fact, the Soviets did place a prominent Russian hypnotist in the front row of the tournament audience.

This was, of course, a classic example of one-upmanship designed to throw Korchnoi off balance, which it did most effectively. Years earlier, Jimmy Grippo, the legendary magician, card manipulator, and hypnotist, was similarly retained by several prizefighters to "psyche out" their opponents. He would stand at ringside, staring intensely at the other fighter, supposedly "zapping" him with "hypnotic powers."

In any case, I decided to challenge both Korchnoi and Karpov when their tournament was over. I would play both of them simultaneously and be blindfolded to boot. A prominent Olympic chess coach who had helped train Bobby Fischer announced publicly that I was just talking through my hat and that if I did go through with this he would eat his!

To everyone's surprise, both Korchnoi and Karpov accepted my challenge and agreed to the tournament. Unfortunately, Karpov had already returned to the Soviet Union and was unable to obtain a travel visa to return to New York, while Korchnoi, the defector, clearly could not return to Moscow. Fortunately, the chess columnist for *The New York Times* agreed to stand in for Karpov, confident of his proven ability to play a half dozen or more games simultaneously.

Now picture me sitting in the United Nations Plaza Hotel with an audience that included some of the world's most famous chess officials and television crews from around the world, and I was suppose to take on two of the world's leading chess experts while blindfolded! An eye surgeon was brought in to provide the blindfold. She had devised and tested a method of blindfolding herself securely, and she applied this same blindfolding method to me.

Now let me point out that I did not expect to win both games under these conditions. Having played chess a half dozen times in my entire life, I was simply hoping to hold my own for a respectable period of time. In fact, I found out later that Korchnoi had wagered that the contest would be over in less than 10 minutes. More than an hour later, I was still playing both men, although all I could do was announce my moves, being unable to see either board.

Ultimately, I announced a move and lost to Korchnoi. At that moment he jumped up and ran to the back of the room, announcing that he knew how I had done it. He spoke with Mark Finston, a fine feature writer for *The Star Ledger* in Newark, New Jersey, telling him, "Kreskin is reading my thought because I keep thinking that if Kreskin is castled at this point, he would lose the game, and that's just what happened."

Of course, Korchnoi was right. Chess players constantly analyze the board, thinking several moves ahead, anticipating their opponents' best moves. By taking advantage of this, I was able to get the players to play against themselves, until Korchnoi deliberately concentrated on a losing move for me!

Incidentally, though I never did have the pleasure of seeing Bobby Fischer's coach eat his own hat, and though I did not win either game, the one against the chess columnist for *The New York Times* ran nearly 2 hours!

McCARTY: You were interviewed by Maureen Seaberg for her book Tasting the Universe *about synesthesia. What is synesthesia? I have never heard of it.*

KRESKIN: Synesthesia is the stimulation of one sense, which involuntarily will elicit a sensation/experience in another sense. An example would be the smelling of a color or the tasting of a lemon resulting in an image of the color yellow. It doesn't replace the normal experience, but always adds to it. For example, there are people who not only hear sounds, but see images from them as well. They are able to see or know the colors, the sexes, or personalities of letters and numbers, etc. They can feel weight or shape by just tasting something. The bottom line is that there are people who when they see a picture of a city may taste chocolate, or when they hear a piano they may feel a sensation in their arm or leg, or when they think of a date or a day of the week like Sunday they may think of them in bright red. It is when one sense perceives something and it seems to be simultaneously picked up by one or more additional senses. *Synesthesia* comes from two Greek words literally meaning "joined perception," and it can involve any of the senses.

McCARTY: Very interesting; does this occur commonly in people?

KRESKIN: The reader is going to find that the people of today are on the verge of a "new" and exciting discovery, one that has lain dormant for decades, and that is that a percentage of our culture, say some 5 percent, think differently. I predict that after "savoring" *Tasting the Universe* by Maureen Seaberg when people gather with family or friends they are going to introduce the question, "Do any of you think in color or differently?" With further discussion, it's going to become clear that those who acknowledge such are not on drugs or brain damaged. Science is beginning to realize that they may be possessing a rare gift, if you will, that is now called synesthesia. Words like that scare people, because they're not common and don't fit into the fabric of everyday grammar. But listen to me when I say it is going to become a common word within the months to come, in essence describing a remarkable gift.

McCARTY: Any there famous people with synesthesia?

KRESKIN: Many people are going to find a common bond with such celebrated figures as Itzhak Perlman, Pharrell Williams, Billy Joel, and, yes, Marilyn Monroe.

No matter what a person's walk of life, whether he or she be a scientist or politician, attorney or actor, student or brick layer, just have a few friends or associates gather around a coffee table, bar, or park bench and start to reflect on what synesthesia is. You will find an outpouring of conversation where certain members of the group will contribute their own experiences and realization that, my goodness, they have this gift, never realizing that it wasn't everyone who possessed it, but enough to make it widespread. As Seaberg teaches, there are many of us who can hear the sound of color or who will see waves of color when they hear music. Certain words or numbers may have shading and color to them. Others will have a special taste in their mouth when they hear a certain word or place or name. It is this interchange or min-gling of the senses that is synesthesia.

McCARTY: How does synesthesia affect your abilities or performance?

KRESKIN: I'm not talking about my ability to read thoughts and I'm not talking about telepathy, but I'm speaking of a way that I'm now going to reveal has been part of my life from day one. It can be iden-tifiable to many people, and that indeed there are those, such as Yours Truly, who can hear the sound of color or will see waves of color when they hear music.

Thousands of times I've been asked in interviews and in conversa-tions, how do I think when I'm performing on stage? On some occa-sions, I've been more explicit in explaining, but very often I "hear" people's thoughts, but at the same time I am heavily influenced by color. I have always found black-and-white movies more visually appealing. I get much more color out of them. Technicolor movies have sometimes proved too limiting for me. I can "feel" a person's energy and, yes, I am heavily influenced by color. But then my mother exuded tremendous energy and positivity, which she reflected in wear-ing her favorite color, yellow.

I sat for a few hours with journalist Maureen Seaberg as she was preparing to make me a part of her book. The common denominator that she found in us was this gift of synesthesia. It doesn't surprise me that it is more common in artists, actors, and musicians, since I've spent so much of my life demonstrating how reality can be altered through the power of suggestion. Often potentials can be brought out of a human being through this force, which by now you know I don't consider to be hypnosis or a trance, but suggestibility. In fact, I find that a person who responds to suggestion or is suggestible is often as well empathetic—able to feel the feelings of others—and may tend to be more prone to have one's senses overlap so that they might hear music from a rose or taste a series of words. After all, don't some of us unconsciously describe an idea as delectable? Yes, tasty! Many of us in everyday life embrace something we enjoy because it just "sounds good." Even in a setting that could be distasteful or threatening, we have encompassed in our culture the phrase "it just doesn't smell right to me." It's not farfetched to think that those who originated these phrases have this gift of synesthesia and were reflecting the way they have blended their senses so that one overlaps the other.

McCARTY: Wow, that is truly interesting and unique.

KRESKIN: It's exciting for me to be part of Maureen Seaberg's new book *Tasting the Universe*. I look forward to discussing and sharing my thoughts about these delectable, appetizing, and colorful phenomena as it affects the lives of millions of people in a very personalized way.

McCARTY: Why do you do what you do?

KRESKIN: The answer is very simple; it's a passion in my life. I never knew anything else I wanted to do. I knew what I wanted to do when I was 5 or 6 years old. I was already practicing when I was 9 years old. I'm an adventurer—I don't climb mountains; I don't skydive, although I have done some spelunking in the past and hiked up the Grand Tetons as well as Machu Picchu. My greatest voyage is the human mind. I find it absolutely unendingly interesting.

Also, the money is good (laughs). If I couldn't do it for a living, I'd probably be doing it in the streets for free. It's something I've done all my life. I have no desire to retire.

FINAL CHAPTER 1 THOUGHTS BY KRESKIN

KRESKIN: But there is a test that I did on a television series that certainly was one of the most ominous of my life. Each week of the almost 6 years of my television show with some 26 or so half hours a year I came up with a dramatic challenge of my abilities. This one took the cake. I wanted a person to come on the show with a safe. The person worked for a safe manufacturer, and I wanted their product to be brought on. Such was the case when I arrived in the afternoon before the taping of the show in the early evening. I met the gentleman representing the company, which I will never forget. It was Chubb.

I said, "Listen, the doors to the studio are now going to be shut. There is not any staff here, it's too early. But I want you to go over to the studio and change the combination, so that you can honestly say on the air that you are the only person alive who knows the combination." Then I proceeded to tell him what I wanted to do and asked if he would agree to it. If not, it was his choice.

He looked me in the eye and said, "Kreskin, let's go ahead." I saw him go through the door into the studio, and when he returned there was not a single human being at the CTV station who had any idea of the combination and certainly not me. By the way, after the program he told me that he had talked to the owner of the company, and the owner had advised him not to do this.

He said, "Kreskin, I believe in you. I want to go through with it."

On the air when we came to the last segment I explained what had been done. The gentleman was the only person alive who had the combination within his mind. There was no copy of it anywhere. He had agreed to go into the safe, the door would be slammed, and I would attempt to read his thoughts and unlock the safe. To get into the safe he had to crouch down. There was a limitation of air in the safe.

It was an extraordinarily tense segment. I'm not a fool, nor am I sadistic. I had a gentleman there with an ax, and if a certain amount of time passed and I found I was helpless to open the safe he would proceed to break into it, breaking through the steel with the ax to give the gentleman ventilation. It was one of the most dramatic moments of my entire life. You could hear a pin drop. There were no verbal camera communications on the set. I suspect they were all done by ear phone. It was the quietest setting I had ever heard in my life on television. Every time I knocked on the safe, he was to think of the next digit. I don't recall if it was three or four digits. The bottom line is that I could not open the safe, for reasons I don't understand to this day, as I am able to pick up mental impressions. I finally turned to the camera, I was emotionally drenched, and must have looked like a dish rag, and I told the audience that I can't do it. I can't seem to get the numbers. The man with the ax was about to chop into the safe.

Then we heard a noise, and we paused, and we paused, and we paused. Something was happening. And lo and behold, within a minute and a half or so the doors swung open. The gentleman (and I don't know if he had a flashlight or what have you) knew enough of the mechanics of safes that he was able to maneuver the gears from within and open the safe. I reminded myself that safes were built to prevent someone from breaking into them, not out of them. The show ended with tremendous applause. Actually, I feel more for him than for me, but it was an incredibly exhausting experience.

He agreed to return, and so he came. It was a month or so later. But what I did not mention is in the first scenario where the gentleman in the safe released himself, the guard with the ax told me had he not released himself, it probably would have been too late to save him. The oxygen would have run out before he could break a hole in the safe.

Well, this time I would allow no chance to be taken. I admonished him to tell us the amount of breathing time in that safe. He had a fair knowledge of it. And I said to him, "Understand, if I don't succeed this time within the limited time that we now know, because I'm not going over that amount of time, that ax will come down. You must understand this." And he agreed. He had changed the combination, by the way. It was a new combination. He climbed into the safe, the door was slammed. It was like reliving a nightmare. I had gone through the same process trying to pick up his thoughts. Two or three times I sensed a false start. But the third time I resigned myself to follow through whatever came to me. Slowly I turned the dial. At one point I heard a click, and I opened the door, and there he was able to walk out.

It was exciting to see the enthusiasm of the audience and my television crew of a couple of years cheering. It was not really possible to say much, as the applause was so loud it became deafening. When we came off the air, I said to him that I appreciated his agreeing to come on, even a second time, "I'm sure the boss told you not to do it." He looked at me and said, "Yes, he did." And I said, "But you came." And he said, "Kreskin, I've watched you for years every week on television. I knew that you could do it."

2 | Close Encounters of the Kreskin Kind

In what began as a demonstration of the power of mass psychological suggestion, the world-renowned mentalist known as The Amazing Kreskin witnessed his UFO prediction come true in front of thousands of viewers.

For months, Kreskin predicted that in "May or June this year [2002], the largest sighting to date will take place in the Nevada desert."

On June 6, 2002, Kreskin intended to exhibit the ramifications of the power of suggestion and how it might be used by terrorists or enemies of the free world. However, just moments following his demonstration, an actual UFO sighting was seen and filmed by a cameraman from the Las Vegas desert.

McCARTY: Were you surprised that over 3,000 people attended to witness your UFO prediction on June 6, 2002? In your own words, what happened that night?

KRESKIN: Frankly, no, as I had in public appearances invited people to come and meet me in the theater where I was performing at the Silverton Casino & Hotel. It was there that I met with a large group of people—400 to 500—to explain the event in detail. Since they were seriously interested in attending the sighting, they arrived at the theater on the night of the event before we headed to a site on the desert grounds. What surprised me were the already more than 1,000 other people who mobbed the grounds aside from the "seriously interested group." They had read newspaper pieces, seen me on television, heard radio interviews, and had come to partake in the event for much more varied reasons than I had anticipated.

During the months of February and March 2002, I was touring throughout Ontario, Canada, appearing each evening at the performing arts center in a program that lasted approximately 2½ hours. At the time, a newspaper reported a story saying that in the ensuing year there had been a 42 percent increase in UFO sightings. There was no theory as to why, and many, of course, took place in remote areas, such as parts of Newfoundland and Canada—but again, the increased number of incidents was significant over past years. The press came to me regarding my feelings, as many were aware that the UFO phenomenon had been given my serious attention in the past.

Two years prior, The Learning Channel devoted a full week of documentary specials to UFOs. Each evening, an hour-long show was devoted to a different area. I was one of the consultants for the first two segments, one of which dealt with *Abduction Memories*; the other was *Sightings*. This piqued my interest and brought me to the point of making a prediction that the next sighting of UFOs—in fact, one of the largest sightings ever—would take place not in Canada but in the United States in the Nevada desert during the month of May or June.

When I stated "one of the largest sightings," I meant numbers of people experiencing the sighting. As the interviews continued all over the world, I promised that when I returned to the States, I would add a signature as to how serious I was about the prediction. I could have discussed it on Regis Philbin's morning show or with appearances on *David Letterman* or *Howard Stern*. Instead, I made a decision to release my formal prediction on *Fox & Friends* for the Fox News Network, since I have known Roger Ailes, the head of the network, for some 40 years.

When I made the prediction in March, I wasn't scheduled to appear in Las Vegas; I hadn't even been offered a contract at that time. But I still pinpointed the month and area of the country that the sighting would take place. By May, I was headlining at the Silverton Casino &

Hotel. By the time June approached, I decided to pinpoint the exact day of the sighting: June 6, 2002. I went even further and stated that the sighting would take place between 9:45 and midnight.

McCARTY: Some UFO enthusiasts were angered by the incident, believing they were conned. How do you respond to this?

KRESKIN: They were not conned by me, but rather they had conned themselves. They need to sit down and reexamine their motivations, beliefs, and why they responded the way they did instead of listening to what my real message was. Only a handful of people were aware of what was behind my prediction.

My money was safe because at least in some way the "sighting" was to be guaranteed and certain. I made the prediction because we were at war. It is remarkable how few people heard that remark or even paid attention to it and the ramifications of it. In fact, Colonel John B. Alexander, author of the book *Future War: Non-Lethal Weapons in 20th Century Warfare*, decried it, as you see in the release I sent you. Many overlooked the true reason that I had for creating the "first sighting" on the night of June 6. Those who were seriously interested came to the theater not to see a show but for me to address them and explain what was about to take place. I didn't know there were a thousand more people at the desert site that we picked. We tried to confine the area because of the desert roads not being lit and there being considerable concern on the part of the police and authorities that people could become lost and endangered by roaming aimlessly on their own.

I explained to my audience that I was going to create vividly and realistically in the minds of some of the audience a clear hallucination that would become the "sighting." I also said to the audience, "If anyone feels that they don't want to become part of this, please leave." To the best of my knowledge, only three people left: a couple with their child. I felt it was not a setting for a very young child to be involved in.

As it turned out, 41 people participated in a series of ideas that I suggested to them. They were not put under hypnosis. They were not put into a trance in any way at all. If anyone has reported otherwise, then they were not responsibly and scientifically explaining the events that took place. Before we left, I told the entire audience what was behind the manifestation.

It was a warning. If I could create a vivid, passionate, almost a panic-like experience of the sighting of UFOs, then someone with the same abilities and ulterior motives who could get to a cable television network on a national basis could put themselves in a position to influence people in thousands of cities in the U.S. and create serious social panic that could cause confusion and even a lack of confidence in the government and officials assigned to the national security. It would be even more serious if such a sinister figure were part of a large movement and was doing this to prove that he and his followers were amongst the privileged messengers who were able to communicate with extraterrestrials and, consequently, advise the populace who to follow and who to believe in.

If anyone doubts that such a phenomenon could be created, reflect on the impact of a piece of radio fiction done by Orson Welles in 1938 based on H. G. Wells' *War of the Worlds*. Furthermore, if this possibility is doubted, let some network give me the airwaves to produce this phenomenon on television for viewers at home. There isn't a network in the Western world that would extend such a foolhardy privilege.

We left the theater and went to the desert, where a crowd of people who were already partying greeted us. We could see that liquor was not the only intoxicant causing some of them to become disoriented. It was a strange, festive atmosphere. Then, sometime after 10 P.M., I dropped a handkerchief, and 41 people began to clearly "see and observe and point out" UFOs in the sky. Some became almost hysterical and many held their ears because the noise from the motors of the spaceships was that strong.

If anyone doubted how vivid it was to these people, they only had to talk to them when it was over. They expounded to a great degree on how real these two, three, or four lights were that moved through the sky. It wasn't until just before midnight that some eight or nine young men appeared at the casino. They had run away from the crowd when they "sighted" the UFOs and hid in the darkness. I don't believe any one of us realized that any of these young men had disappeared and for how long.

Clearly, a *sighting* had taken place, and before anyone suggests that I'm playing with words and double-talking, they'd better get their literature out on UFO sightings. They have been described as manifestations that later on could be explained as swamp gas, experimental aerial machinery, refractions of light in the sky, other weather phenomena, hallucinations, hysteria, and on and on go the theories. In fact, if one examines the Condon Report or the studies of the Hynek organization, one realizes that practically every sighting has had some explanation of this type. In the case of Condon and Hynek, both research groups have found no evidence of machinery from another part of the universe.

McCARTY: Shortly after you left that night, around 11 P.M., a group of 75 people observed a green light in the sky. A local Las Vegas television news station aired a live feed of this. Did this even amaze The Amazing Kreskin?

KRESKIN: There were those who were "disappointed" that everyone didn't see UFOs in the sky. Well, I have very little sympathy for those who expressed such disappointment. After all, I publicly reported that the manifestation would take place between 9:45 P.M. and midnight. By 11 P.M., all but 75 or so people had left, and many of those remaining were the technician crews packing their equipment. At 11:03 P.M., a gentleman who worked at the Silverton Casino & Hotel happened to look up and saw a green light moving slowly across the sky. He screamed to those around him, and by 11:04 P.M. a second green light appeared.

Fortunately, Steve Crupi of the NBC-TV affiliate Channel 3 had his camera on and got this on the 11 P.M. news. Some of the people who were packing immediately picked up their cell phones and called their families and friends to tell them to go outside and look. Many responded that they were already watching it live on television. In the interim, Las Vegas Boulevard became jammed with cars, as people not watching TV looked up to the sky towards the desert highway and saw the same green lights. One can only speculate between outdoor witnesses and those watching TV how many thousands witnessed the *sighting*.

There were scores of messages that I received via telephone, fax, and e-mails of people who saw UFOs within the same time frame, with delays of approximately 10 minutes or so. Many of them were unaware of my prediction. You ask, "Was I surprised?" In truth, I was very specific about the time the sighting would take place. Furthermore, for a number of evenings before June 6, I had a vivid dream that a second sighting would take place. Indeed, a friend visiting me from Indianapolis told me of a similar pattern. Steve Crupi of NBC-TV felt that it was an airplane, but everyone I have spoken to has discounted this, including John B. Alexander, an authority on UFOs, who checked and said there was no such plane flying over at that time. None of the people who saw the lights heard engine sounds, and with the airport only 2 miles away, that would be hard to believe. As of now, the exact nature of that UFO "sighting" is unknown. I'm not saying that it will never be explained, but to have two sightings take place on the night and during the time frame I predicted has even boggled my mind!

But the real message has been blurred in the excitement created by those UFO believers and nonbelievers. The skeptics felt that I was trying to prove the existence of UFOs, and the believers—either for scientific, cultural, mystical, or religious reasons—felt that I may be trying to debunk UFOs. Neither was even close to the truth.

The initial sighting was a warning. It is a warning to the Western world of how the power of suggestion can grip masses of people, and not always in an advantageous way.

McCARTY: Do you believe in UFOs? What are your thoughts on alien abductions, crop circles, cattle mutilations, and Roswell/Hangar 18?

KRESKIN: This will surprise those who did not hear my endless remarks in interviews for almost 2 months. I have long believed in some kind of extraterrestrial intelligence. God forbid if the only form of intelligence is here on Earth. If that's the case, the universe is in ghastly trouble.

I have long believed there is something physically significant about UFOs. As a young man, I was assured by the legendary radio and television communicator Arthur Godfrey, who was also a highly qualified pilot, that his plane had one time been tracked by a UFO that could not be explained as some military research vehicle. I have, furthermore, many times sat in the cockpit with commercial pilots during a flight and have been told about sightings they've had which they were not about to make public lest it jeopardize their job.

I evidently rankled others with the comment I made about alien abductions. I observed that many sightings seem to take place in limited areas, like among a group of guys fishing in the swamp after drinking vodka. It seems that sightings are less frequent or popular where there are large groups of people. Cattle mutilations I find to be an intriguing phenomenon, but I don't think it needs to be blamed on outside enemies. I also feel the same way about crop circles. As far as Roswell and Area 51 are concerned, those are remarkable phenomena, which have significant social, sociological, psychological, and scientific ramifications. I don't think that the Roswell or Area 51 phenomena can just simply be explained away as hallucinations.

I've had hundreds of hours of experiences and discussions regarding UFOs. I appeared often on Long John Nebel's radio show, heard on the WOR mutual broadcasting system out of New York—Nebel being one of the great radio personalities of the 1950s and 1960s. He would cover not only the paranormal and mystical, but UFOs, as well. He dealt with more UFO people and subjects than any other human being alive today. Everyone appeared on his show at one time or another: the early UFO promoters, pioneers, and romanticists, as well as scientific minds, such as J. Allen Hynek.

What many people don't know is that Dr. Hynek came to me and asked if I would become a partner with him when he finally established his research organization; an invitation that I declined. He was to be much respected because he neither accepted nor rejected but open-mindedly and brilliantly researched UFO phenomena.

With Nebel, I heard it all: people who traveled aboard UFOs, you name it, and not all of those people were lying. There was no doubt in our minds that many believed the stories they were telling, and Long John was very accommodating to them, although those of us who knew him well realized he didn't buy into any of the visitations, travels, abductions, and what have you. He introduced the listening audience to a wide range of characters, who had only been read about in earlier years.

McCARTY: Let's talk about the famous Orson Welles radio broadcast of H. G. Wells' War of the Worlds. *Have you heard tapes of the show? What do you think attributed to the mass hysteria of the broadcast?*

KRESKIN: Not only have I listened many times to the tapes of the broadcast, but I also spent many hours discussing the program with Orson Welles. How real was the panic that was created by his broadcast? That Sunday evening, my father was getting a haircut in a small town in New Jersey. The barber was a friend of his, and since the shop was closed it was a chance for my father to visit with him and have his haircut. He looked outside the window and saw cars racing down the quiet street with furniture on them, including, in one case, a mattress. He hadn't heard the radio and couldn't figure out what was going on. There are thousands of such stories.

As to why the episode caused such mass hysteria, it became a social delusion of the 20th century. In 1938, it should be realized that the United States knew and feared a World War on the horizon. Even back then Americans were seriously occupied with the threat of chemical and biological terrorism, a subject that rarely comes up during discussions and analysis of Welles' *War of the Worlds.* The mass media during this period was influential in creating and spreading the concern of this danger. The German aggression in the war in Europe was giving greater credibility to the use of such biological weapons. With that kind of backdrop, Welles' presentation became more easily accepted.

I once asked Welles if he had any idea that his broadcast would have such an impact. He told me that many calls came into the CBS switchboard during the broadcast asking what was going on. It soon became apparent that people were panicked. Network officials came to the studio wanting to interrupt the broadcast to placate the public. But they couldn't get in because Welles had the doors locked!

FINAL CHAPTER 2 THOUGHTS BY KRESKIN

KRESKIN: As I've explained, the reason for my demonstration was to alert and forewarn the Western world. I look back upon the brickbats that were thrown at me with somewhat jaundiced, almost removed, reflection. It does remind me of a time 20 years ago when I campaigned for my conviction that hypnosis, the hypnotic trance and the hypnotic state, simply do not exist and that there is no such thing as hypnosis.

Twenty years ago, the criticism became so scathing that no one paid attention to the fact that I was pointing out that while there was no such thing as a trance, the power of suggestion was so strong that it could create changes in the human body, cause people to hallucinate phenomena, and so. That has all changed. My position has been heeded in much of the world today. The credibility of witnesses who remember better under hypnosis regarding the details of a crime needs to be questioned. UFO sightings or abductions should be looked upon with tremendous skepticism. The idea that repressed memories can be brought forth under deep hypnotic trance can be looked upon as scientifically potential hogwash. So, the treatment I have experienced from UFO enthusiasts causes me to question their real belief and how legitimate it is. If I believe in something strongly, there isn't too much that can disturb me, especially if my belief is legitimate. But there is a warning that must be heeded, especially in a war that I predict will continue far beyond what most people will envision. The understanding that our intelligence services have of "psychological warfare" is, in my opinion, pathetically shallow and archaic, lost in the last century. They need to wake up!

3 | Famous Icons of the 20th and 21st Century

KRESKIN HAS KNOWN HUNDREDS AND HUNDREDS OF PEOPLE FROM THE 20TH and 21st centuries. In fact, he once wrote an intriguing book, still one of my favorites, called *The Amazing Kreskin's Future with the Stars,* which featured reflections and predictions of Kreskin and leading celebrities and opinion makers in the fields of entertainment, sports, health, and science. Kreskin is currently working on another related book called *Kreskin and Friends.*

I just picked 17 people who I thought the world's foremost mentalist might have some interesting things to say about. Kreskin could have written a whole book about some of these people. Prepare to be amazed.

McCARTY: Let's start off with one of the most beloved and respected entertainers of the 20th century, Bob Hope.

KRESKIN: I don't have any notes on what I'm about to tell you, but I do have some special memories of Bob Hope. I was appearing at the Waldorf for a special dinner in his honor. We had never met before. I was the entertainer for an hour, as he sat on the dais. My check was hidden; this is a feature in most of my performances, and I will expound upon it in greater detail later on. But the bottom line is that I proceeded to roam the auditorium as the committee concentrated on where they had hidden it. For me the drama was the discomfort I was experiencing in even approaching it. Here we had an audience of some 1,500 newspaper, radio, and TV people, and I'm on the dais. I kept lifting a tray which had extra meat on it. When I was lifting the tray, there was no check under it. Hope told me later he was gazing at a chandelier throughout this whole thing. He didn't want anybody in the place to think that he was involved in helping me, since the tray next to him on the dinner table of the dais was not so far off. I remember looking at the committee and asking if they really knew where the check was hidden. One of the ladies on the committee with a proper annoyance said to me, "of course we do, Kreskin." I had no right to ask such a question since they were the committee, but I was perplexed. I backed away, and suddenly an expression changed and I looked at the committee. One of them said, "do whatever you need to do, Kreskin," which was, of course, telling me nothing. At that point, I took my jacket off, rolled up my sleeve, and shoved my hand into the stuffing of the turkey. That's where the check was hidden...you got it...in the turkey stuffing!

Well, some years later I was a surprise guest in the Dallas-Fort Worth area where a private performance was being given by Bob Hope. The audience must have paid thousands of dollars for each ticket, as it was for a special fundraiser. Hope finally brought his wife on, and they were singing Hope's theme song, "Thanks for the Memory." Backstage one of the people provoked me to go on. I said, "I cannot go on and interrupt the performance," and they said, "Kreskin, this is why you're here." You don't interrupt a person's theme song, especially if it is Bob Hope, Liberace, Bing Crosby, Dean Martin, or any such legendary figure. Nonetheless, as instructed, I walked out. Bob looked at me; he didn't look annoyed, but he looked visibly surprised, and he said, "Kreskin, what are you doing here?"

I said, "Bob, they sent me to read your mind," and his remark was, "Kreskin, now we'd both go to prison." The man couldn't be thrown by anything—nor was his ego hurt. He was too great of an entertainer to let his ego interfere with the test. For I asked him if he would concentrate on some incident in his life that he felt that no one in the audience would know, and he reflected and said he had something in mind.

I borrowed a watch from a woman in the audience and I asked him if there was a clock anywhere within the setting he was picturing.

In some way he said there was, either that he could imagine a clock or that he knew the approximate time. Anyway, I turned the dials of the watch. I had a witness on stage with me standing next to Hope and his wife, Dolores, and I laid the watch on her palm, and then I began to describe the scene. There's a woman in the scene, and she seemed to be dressed in white, but I could not comprehend what the outfit was. It didn't seem like an evening gown or an especially glamorous outfit, but the one thing that struck me was that over the left side of her blouse or what she was wearing was a heart, whether it was a pin or what have you. Bob Hope gasped. He said to the audience that he doesn't know of anybody, certainly none who he had contacted in recent years, who had any idea of this experience. It was during World War II, and he was in an army hospital. A woman patient was lying on a bed in a white smock and the pin she was wearing was in the shape of a heart. I asked Hope what the time was, and he was very matter-of-fact about it. He knew, but didn't explain to me why. The lady holding the watch gasped out loud, because I had set the watch to the very minute that Hope had in mind. Hope told me later on, "Kreskin, I don't know of anybody that knew about that incident.

McCARTY: How about Milton Berle, also known as "Uncle Miltie" and "Mr. Television" to millions during TV's Golden Age? He was the first major star of U.S. television.

KRESKIN: A few years later I was to appear on a radio show that was extremely popular in Los Angeles. When I got to the studio I was overwhelmed. There was a guest before me, and it was Milton Berle. The last time I had seen Milton was when I was one of the panelists on *What's My Line* and had managed totally blindfolded to guess him, not because of telepathic ability but because of his answers to questions. I couldn't wait to see him, and the producer, seeing an opportunity, suggested I go on the air while Milt was still on. I didn't want to intrude, but they urged me to do so, and I walked on.

Berle was delighted, and we sat and talked on the air, and I told him those exciting memories of my earlier days as a kid, not having a television set, but walking on Tuesday nights to my aunt and uncle's house, which was a couple of miles away, to watch at 8 P.M. *The Milton Berle Show*. I knew then that it was broadcast live. There was no such thing as taped television at that time. It was spontaneous. I remembered hilarious scenes that he popped in and out of. Whether it was a skit, or a singer, or a chorus, or a magician with assistants, he suddenly appeared.

Berle explained that these were the early days of television. Nobody was trained in directing television shows, in timing television shows, or choreographing them. It had come out of vaudeville—live entertainment—and for that reason he took over the show. From out of nowhere he added, "You know, I paid for the crew." He went on and on and said, "It would surprise people what my original salary was, what NBC paid me." Then he started to stutter and stammer, and obviously was experiencing a memory block, which could happen to any of us at almost any age. For some reason an image flashed in my eyes, and I mentioned a sum of money. It was not a lot of money for this day and age, and he gasped and slammed his fists on the desk. He proceeded to say he had seen many mind reading acts in his life and was a magician himself, but "I want you to know that this man is for real. I want you to know that Kreskin pulled through his unconscious the exact amount sum I had in mind."

McCARTY: How about actress Bette Davis?

KRESKIN: My one meeting with Bette Davis was on *The Mike Douglas Show*. That show was broadcast mainly out of Philadelphia, Pennsylvania, on KYW. It was an extraordinarily successful 90-minute show which went on live at 12:30 P.M. in Pennsylvania but was seen around 4:30 P.M. in much of the rest of the country.

I did 118 shows with Mike Douglas. Amongst his earlier producers were Woody Fraser, who now produces *The Mike Huckabee Show*, and the legendary Roger Ailes, who is now the head of Fox Television broadcasting. The format for my appearances was really instigated by a couple of the producers, including Roger Ailes. Usually, some 18 to 22 minutes was given me in three segments. That's right, three segments. But first I would sit down and Mike would ask me some questions about anything. I usually told some dramatic experience regarding ESP.

A popular question was why people have a feeling they've been somewhere before and they never were. There was a policy instigated by Roger Ailes that I would be asked a question that was not mentioned to me before the show. There were interesting topics. The topic could be about a person who spoke passionately about some world issue or some strange occurrence in a part of the world, an unusual movie, and so on. They wanted me to think on my feet and trusted me to do so. We had some fascinating conversations.

The second segment was one of Mike Douglas's favorites. It came from my concerts and was an important feature. I would sit in a chair by myself and tune in on the thoughts of members of the audience whom I've never met before. I would reveal to them names, dates, addresses, experiences that they were certain I could not have known. Mike was always my aisle man, walking around with a microphone. We had a ball doing this.

The third segment was usually with the co-host, and every week Mike brought on a celebrity who stayed the entire week. This particular show had Bette Davis. I was ecstatic. I had admired her all through the years. I could name film after film. On the air, I handed her a book. One of the other guests was given an envelope with a single piece of paper in it, a large business envelope, which he then pocketed. I urged Bette Davis to turn through the book and think of any page and some phrase on the page. She did. I was able to perceive her thoughts. But before I even did that, I asked her if she had memorized the page number, which she did, and she held on to the book. I never touched the book once I had given it to her. And I proceeded to read her thoughts, which enchanted her.

And it was obvious in that Bette Davis look and the cadence of her voice that she was taken aback, and then oh, I had an ace in the hole. I asked her to turn to the page and show us the exact phrase that I had perceived. She turned to it and there was silence, and Mike said, "Is everything okay?" At first she didn't answer. She was asked again, then she turned the book to Mike, and it was clear the thing she had thought of was not in the book, it had been ripped out. She kept saying, "That's impossible, that's impossible." I asked the other guest to take out his envelope and remove the contents. Lo and behold, there in the envelope was the very page that she chose, and when he handed it to her, she fit it in the book and it fit exactly in the ripped place. What is interesting is what happened in the following segments before the show ended. Mike would be in the middle of a conversation with another guest, and suddenly Bette Davis would say, "That's impossible." She must have said it a half a dozen times, and the remark stole the show.

If you really want to know what happened, the page that she "saw" was never there to begin with. She never truly saw the page number nor the phrase. I had programmed her to think of and also to "see" it. That's the real reason why she and everybody else on the show were stunned when there was no trace of the page in the book. Talk about the power of mental suggestion!

McCARTY: Let's converse about comedienne Phyllis Diller.

KRESKIN: I've known Phyllis Diller for a number of years and admire her. A bond was created between us when one day she sent me a picture of one of her pets. She had known of my love of animals, as I had sent her once before a picture of one of my pets. It turns out they were cats. Her cat's name was Miss Kitty. My cat's name was Miss Kitty. When Phyllis learned that Miss Kitty had passed on, I received a very poignant note from her. We both share a very great love of the animal world. I've appeared with her a number of times on broadcasts. Indeed, these are special moments she added to my career.

Years ago when the CTV network was interested in doing a series built around me, one of the pilots had as guests Marty Ingels and Phyllis Diller. On the air, I had them think of playing cards, any playing cards. There were no decks there, they were just thinking of cards. I had one of those jumbo decks of cards. I took two cards out and nailed them against an easel. Oh, by the way, the cards they had decided upon they thought about individually. Before the show they had been given a deck of cards and told to go into a dressing room.

Each decided on a card which they then put in a separate steel container which, in turn, was submerged in a giant clear glass container of water that had a lid sealed over it. When the show went on the air, they were the only ones who knew the cards in those containers.

Nobody had touched the containers. When they took the cards out of the submerged containers and opened the sealed lids and unrolled their cards and showed them to the camera, I then ripped from the easel my two giant cards, showing them to be the particular cards they thought of. This particular pilot proved to be the pivotal point in my career, for it was at this moment that the CTV network in Canada decided it was a go with the Kreskin half-hour series, which went on for 5½ years. I remember the enthusiasm and the joy of my two guests, especially Phyllis Diller. She said to me once on the air on *The Mike Douglas Show*, "Kreskin, you're a male witch. You ought to be burned at the stake."

McCARTY: You have met Hugh Hefner, publisher and editor of Playboy *magazine, many times. His magazine has been a big influence on my interview skills, so we have to include the flamboyant Hef.*

KRESKIN: Regarding Hugh Hefner, boy do I have a story to relate. I had done a number of appearances at his Playboy Clubs. At one time, this was the place for men to go to meet interesting women and waitresses called Playboy Bunnies, who always dressed in provocative but neatly coifed outfits. I was asked to appear on his TV series *Playboy After Dark*, and aside from demonstrating my abilities as a thought reader, I had a game released called Kreskin's ESP game. Amongst the properties of that game were not only packs of special cards with ESP symbols on them, but a pendulum and a small tablet over which one held the pendulum by the end of a chain. The weight was held over the middle of the board and would intrigue people who bought the game or saw it demonstrated on TV. Some would participate on their own when I demonstrated it with groups. If they held the pendulum an inch or so off the base and thought of questions, the pendulum would start to move. There was a vertical line that had the word YES on the top and a horizontal line that had the word NO at the bottom. If they were asked a question for which they knew the answer to be NO, without saying anything, the pendulum would start to swing in a NO way. If the answer was a strong YES, as much as they'd try to hold the pendulum still, it would start to swing forward and backwards. To stop it, I would have the group or individuals lower the pendulum so it touched the board. Hugh Hefner was one of the subjects, and there were other guests who were entertainers. I asked intriguing questions: Do you enjoy ice cream? Do you like chocolate? Is your favorite color blue? And on and on. But this was a show run by a man who owned *Playboy* magazine, and I simply asked the question, "Are you in love?" It was an uncomfortably dramatic response, as Hefner's pendulum started to wobble front and backwards, and then before you know it, it was swinging right and left, right and left, NO. The camera suddenly pulled away from Hugh Hefner, because during the period the show was on the air Hefner was having a rather passionate love affair with one of his prominent girls. At least that's what the public assumed.

McCARTY: Let's talk about one of my favorite British actors, Peter Cushing. What are your thoughts?

KRESKIN: As my series developed on the air as a weekly half-hour program, it took on a life of its own. It was not seen only in Canada and the United States, but all over the world. It was rather dramatic to see it dubbed in Japanese. As a result of tremendous interest, 2 years of the series were recorded in England, during which I had a ball. I have a great passion for the British people. And if I am with a Britisher old enough to have been living in London in the Second World War, I will get out of my chair, no matter how well dressed I am, and sit at their feet and say, "tell me how you survived and how you handled the nights of bombing." Today, many fellow Americans are suffering tremendous economic problems, but thank God we are not in the situation that the British people went through day after day, leaving their homes and finding their neighbors were not there anymore. Peter Cushing was a wonderful guest, and I couldn't wait to have him on. After all, he had done the great Hammer horror movies and he appeared with Christopher Lee in the *Horror of Dracula*. It was an exciting program.

On the air I asked him to think of someone in his life, and because of the spirit and the gothic nature of the interview I decided to dramatize it in an unusual way. There was a bowl of ashes on the table in front of me, and I said I was about to show him something that was done by the old-time fake mediums in England and in the United States but not in the way I'm going to do it. The fakes rigged things and used gimmickry. Peter Cushing had someone in mind, and I proceeded to tell him the person's full name, but in a unique way. I rolled up my sleeves and poured ashes on my bare wrists. He and I rubbed the ashes, and as we did so some of the ashes were clinging to my arm, and there appeared the name of the person he had in mind. I said to him, "Who is this person?" He mentioned that she was his wife and that she had passed on a couple of years ago. I expressed my sympathy and as we were looking at the ashes he said, "Don't worry, Kreskin, it won't be too long before I'll be joining her." A few seconds later the time on the show had run out. No one could have predicted a more dramatic moment. And years later when Peter Cushing's biography appeared, I was deeply touched to find the pages in his book wherein he spoke about me. He said as he had written on the Internet through the years that what I do is legitimate, and the experience he had with me was done absolutely legitimately. His remarks meant so much to me, and my admiration for him increased from the day that we bonded.

McCARTY: Let's talk about your longtime friend, the Chairman of Fox News Channel and Fox Television Stations, Roger Ailes.

KRESKIN: Roger Ailes has become a giant in broadcasting. He is President of Fox News Channel and the Chairman of the Fox Television Station's group. He is one of the most remarkable men I've ever met in my life and as powerful a person in broadcasting as you can find. Intriguing is the evolution of this man. In the 1960s, he was one of the producers of *The Mike Douglas Show* out of Philadelphia, Pennsylvania. The show was on 90 minutes a day in the afternoon around the country and was a tremendous success, with high syndication. Ailes came to see me at a performance in the Lehigh Valley area of Pennsylvania. That was the first of 118 Mike Douglas Shows. It's a shame that some of them were lost, for like Johnny Carson with NBC, Westinghouse, which was syndicating the shows, did not keep a great many of the tapes at that time. They were lost for good.

A bond grew between Mike Douglas and me. He was very unassuming. He relied heavily on his crew to direct him, but he related just easily and naturally with any guest and was a wonderful supporter of my work. What he loved to do was to be in the audience during the audience readings. This is an integral part of all my public concerts. Indeed my television series, *The Amazing World of Kreskin*, had this as a feature of each half hour show. In fact, the head people at the CTV network insisted that I retain the audience readings in my programs, as they knew the viewers related to my revealing what was on the minds and the thoughts of the total strangers in my audience. Mike Douglas loved to hold the microphone, and when I announced a name or a date and someone in the audience recognized it, he'd go into the audience and verify that the person never met me, as I then proceeded to tell them further thoughts in their mind.

I came to know Roger Ailes in greater depth. I would often drive from northern New Jersey to Philadelphia and sit down with Roger and talk for hours, sometimes until one or two in the morning. He often had me reflect what I planned to do as my career grew more and more. I found so intriguing his comments and reflections of the people he came to know in the broadcast field and the various celebrities, from politics to show business. We visited each others' homes. A very genuine rapport grew. Roger finally left the *Douglas* show, and, talk about a giant step, became the Public Communications Advisor for then President Richard Nixon. Lo and behold, he became a similar advisor for President Ronald Reagan and continued and became advisor for President George H. W. Bush.

While building a public relations firm in the interim, Roger Ailes became the campaign manager for Rudy Giuliani's first mayoral campaign in 1989. But it didn't end there. Here is a man who amassed tremendous understanding not only of audiences for television, but the thinking of giants in public office, so he was well prepared when after being involved in other television corporations he was welcomed into the Fox organization, inevitably becoming the head of Fox, whose success clearly can be credited to Roger. Because of his remarkable knowledge of the way the viewing public thinks, what is on their minds, and what is of concern to them, he has an equally challenging ability to discover the right people for television formats today in the area of news. He is the one who realized from the very beginning that Bill O'Reilly's nightly 1-hour broadcast would have tremendous audience pull. Incidentally, it has become the most popular in all of cable television.

There's a story that Roger Ailes tells, and it's a message that I want to leave in the hands of those young readers who want to go into broadcasting, public relations, or related fields. When Roger completed his college education, he applied for a job to work on a new television series, at that time originating from I believe Cleveland, Ohio. The producer, who he became very close to, asked him his background. Roger mentioned his education and studies in broadcasting and the fact that he'd done some in college. The producer shrugged his shoulders and said in essence, "Come on, Mr. Ailes, what real experience have you had?" And then he still offered Roger a job at 25 dollars cash a week. Roger accepted that job. He has said many times that it was one of the wisest decisions he ever made in his life. The experience he had there enabled him to understand all areas of television production, from the man behind the camera, to the person who delivers the mail, to the person who sets up the microphone, to the individuals in the control room who pick the best shots, all the way up to the writers behind the scenes, makeup people, and all others involved, and yes, the performers and broadcasters themselves. I might add that in the scores upon scores of people I have met who have worked with Roger Ailes there is one common word used in describing his attributes that I hear over and over again, his "loyalty."

McCARTY: How about one of your icons, Arthur Godfrey?

KRESKIN: Michael, this is not a biography of Arthur Godfrey. Peter Lassally, who has worked for David Letterman for years and worked for Carson before that, and before that for Arthur Godfrey himself, said to me one day that I should do a biography of Godfrey, since I've obviously amassed more material than anyone he's known. He had worked for Godfrey for a number of years. I have some 200 pages of material and have heard hundreds and hundreds of his TV and radio shows through my childhood and later years.

Arthur Godfrey had a greater impact on me than any broadcaster in history, since when he came on radio and television in the late 1940s and early 1950s he knew that there was probably only one person at home listening on the radio. His radio shows were in the morning, and those were 1½-hour shows 5 days a week. In addition, he had his hour-long Wednesday night television show and on Monday night a half-hour talent scout show, both of which were rated nationally amongst the top 10 for some 10 years.

He knew something, and it changed the whole foundation of broadcasting, He learned it while being bedridden after he was struck by a truck that went off the road. Almost every bone in his body had been broken, and his heart had been shifted temporarily to the other side of his body. He lay for endless weeks listening to the radio, and in the 1930s and certainly the early 1940s, the announcers were very formal. In those days of radio, when you went on the air you were dressed in tuxedos or evening outfits, even though you were never seen. Godfrey thought this was ridiculous. He was not speaking to a theater audience, he was really speaking to one person, and that's the way he spoke. He changed the whole foundation of broadcasting, and became the most powerful single figure in the history of broadcasting. He influenced presidents. He had the president and vice president fascinated. When a catastrophe hit, Godfrey was the person to go on the air, because his voice was more familiar than even the president's. Roosevelt admired him. Roosevelt's wife Eleanor wrote him a letter almost every day when she heard him on the air, and the stories are endless of the power he had.

Lucille Ball on national television said the only reason her show with Desi Arnaz made it was because of Arthur Godfrey. Her show followed him on Monday nights at 9 P.M., but it wasn't getting an audience. People were turning to another show which was a sob/sympathy-type show where people came on with afflictions or problems, and whatever the contest was or however it worked, they would be given some money to take home. It wasn't an awful lot of money, but they were able to leave with some kind of money to help them with their plight. It had drawn a remarkable audience. Lucille Ball and Desi Arnaz were not doing well at all. Then somehow the message got to Arthur Godfrey, and as he was ending his live simulcast broadcast on radio and television on Monday night, a half a minute before 9 P.M., he said, "Listen, I know you're used to listening to another show with all the tough stories that people are going through, but I want you to do me a favor. I want you to watch the program that follows with a woman that I just think is fantastic, Lucille Ball." Then he went off the air, and a few weeks later *The Lucy Show* was set for an entire season.

My first meeting with him was when the *Mike Douglas* people found out he was going to be a co-host and they immediately booked me as one of the first guests. They went to Godfrey and said, "We've got a special guest for you, The Amazing Kreskin." You've got to understand, here's a man I revered throughout his career. Godfrey's response was, "Who the hell is Kreskin?" and they didn't get me on at first. But they finally talked him into it, explaining that I was an admirer of his. Godfrey didn't watch television. He never went to the movies. He had always been busy as a broadcaster, and as such was either performing all the time on the air or in concerts and had no time to watch television.

I appeared on the air and he took a grandfather watch, an old fashioned one, which we reminisced was the kind of watches that businesspeople were awarded after a number of years. He got a kick out of that. He was trained in aviation as well as in radio and television so he knew the importance of timing. He proceeded on the air to set the watch he was holding, unlike Bob Hope who had a time in mind mentally. I took the watch and handed it to someone who read the time, turned the watch face down, and started to turn the dials, and stopped whenever he wanted to. I asked Godfrey what time he had set the watch to, and he gave me an answer in French, which most people didn't understand. When he realized the key person holding the watch had set it to the very same time he had in mind, it flipped him out. He had seen everything, but this took him aback, and he kept thinking if there are no electronic devices, if there's no hidden radio in the watch, which of course there wasn't, then there's no other explanation but some telepathic ability.

Off camera he was a bitter man, because he had lost his series and a television career that had been legendary. My admiration, opinion, and reverence for him then or since have never changed.

If there was ever evidence of the impact that this forgotten giant has had in the industry, it was the coverage of the funeral of Franklin D. Roosevelt. The recording of his broadcast has become a classic in special events in broadcast history. When I was a little boy in school, our teacher played some highlights of broadcasting and it included this moment.

A producer at CBS asked him if he would give them permission to include in their album, as a moment of his broadcast histories, his coverage of the funeral of FDR. Godfrey choked up and without any request for contracts or anything he said, "You can use it any way you want" and never spoke about it again. It had been a live broadcast. A president who had been elected for a fourth term and had carried a nation through the Second World War had died. He did not live to see the end of the war. Godfrey was asked to describe the funeral. He had a tremendous bond with President Roosevelt for a reason that I will not go into at this time, but it was a solemn period that can only be compared to the funeral after President Kennedy's assassination.

The entire nation, no matter what their age, was in deep mourning, and Godfrey spoke in his deep voice, one which everyone could relate to as that of an older father or grandfather. We all heard him speaking. And then came the coffin pulled by the horse, and Godfrey eloquently and in very few words started to describe it. He had difficulty continuing, and finally in a couple of minutes said, "and traveling behind is our President Harry S. Truman," and Godfrey in essence said, "May God give him all the strength to continue on, but I know many of you feel the way I do now," and started to sob on camera. He was so emotional he sent the broadcast to the network station, at which point music was played. That is the only real description of the president's funeral in radio history that has held up through the decades. When one hears this radio broadcast played back again with the sorrowful ending where he says he could not go on, it is a reflection of how this man was able to think and share the feelings of his listeners.

McCARTY: Let's shift gears and talk about Bishop Fulton J. Sheen.

KRESKIN: In the early 1950s, Milton Berle was king of Tuesday night television until a few years later when his ratings started to drop. It was not because another variety show was competing with NBC. It was because on a local New York station, Channel 5, a single figure was appearing for a half hour every Tuesday from 8:00 to 8:30 P.M. It was a Catholic priest, a bishop prominent in New York who had been heard on the radio for many years, Bishop Fulton J. Sheen. This was his first appearance before a large television audience, and it was the beginning of a series. He didn't really preach on the air, although at times he reflected on his Catholic discipline and belief and training, but his audience were not only Catholics, they were Protestants, Jews, and atheists. I knew all such people, and they were fans of his, because he didn't preach a specific religion. He just preached the good word, and furthermore he had a fantastic sense of humor. He spoke without any notes or note chart held by the camera. Teleprompters didn't exist in those days.

I got to meet him on a number of personal appearances. One day we were appearing before a corporate group. He was speaking earlier that day and I was performing at night, so he was attending my show. But during the day, he and I met and sat for a couple of hours and conversed. Bishop Sheen had a remarkable sense of humor, and he loved to tell a story about me, because he had seen me perform publicly and from our conversations he knew something of my past. His favorite story was that my family originally thought I was going to become a priest, and it is true.

My career was well defined by the time I was 5 years old and nothing could draw me away from it. I was most interested in my faith and got to know the priests and performed often for the nuns and indeed did so later on in my teens after high school. Even though I was traveling, I managed to attend Seton Hall University, a Catholic university in New Jersey, where I minored in religious philosophy and majored in psychology. Years later I received an honorary doctorate in psychology as well. Sheen commented on my Catholic background and that some in my family thought I would be a priest. He philosophized in his storytelling voice, "Imagine Kreskin in a parish, and it's Saturday afternoon, the day before a holy communion, where these youngsters that are going to confession, because they have been studying with the nuns preparing for First Holy Communion. It's a special moment in all Catholic youngsters' lives. Little Johnny goes into the confessional and closes the door behind him, which plunges the confessional in darkness as he kneels in front of the panel. He hears the panel move. At this point he says, 'Bless me Father, for I have sinned.' And Father Kreskin says, 'young man, tell me your sins.' And Johnny says, 'Well, Father, I lied to my mother twice.'" And Bishop Sheen says Father Kreskin interrupts and says, "Young man, you're lying again because you lied six times and you know it." And that was one of Bishop Sheen's favorite anecdotes built around me.

McCARTY: How about one of my favorite film directors, Alfred Hitchcock, who has done some of my favorite films, such as Psycho, The Birds, Torn Curtain, Vertigo, Rear Window, The Trouble with Harry, Frenzy, Family Plot, Lifeboat, To Catch a Thief, Notorious, Dial "M" for Murder—*I could go on and on.*

KRESKIN: I'm an unabashed fan of Alfred Hitchcock, who *Entertainment Weekly* years ago picked to be the greatest director of modern times. The thing about Hitchcock was his ability to get into the skin of the audience. He knew how his audiences thought. The camera work and the actors, whom he often with humongous tongue in cheek called 'cattle,' were putty in his hands, if, of course, they were up to the role they were playing. In my mind, I often feel sorry in a small way for people who never got to see *Psycho* when it first came out, since no one knew what the movie was about. You were not allowed to enter the theater once the movie started, and you were admonished when the movie was over not to talk about it. The only way I can describe it, seeing it for the first time as a college student on a Friday night with an adult audience, is that after the first murder took place, we all were in a state of shock. Almost every scene where a door was open, or an actor walked around a corner or to another side of a room, one shuddered to think that his grandmother would lurk out again with her knife. It was such a frightening scenario, that first murder in the shower, that many people who only saw the movie once remember red blood, even though the movie was in black and white. Hitchcock did not want the movie in color, for it was not a slasher movie, but much higher class. It was a dark, black-and-white, gothic horror story.

I never met the man, but I revered his work. After the movie appeared, I got a kick out of how his image changed forever. He was no longer to be thought of as just the master of suspense. What he had done with *Psycho* was to make one of the greatest horror movies of all time, and to soothe his public, with his tongue in cheek, he said that his next movie was to be a fairy tale. And out came the movie *The Birds*. But with *Psycho*, he clearly revealed one of his greatest skills—how to throw his audiences a curve. Who would have ever thought that the star of the movie, Janet Leigh, would die within the first quarter of the movie? It was unheard of for a star.

And what a stroke of brilliance was his movie *Rear Window*. Here, Jimmy Stewart, with broken legs, was confined to a wheelchair, pretty much immobilized. All he could do was to look out the window of his room and see a connected array of apartment buildings. He was claustrophobic. In essence, his life at that time was watching the world of windows and the people behind them. Everyone in the theater could identify with the helpless limitation he was beset with.

You could read between the lines what was going on in these people's lives, and some of it appeared rather surly. And through this eavesdropping, you surmise that evil was at stake. Almost helpless in a wheelchair, Stewart was watching the murderer who just then happened to glance towards the window and spot Stewart across the way looking at him. Talk about horror and terror. You knew this monster in the movie, played by Raymond Burr, was going to find Jimmy Stewart and kill him.

*McCARTY: Let's talk about another great actor, director, and writer— Orson Welles. He has done just as many great movies as Hitchcock, including some of my favorites—*Catch-22, *the original* Casino Royale, Is Paris Burning?, A Man for All Seasons, Moby Dick, Touch of Evil, The Muppet Movie, Black Magic, Citizen Kane, *and so much more.*

KRESKIN: I came to know Orson Welles in the latter part of his career. When I was appearing in England at the New London Theater one summer, Welles came to see me. We spent an entire afternoon talking across a dining room table at a restaurant. Of course, he had opinions on everything, including movies. He predicted that to fill time, movies, including television movies, will be replete with car chases; never realizing those scenes may be replaced by sci-fi spaceships. And on and on the stories would go. He felt that one of the worst things to happen to movies was color. At first I was startled, and then he continued to explain that color is such a strong stimulant that it can detract from a movie. He wasn't talking about *Doctor Zhivago* or the *Wizard of Oz*, but I could imagine the darkness of *The Lodger* with Laird Cregar, a Jack the Ripper movie, being made in color. How it would have lost so much of this mystique of shadows. He loved hallways, walking down long stairs in movies. It was a great entrance.

Welles was also somewhat of a magician. Not a great one, but as an actor playing the role of a magician, he was outstanding. Most actors I have seen perform as magicians were rather second rate.

One of the untold disasters in Welles' career was an incident which destroyed his relationship with Johnny Carson. He was a guest on Carson's show, and they were in a commercial break. Welles was scheduled to return the following Monday and host the show. Carson often took off on Mondays. Understand, the conversation was not being heard by the viewers, and Johnny rarely engaged in conversation during the commercial breaks. But as Fred De Cordova, the producer of the show, recounted to me, Welles turned to Carson and said, "You know on Monday, I'm going to do a Kreskin." Johnny did a very slow take and looked at him and said in essence, "What do you mean?" Fred was uncertain of the exact remarks, but basically he had told Carson he was an admirer of mine. He was going to do a dramatic mental test legitimately, the way Kreskin would do it. Evidently, that was all that Carson needed to hear.

The bottom line is that Welles did come in on Monday to do the show. What he did not know, and never knew, was that Johnny came in as well and admonished his crew not to alert Welles of this. Exactly where Johnny sequestered himself is not clear to me, but let's get on with the disaster that Welles created. Welles proceeded to ask people in the audience to give him lengthy numbers, perhaps even in the millions, which he proceeded to write on a blackboard. At the end of this situation of calling out numbers, he totaled them and asked someone from the audience who'd been given a sealed envelope to come forward.

Lo and behold, as he tore open the envelope, what Orson had predicted the total to be was completely wrong. I remember watching that night because someone from *The Tonight Show* called me and told me to watch the show from LA. The shows were delayed, and they tracked me down to have me look in.

Vincent Price was the next guest and walked on the show and said, "Orson, you just laid the biggest bomb of your career." It wasn't just the failure that irked Carson; it was more about what he learned and what a percentage of the audience saw. The man who came forward with the envelope had been sitting in the audience with an adding machine or calculator, and as the numbers were placed on the blackboard he would add the numbers. When he got a total, he quickly wrote it down, put it in the envelope, and sealed it. Only he got the numbers wrong. Not only was the result a failure, but the whole stunt had been faked, since Welles had used a stooge.

Carson never again allowed him to perform on his show, though occasionally he would have him on to talk. Understand that Johnny Carson had bonded with Orson Welles. He had taken him out to dinners and shows, but you could only double-cross Carson once, and that was the end of their relationship.

McCARTY: How about William "Captain Kirk" Shatner. Would you like to share a story about him?

KRESKIN: I was pleased when William Shatner agreed to appear on my TV series *The Amazing World of Kreskin.* He is Canadian and had become a fan of my work. He ended up doing four shows with me and asked if he could come back and appear as the celebrity guest for another show. The first show had an unforgettable moment. Though I never rehearsed the show, we did a very brief walkthrough, since

I was going to place myself in a telephone booth outside the studio and Bill Shatner, whom I had not previously met, would be indoors. When he came on the set, which was being broadcast before a studio audience, he told the story that before the show he had been told by my producers to buy a book that he could honestly say was not looked at or tampered with by the staff. He went to a store in downtown Ottawa. It turns out it had just closed and he proceeded to knock on the door. He was knocking so incessantly that the owner came by to tell him that the store was not open. The owner must have taken a double take, quickly opening the door as he recognized Bill Shatner, and said, "What can I do for you?" It was at that point that Bill bought a book or two from the owner of the store and came to the studio. I did not meet Bill Shatner until he came on the air, and he brought at least one of the books he purchased with him. I asked him to turn to any page in the book and concentrate on some scenario. As I recall, I pictured a person slumped over with a knife in his back. It turns out what Shatner had purchased was a murder mystery story and the scene he was reading was the scene I had described.

But the climax of the program came that night when I left the studio and called Shatner on a phone line which was set up for me to call the studio. However, it wasn't quite the clean-cut setting that we had that afternoon. It was nighttime. A blizzard was hitting the town. I was finding it difficult to see. I could hardly see those who were photographing me. I was also finding it mighty damn difficult to stay warm.

A padlock was given to Shatner by my wonderful announcer Bill Luxton and also about a dozen keys. Shatner picked about 12 people from the audience, handed them each a key, and tried them all on the padlock. Only one key fit the padlock, the others did not, and they kept trying. Each person sealed their key in a small envelope, and they were mixed up so that when they were handed back to the different people no one knew which key opened the padlock. I proceeded to have Shatner talk to each of the members of the audience that were on stage. Bear in mind that I could not see them; I couldn't see anyone in the studio. All I could do was hear what was piped into my telephone hookup. As I heard each name, I finally stopped at one person and said to Shatner, "That is the individual who is holding the key to the padlock. Would you gather up the rest of the envelopes?" Shatner did, and put them into another larger envelope. Someone was coming by to gather the keys. But one thing, parenthetically, before the padlock was locked Shatner was made to take off his jacket. A chain was fed down Shatner's left sleeve, around the jacket, and down the right sleeve, so when he put his jacket back on a single chain was hanging from both his wrists. The padlock was wrapped around his chain. The only way he could take his jacket off without ripping it was to unlock it with the padlock. There he stood constricted. Not only was the padlock locked, but his limbs locked, and I now proceeded to name the person I thought held the key.

Oh, the other keys. Bill Luxton helped gather them, put them into an envelope, and hand them to a man, who proceeded to seal them as he walked out of the studio, and the camera followed him. We saw the man get into a truck and drive away. He was a post office official, with the rest of the keys to be mailed to my office in New Jersey. The audience went into pandemonium, and Bill Shatner gave a classic smile. Either this key would do the trick, or a pair of scissors would extricate him. The envelope was given to Shatner, he opened it, took out the key, tried the padlock, and sprung the lock. Shatner has never forgotten this scenario.

McCARTY: I am going out on a limb on this one—Lenny Bruce, the counterculture comedian who paved the way for modern stand-up comedy. Did you ever meet Lenny?

KRESKIN: I never knew Lenny Bruce. I never saw him work. I only knew of him through Steve Allen, who was one of the great wits of early television, a tremendous comedic mind, a very talented musician, and a great, great writer. I became familiar with Steve Allen, in the 1950s and 1960s when he had a regular television series. That's the period when Lenny Bruce not only reached some popularity, but became highly controversial and censored in many cities. It was Steve Allen, though, who thought the man had a stroke of genius. He just didn't use four-letter words for the sake of four-letter words.

McCARTY: How about bestselling horror author Dean Koontz?

KRESKIN: The passion that Dean Koontz has for writing simply exudes on every page. But I feel an even closer bond with Koontz when I realize his revulsion for Freudian theories. How wearisome it has become over so many years that each character or subject of a movie, play, or novel had a traumatic past which would shape what he became. What a joy to know that Koontz thinks of the human personality as much more than a cause-and-effect mechanism and rather one with great depth. His works are not only a wonderful antiseptic to the infections that Freudian thinking has created in life, but, moreover, his writings are among the most spellbinding and riveting that I have ever read.

McCARTY: You had a dramatic demonstration on The Carson Show *in which Bette Midler, the "Divine Miss M," played a part.*

KRESKIN: Through the years on *The Carson Show*, I never rehearsed anything. Before the show I might go out and tell the camera crew where I'm going to walk, where I might stand, and if there was a lot of motion involved in what I intended to do, but I never really did a rehearsal. I didn't rig anything with guests, and if the studio audience was involved, they were truly strangers to me. In this particular case, though, I planned a test with Carson, which it turns out NBC vetoed.

I was going to come on the show and point out to him that what I was going to do was associated with hypnosis. But since I have advocated strongly that there is no hypnotic trance, I emphasized that it is through the power of skillful suggestion that some very dramatic things can be done to influence a human being. Then I asked the director, Peter Lassally, to go back and tell Carson what I was going to do.

He returned and said it was fine. Johnny would go through with it. A few days later I received a phone call from an official at NBC telling me, "No, you are not to do this." They were evidently fearful of what I was going to do and fearful of any harm being done him. After all, he was one of their prized products, and they didn't want anything threatening to happen to him. Well, you don't argue with NBC any more than you do perhaps the president or the Vatican, and, oh boy, I didn't even consider doing it. Except a few days later while I was on tour in the Midwest appearing at a university I got a call in the evening from one of Carson's private secretaries. She said Johnny wanted to speak to me. It surprised me, as I never spoke to him before a show. Johnny got on the phone and used some very colorful language in describing the person who vetoed the test at NBC. He said, "Understand, we're going to go through with it."

The day of the show I arrived at the studio late as I had been delayed in route. There was no time for a walkthrough. This was the one test that I would ever do with Carson for which I knew I would have to do a run through before actually attempting it with him. It was just that kind of test. I had to know that he was capable of responding, but it was too late. I came in and was very preoccupied, very nervous, which is not like me. I got a hold of Fred De Cordova, the producer, and told him I must see Johnny before the show. Fred looked at me as if I was insane. I talked to the directors and said, "I have to see Johnny."

Finally, I said to them, "I can't do the test unless I talk to him!" I knew there was no time for a run through. If we couldn't do a run through I had to at least just talk to him. I will tell you that literally about 15 minutes before the show someone came to see me. The audience was there. Ed McMahon was ready to announce the program. I was walking to the hallways towards Johnny's dressing room when a secretary said, "Kreskin, this never happens. Before going on the air, Johnny does not have someone in his room. He's quite nervous." But she said to go ahead, and she would wait out there. I opened the door and walked in. It looked like a scene out of *The Godfather* or *The Sopranos*. There sat the man, Johnny Carson, at a desk. There was a tilted lamp with a bare bulb pitched over the desk so it shone only on the papers in front of him. I realized it was his monologue. This was something that Carson cherished. I couldn't see the rest of the room. If there were people in it, there was no way of knowing, but it was clear that it was only the two of us. He looked at me and said hello, but that was it. I said, "Johnny, please trust me. Listen to me. Listen to what I'm going to say to you. Hear my voice." And I looked at him, gazed in his eyes, and said, "During this test I'm going to mentally count from 1 to 10. I'm going to be talking to you. When your eyes close, listen to my voice." I spoke for about a minute, a minute and a half. When I finished, I said, "Thank you, Johnny." He looked at me and said, "Kreskin, don't worry. I know it will work." That was all. It was an incredibly dramatic scene in my life, which I have never really made public. Finally, when my time came to guest on the show, I sat down as I always did with Johnny before I performed. I reflected on my work and about my position of there being no hypnotic trance. But we were going to do the catalepsy test associated with hypnotism.

We walked to center stage. Ed McMahon and Doc Severinsen were called over. They didn't know what I was going to do, as there had been no run through. There were two chairs there. I started talking to Carson. As I did, his body became rigid, and I admonished Ed Mc-Mahon and Severinsen to help me lift Carson and stretch him between two chairs. They looked at me as if I were insane. I said, "Listen to me." They lifted him and stretched him between two chairs, his head and shoulders were on one and his feet were on the other. We let go, and there he was stretched between the two chairs. Oh, one more thing. The prior guest was still on stage. I invited her to come over, and she did so very sheepishly. She was extremely nervous. She was shaking. It was the Oscar-nominated actress Bette Midler. I told her to sit on Johnny. After much encouragement, she sat on Johnny's middle, and lifted her legs off the floor. The audience reacted with a crescendo of applause. We finally got her off of him and lifted him. I counted backwards mentally. Carson told me later he knew what I was going to do, because I had warned him. It felt like a little baby was sitting on him, not a human being. A picture of Midler sitting on Carson hit the centerfold of *Parade Magazine*, the Sunday supplement, and was seen all over the Western world. It is one of the dramatic moments of my career.

The first time I appeared on *The Jimmy Fallon Show*, the producers met me outside in Rockefeller Plaza. I was flattered that they had taken the trouble to meet me and take me up to my dressing room. They said, "Kreskin, would you be interested in seeing the studio?" I said, "of course, I would always like to see the setting before the show." I walked in and I realized why they had asked me this. It was the same studio where I did scores of *Johnny Carson* shows before he had moved to LA. It brought back a flood of memories, and I stood there almost shaken. The director said, "Would you reflect on this when you come on the show?" I said, "You don't know how much I will...I can describe every corner of this studio, things that happened, and what have you."

When the show was over, I reflected on one of the most dramatic incidents of my life, namely the Bette Midler/Carson thing. I said I believed I could do it with Jimmy Fallon. My next appearance was extremely powerful. We talked about Carson and the show and what happened here, and, some 30 or more years later, for the first time I am in the same studio doing the same test.

Fallon walked out to me at center stage. He had great trust in me. Within a few seconds, his eyes were shut. He could not open them. He tried, but he could not. I caused him to make his body extremely rigid, and his musicians, The Roots, lifted him. There he was suspended. Oh no, no one sat on him. A chair was brought behind him, and I stood up on it and ended up putting both my feet on Jimmy Fallon and stood on him as he lay suspended between two chairs. That broadcast was repeated the next night on *The Jimmy Fallon Show* and was discussed the third night on the NBC show. That was the extent of the impact of reliving a past moment of my work with Johnny Carson.

Basically, in the catalepsy test with Carson and Fallon, through mental suggestion, I successful tapped into their full muscular usage, locking their muscles and creating what we call a cataleptic response of complete body rigidity.

4 | Would You Play Cards with Kreskin?

Everybody knows that Kreskin does amazing feats on the stage and on TV, but not many are aware that he also is an "amazing" gambler, too. He once won an unprecedented 22 consecutive blackjack hands—statistically the chances of doing something like that are improbable, bordering on next to impossible. He is so good that his picture is in the rogues' gallery of almost every casino in the Western world. That picture is for those working at the casino to look out for certain players that could possibly be threats to the success of the games, including table games. The real issue is his playing poker, not so much blackjack. Bear in mind that today when blackjack is dealt the cards are pulled out of a shoe. Not only is the dealer not holding the deck of cards in most blackjack games, but the dealer does not even see his or her down cards. However, in the case of poker, not only are the people involved seeing the cards they're holding, they are concentrating on their cards, so their minds are focused.

McCARTY: Kreskin, you are known for your blackjack expertise. What are the secrets of playing blackjack or 21?

KRESKIN: There really are no secrets. The basic formula for succeeding at the game of blackjack is to realize that a deck has a memory. Even multiple decks have a memory. By that I mean that as cards are taken out of the deck into play, the cards remaining offer either a potential plus for the gambler or a negative situation. You are trying with the cards dealt you to get a hand that's as close to 21 as possible, because that's the highest score of combinations and the strongest way of winning. And you don't want to bust, and neither does the dealer. Busting means you're dealt a card that gives you a total over 21. The problem is that the more small cards, say 2 up to 7, there are in the deck, the less chance there is for the dealer to bust. If there are mostly high cards remaining in the deck, the player has the advantage. Card counters try to keep track of low versus high cards that have been played to determine if the deck is now favorable to them. Casinos use multiple decks to make it harder for the card counters. Now that is an oversimplification, because one needs to study the mathematics of the game, which is a story in itself.

The other skill that so many people playing blackjack don't understand is how to handle your finances. You don't increase the amount of money you're betting on a hand, whether it's $2, $5, $10, $50, $100, unless you've already won a couple of hands. So that in essence after a while you're betting not with your own money, but with the house's money. When you are in a losing streak and you're betting your own money, you bet as low an amount as possible, that's going to be your minimum starting bet. One rule, which I advise many people of the game to follow, is if you lose four hands in a row, get up and leave the table. The decks may not be in a "positive" state for you to continue to play without losing more.

Let me give you the strongest, positive advice I could ever give anybody in a gambling setting. As dealers and pit bosses have admitted to me through the years, there are probably only 1 percent of the players who ever follow the rule. You have to have the sense to know when to get your carcass off the chair and leave. If, when you're gambling, you've lost so much that you decide to gather more funds than you originally intended to bet, whatever the game, you're doing something which has been known for hundreds of years—you're chasing your losses. When you do that, you're almost guaranteed to end up in disaster. Remember again the most important truth of all, and that is "casinos were not built by winners."

It has reached a point now where gambling has entered the Internet. Computers are very hypnotic, and, as you know, the passage of time can be very extensive without even realizing that time is going by. It's like being engrossed in a good movie. I can say from experience that you can sit at the computer and suddenly 4 or 5 hours have gone by. I know that the casino companies are going in the direction of Internet gambling. That is going to be a great danger to the players since they will be unaware of the passage of time.

McCARTY: You once won a record 22 straight hands of blackjack. Tell us about that experience.

KRESKIN: In November of 2003 at the Resorts International (Hotel/Casino) in Atlantic City, I won 22 straight hands of blackjack against an 8-deck shoe. I'm told the odds of winning that many hands in a row against a shoe are in the millions.

That night, I had around $200 with me, and eventually lost all but $20. Since I was at a $25-dollar minimum table, I moved to a blackjack table that had a $15-dollar minimum and decided that as soon as my money was gone I'd be out of there. I was tired and long overdue to drive home.

Suddenly, I'm winning hands, so I started to wake up. I started increasing my bets to $100, then $300, and then $500. The crowd around the table grew to more than 200 people. Security guards, players, everyone was screaming on every move. This would never play in a movie—it's not convincing.

Incidentally, I broke a record. A few years earlier, someone had won 18 straight hands...it was me.

I walked away with nearly $10,000. I guess you could say it was a good night.

McCARTY: You were banned from a casino. Why?

KRESKIN: Gambling is not a right; it's a privilege, and as such, it is a privilege that can be denied a person. I have been banned in some casinos. I had gone over to the MGM to visit Siegfried and Roy, the magicians, where they were headlining. They're wonderful people, and their love of animals is something I share.

Since I was asked to wait a bit while Siegfried and Roy changed from their performing clothes, I proceeded to sit down at a casino table. An entourage walked into the casino, right into the center of the pit. I was sitting there quietly, and they approached me. I have to say in retrospect it was like having flashbacks of seeing *The Godfather*. The guy that was talking to me almost looked like the late Marlon Brando... it threw me. He said, "Kreskin, you are not to play here. You can approach any game of chance within 8 or 10 feet, but you are not to play." They banned me. I was banned, not because I was winning, but just because of who I am.

McCARTY: You have gambled at famous international casinos. Is there much of a difference between casinos in the United States and those abroad?

KRESKIN: A major incident took place in Aruba about 10 years ago. Of course, Aruba is a remote area. The people who came to see me were not the people who live on the island, but people from Europe and America, who went to see my shows. The natives were not too aware of who I was and I played quietly. I usually left when I'd won a couple of hundred dollars. This story is one that I have never previously told. My road manager, who at that time was Chris Light, has described it to be like a scene out of an old Tyrone Power movie.

My last night in Aruba, after my show closed, I walked into a casino at another location and started playing. I walked in with exactly $37 with which to play. It was late, but the casino was remaining open after its normal closing time. I asked why, and they said that if they have action they keep the game going. I was the only one playing. Other casino people were standing behind their tables and watching. I had nothing but $100 chips on the table. It was like a game, a board game, because the chips didn't mean anything after awhile.

My road manager would come in every half hour, and I would give him a dirty look, meaning get out of here, don't shake the bush. I finally left at 3:00 in the morning, which is way beyond closing time. I had to fly out at something like 6:00 or 7:00 the next morning. I just packed. I didn't go to bed.

I called the entertainment director at the hotel and said you should see what I'm carrying on me. They had paid me in cash. It was $22,400. That was what I was packing into my jacket pockets. It looked like I had a tremendous weight problem. If I'd been searched, I'm sure they would have thought I was a drug baron. There was an incredible excitement about the whole scenario.

McCARTY: What was Nevada gambling like in its infamous early years?

KRESKIN: Bill Harrah and Pappy Smith founded Reno and put it on the map with their two casinos. They created the practice of bussing people in so that people who didn't drive could come in for the day and then go back.

Pappy Smith had a philosophy for all the dealers—"Let them leave winners." He didn't mean that everybody left winners. He just didn't want people leaving having suffered serious losses. He wanted them to come back. In those days, he would go up to people or have some of his people go up to them and say, "Do you have enough money to go home?" "No, I flew here, or took a bus, and I'm too low on cash." He'd make sure they got home. They never forgot him because he had the personal touch.

The bottom line is have your limits set ahead of time, and when those limits are gone don't think that suddenly a star has come out with Judy Garland sitting on it and you're going to make it back. Come back the next time.

Don't you think that rule is kind of pertinent in this day and age with all the casinos around? I'm not knocking the casinos. I'm supportive of them. They have been good to me. They pay my wages, my fees, and they've been darn good fees. I've had good tie-ins with them.

FINAL CHAPTER 4 THOUGHTS BY KRESKIN

KRESKIN: John Romero said something interesting about me. He is a very prominent authority in the gaming industry. He is not one of those people who just write books on how to play to gamble or how to win.

He instead writes for the industry as a consultant all over the world on tournaments and special gaming events.

Romero knew about my skill in manipulating playing cards and had seen me in performances as a thought reader using playing cards. He said, "Kreskin is the most dangerous man in the world with a deck of cards. The casinos would rather deal to Willy Sutton." Willy Sutton was the legendary bank robber in the early half of the century to whom was attributed the statement, "I rob banks because that's where the money is."

5 | Love and Hypnosis

You fall when you get struck by Cupid's arrow. You fall in love, and your world changes. Everything seems more special; life is suddenly brighter and happier. Love is magical, sometimes even hypnotic, but can you hypnotize someone into loving you? We asked these questions of the heart to Kreskin.

McCARTY: Have you ever used your powers for seduction?

KRESKIN: (Laughs.) If I *did* use them for seductive reasons, I would say that I didn't. So I am going to say, no I haven't. I really feel people in sexual situations often give off very strong vibrations that you often can't detect. You could almost call them telepathic.

McCARTY: Did you equate hypnosis with love?

KRESKIN: Actually my equating hypnosis with love is not of my own origin. I have simply amplified something that the legendary psychoanalyst Sigmund Freud espoused over a century ago; namely that the people in love, in deep love, in passionate love, have a pretty similar relationship to people who are under hypnotic influence.

Freud was introduced to hypnosis by Dr. Josef Breur, who felt that people in this special mystical state could better remember details from past experiences. This would help Freud and get to the early seat of the emotional problem. But there were some unnerving experiences occurring with analysts, doctors, and therapists. Sometimes patients, particularly women, would lunge forward out of their hypnotic condition and try to embrace the therapist, like they became "in love" for that moment. Or more, it was suggested that there were sexual factors involved in the relationship, and the "transference" of a special quality was building up between the therapist and the patient. Freud abandoned hypnosis not only because he was a rather inept hypnotist, but he found it was not necessary for what he sought to accomplish. Even without hypnosis the same relationships built up between the patient and the therapist.

When you fall in love, you set aside many of your barriers. You don't really stop to analyze things like your assignments for tomorrow, what you're going to do about that chronic postnasal problem, how you will get your homework done, and so on. No, you find the person you're with is beginning to take on a mysterious and, yes, rather unscientific relationship with you. After all, would simply being touched ordinarily arouse erotic feelings? Not necessarily, except look at the induction that you've gone through. No, you are not under the control of a hypnotist; you are not being told to relax and listen to slumberous words; you are not watching a rotating disc.

There are other tools that are helping to bring about an extremely romantic, noncritical frame of mind and body. The quietness of eating dinner with soft lighting; the occasional touching of two glasses may symbolize unconsciously something that's clicking between you. You may even take advantage of another way to harmonize with your partner by dancing with them, especially to romantic music—the swaying, the motion, the fact that the bodies are in synchronization. This, along with the thoughts between each other, and the words, tend to magnetically draw a person closer. What is interesting is that unlike traditional hypnosis, both partners are becoming mesmerized. I have said for many years, "It's a wise hypnotist who knows who is hypnotizing whom." In my opinion, in many cases the hypnotist is as much hypnotically influenced as the subject.

McCARTY: How does suggestion work into all of this?

KRESKIN: The key is suggestion. People who are apparently hypnotized are responding to the power of suggestion. They are not really in a trance. They are not really asleep. In fact, they're not in any special altered condition at all. I stress this in spite of what most stage hypnotists might suggest, let alone doctors, psychologists, and so on, who propose to put people in a trance and activate some psychotherapy. The trance is BS. There is no trance. It is the fact that under certain conditions we can be so convinced of a set of ideas that they can bypass our reasoning. The people who are described as hypnotized are responding to ideas without analyzing them. Remember, when mommy kisses little Billy on the forehead when he walks in crying because he has hit his head, Mommy simply says, "Let me kiss the booboo and it will go away." Suddenly Billy stops crying and goes out to play. He is so reassured by her remarks, trusting them, that he ignores the pain that is still there. By ignoring it he lessens the pain.

McCARTY: Can you give an example of this?

KRESKIN: In the same way, is it not remarkable that we can watch a horror movie or read a Stephen King novel in a warm room and still get goose bumps? Do we ever stop to think how remarkable it is that the way we think can alter even the surface of our skin? If we watched the movie and kept dissecting it, thinking about the camera men behind the camera, the people off to the side, the way the movie's structured, we would not envelope ourselves in the story, and horror or fear would not touch us.

But then again, a fictional story can cause us to cry, such as when you watch a tear-jerker motion picture. I, myself, can think of *An Affair to Remember* and cannot help but be in tears at the end of the movie. So in spite of common sense telling you that this is only a movie, it's not really happening, no one had died, and so on, we still react. By enveloping ourselves within the story, we don't stop to analyze. We've trapped ourselves sufficiently with the dialogue, the movement of the characters, and the music. We are responding in the same way as a supposedly hypnotized person who's been told that they're watching a sad movie and within a minute the subject is crying on the stage. In the same way, when you're falling in love, you have dropped many of your guards, including your critical thinking.

Know if you're going to get more deeply involved with another, speak the person's language, move the way they do, use some of the key words that they like to use when they're expressing themselves. Not overly so, but from time to time, as it touches on greater meaning within them. If you find that when you touch them, their expression is comfortable and you get the feeling that they're comfortable, then that area of touching can be repeated from time to time.

And if you're really a master and fully at home with this process, you can remember the music that was played either at dinner or some particularly meaningful moment and reuse that music; play it again. After all, it tends to reawaken some of those same feelings, like a post-hypnotic suggestion. Let yourself move with the flow, and neither of you really leads the other. What you're doing is emotionally dancing together. Then you guide each other simultaneously, until you really experience a true romance, where for the minutes and hours reasoning and analyzing are not important. But if you don't feel that way, or you don't feel the way your partner does, you're only conning yourself. No, you don't need any pendulums or watches or rotating discs or a glaring eye, but sometimes you do need a hypnotic focal point. In this case, take advantage of what has a romantic symbolism, something in the shape of a heart, a box of candy, a broach, or a simple picture. Oh, yes, I repeat there is a gigantic similarity between hypnosis, true hypnosis, and love, true love.

McCARTY: Can one determine if someone is lying when he or she says 'I Love You'?

KRESKIN: In modern society today it has been found by many analytical researchers that one of the most difficult skills to teach is how to detect if someone is lying. Perhaps as little as 1 to 5 percent of humanity can ever learn this. Part of the reason is that we've become basically so dishonest in some of our expressions and comments to others that lying has become a common skill, so natural that there is no guilt felt anymore. The polygraph or lie-detector test doesn't really work unless a person has emotional reasons for holding back on something, so lying is too much an intensive part of our culture to be detected. As a lover you are in an uncritical frame of mind. So, too, is the person you are enraptured with, so you tend not to think in a critical way. Let me have you understand this...if you're going to analyze whether or not a person's lying to you when you're in love, then you'd better step away from the experience, get out of it, because you do not have the same frame of mind as the person has that you're with.

That's right, there's a price to pay, because love is an expensive experience. Oh, you might later on look back and analyze things when it is all over and you are not with the person. One way would be to mentally relive some of the experience, listening to what you remember, including the sound of the person's voice. Is there something strangely different? Also, is there any feeling of uneasiness that you experienced when that person said they loved you? That could be a signal that all is not what it's cracked up to be. But remember this, love is a two-way experience. Whatever is put into that experience is as much your responsibility as the other person's, so don't play the blame game. Keep in mind the next time you're hypnotizing your partner, if it's really working, that partner is also mesmerizing you...of such is love.

6 | The Great Houdini

KNOWN AROUND THE WORLD AS HARRY HOUDINI, HIS REAL NAME WAS Ehrich Weiss, born in Budapest, Hungary, on March 24, 1874. Houdini's magic career wasn't very successful to say the least. He performed at dime museums, sideshows, and the circus. He focused on traditional card tricks, billing himself as the "King of Cards." Then he began experimenting with escape acts, and the rest, as they say, is history.

McCARTY: Harry Houdini was a professional magician by the age of 20. He started out doing card tricks, and then moved on to doing vanishing acts. By the time he was 25, he was a worldwide sensation because of his escapes. How would you rate him as a magician?

KRESKIN: When we think of magic and magicians today, we often think of Houdini. Such was not the case in the 1930s, certainly not in the 1920s or the 1910s, those last two decades during Houdini's heyday. Indeed, it wasn't until perhaps some 20 years after Houdini's death that people really started to think of Houdini as a great magician. The truth of the matter is he was a second-rate magician—let me correct myself—a third-rate magician. He was terrible in handling magical effects, was not a good sleight-of-hand artist, and was extraordinarily clumsy in most of the magic that he performed. I could never figure out why my dad, who loved magic and knew nothing of the secrets of the art, was never impressed with the appearances that he saw of Houdini in vaudeville. He had revered Howard Thurston, who in my dad's mind was the greatest magician he had ever seen.

McCARTY: That is surprising because when people think of Harry Houdini they think of his magic, as well as his escapes. Please elaborate.

KRESKIN: Before people read this and become irate, don't misunderstand me. Whatever we say about his skill in traditional conjuring, Houdini was unquestionably the greatest escape artist of all time.

There is not a single performer of escapes today that can even begin to remotely approach the achievements of Houdini. In that specialized area of conjuring, Houdini is synonymous with the word. In the last few years of his life he fulfilled a lifelong dream. He finally got to do something he had wanted to do for many years, and that is a full-evening stage magic show; that is, a 2-hour or more performance in which great magic and mysterious magic is presented with illusionary qualities, such as disappearances, changes of one person for another, the passage of an object disappearing from one part of the stage to another, all these and a number of other specific areas intrinsic to the true visual beauty of magic, the stage illusionist.

Houdini divided his performances into three areas. The show began with traditional magic. It was followed by escape work and climaxed with his exposure of fake mediums. The last two parts of the show really saved the program, for Houdini's sense of stage theatrics in which romance and mystery could be created in vanishing a ringing alarm clock or causing a person to disappear from a cabinet simply was not in Houdini's makeup. The reason is that the skill that he was truly able to capture was that of challenges. After all, where did he make his name? Escaping from restraints, handcuffs, being tied up, being placed in a cabinet, being placed in a sack, hanging upside down over a square with hundreds of people looking, hanging by his feet as he proceeded to escape from a straight jacket, and his great stage escape, a Chinese water torture cell, when he was lowered with his legs in stocks into a glass cabinet filled with water. The curtains were closed in front of the cabinet as one assistant stood with an axe and a second-hand dial of a clock started moving around, the audience wondering how many minutes could he manage to hold his breath.

If he had trouble, how long did he have before the escape had to be successful? Houdini admonished his audience to hold their breath when the mystery started, and the audience was enchanted. There you see the genius of Houdini. He would come into town after town and bring up on stage the local locksmith or perhaps some law enforcement official. Whatever they were, they brought a restraint that they had designed which that they hoped would prevent him from executing an escape. Many of the townspeople flocked to the theatre to see their local locksmith and see if he could prevent Houdini from escaping. Houdini would be handcuffed or tied or put in a chest or a box, and usually the box or chest was put into a cabinet and the curtains were closed.

Behind that cabinet was going on some mysterious phenomena of which the audience could never expect to understand. It was during that time that the audience would hear music, while Houdini was trying to escape. Understand that this was vaudeville. The usual acts had only 10 to 15 minutes a turn, or if they were the headliners, maybe 20 minutes. Some big stars like Al Jolson might get a half hour. But could Houdini always be relied upon to escape in the exact amount of time? No. Sometimes, he would go beyond his expected time and 15, 20, or 30 minutes may have gone by. That's right. What was happening on stage? Nothing. It was all in the imagination of the audience, who at times were at the edge of their seats. Some would be on the verge of panic, screaming out loud to get him out, and the guard with the axe and perhaps the other assistant both continued to stand outside the cabinet. When Houdini escaped, pandemonium often broke out within the audience...from the relief from the tension.

McCARTY: If Harry Houdini wasn't much of a magician, was he more of an entertainer?

KRESKIN: Houdini knew how to play his crowd. This kind of entertainment and skill would be hard to employ in today's day and age.

Not just because of the MTV-type limited attention span, but because so little in television is live. If live, there would be no opportunity to go over time, should the escape not go as readily planned. Houdini enjoyed looking at comic books or trivia magazines. If he had a flashlight he could sit inside the darkened cabinet or chest and read and kill time, until he felt the audience was ready for him to walk out.

McCARTY: It was said that he made a full-grown elephant disappear from the stage by dropping it into a swimming pool. Can you give some more insight into this magic act?

KRESKIN: For a short period of time, Houdini appeared at the Hippodrome in New York. The months he was there he had gigantic audiences developed basically through word-of-mouth. Bear in mind his performance was not being filmed; it was not on television; it was not being made into a movie. So the only witnesses were those who attended the show. He did one remarkable piece of stage magic, the legendary illusion known as The Vanishing Elephant. Houdini stood on stage while an animal trainer walked out an elephant and guided it into a long cabinet and closed the doors. Music played and then one door was opened. It didn't give a completely clear view of the inside of this long cabinet, but from what the audience could see, there was no elephant in sight. What was disconcerting is that two men had wheeled the cabinet onto the stage before the elephant climbed in. After the elephant "disappeared," 12 men wheeled the cabinet off the stage. It was not one of the great illusions in magic history. The fact that the illusion was done over a swimming pool so everybody knew there could be no trap doors is not the point. The significance is that so few wheeled the cabinet out and so many wheeled the cabinet off stage.

There are many commentaries as to why Houdini's escapes so enraptured audiences. First of all, they had never seen anything like this before. In the days of vaudeville, which was live entertainment, he was challenging those who came forward to restrain him, but in the same breath he was risking—or apparently risking—his safety and at times his life. When a tightrope walker walks across a wire, he is certainly challenging all the laws of gravity and balance as the average person knows it, but he's competing with himself. No one has put him in that position. Houdini somehow was using his gift to overcome a physical adversary. He was being confronted with the ingeniousness of a person or a group who plotted to stymie him. It was not unusual for him to enter cities, go to its jail, and receive headlines the next day that he had escaped from his jail cell.

To my way of thinking, Houdini's greatest piece of magical escape was the underwater escape. He realized the impact it had on audiences. A milk can large enough for him to submerge his body was brought on stage. He climbed into it, water was poured in, and a lid was screwed on. It was clear to the audience that only a certain amount of air was available for him to survive. An even greater underwater escape was The Upside Down Escape. His feet were locked in stocks, and he was lowered head first into a cabinet that had glass fronts. It was filled with water, and before the curtains were closed the audience saw the lid of the cabinet being locked. Everybody watching could not help but gasp at how—even for seconds—he could maintain the ability to escape. For years it was the climax of many of his vaudeville turns.

But in the challenge area, probably nothing publicity wise could compare with his underwater escape, where he was handcuffed, stood on a bridge or a boat, and jumped into a river while reporters and viewers stood by the bridge's edge or the edge of the shoreline waiting for him to come forward, often with handcuffs in one hand, but obviously surviving and able to swim to a boat or to the land for help. One famous story took place in Detroit and was depicted in the Tony Curtis/Janet Leigh movie *Houdini*. They broke a hole in the ice of the frozen river, and the shackled Houdini was lowered into it. When he finally escaped from his shackles, he found out that the current had driven him farther downstream, so his further challenge was to find the space of air between the water and the ice itself, until he found the opening to free himself.

It is one of his greatest escape stories, and it followed him around the world. The only problem is it never took place. The day that he did the escape it was so warm in the state of Michigan there was no ice to be found in the Detroit River. But we must remember that television and radio were not as immediately available, and by coloring the story he created his own legend. But let's not deny him the basic stunt of escaping from a cabinet, a chest, or simply handcuffs and being thrown into a river. The question, which many people ask, is did he invent this escape?

Well, that's an interesting story because another magician was stopped from doing the underwater escape. He was not an escape artist. He was a very fine illusionist, whom I remember seeing as a kid when I was 9 years old and then a few years after that, doing a shorter turn in movie theatres. The magician I speak of is Harry Blackstone. Blackstone looked like a magician with bushy hair. He didn't look like an escape artist. When you saw him, you thought he had to be a magician, but he garnered publicity by escaping after being thrown into lakes tied up or encased—and Houdini stopped him. In those days of vaudeville, there was an organization that tried to protect performers, although I doubt if they were extraordinarily successful. They had certain codes, and Houdini sought to stop Blackstone from performing the stunt because he, Harry Houdini, had originated it. That's all Blackstone had to hear. Blackstone took a crew of people to a warehouse in a certain town to show the chest that he had used in the escape. Since these were officials from the vaudeville organization, it was important that he be able to reveal that this chest had been dated years before Houdini ever did escapes. When they arrived at the warehouse, much to Blackstone's chagrin, there was no chest there. This left a bad impression in the minds of the vaudeville officials. The bottom line was Blackstone was advised never to do the Houdini stunt again, and so ended the story.

In the years that went by, Houdini continued to do the underwater escape. Others may have as well, but he couldn't stop everybody. A few years after Houdini died in 1926 a friend of Bess and Harry Houdini's, a famous show business mentalist, Joseph Dunninger, came to visit Bess. She'd always remained friendly to people in show business, and when Dunninger inquired about materials in the cellar, Bess told him, "Joe, go downstairs and take whatever you want." He found books and other items. Houdini had vast collections, and often stuff was thrown here and there in piles. But he had nothing to take it in, and he was taking a number of packages. Bess told him if he could find a box, just take it and pack it up, which Dunninger did. As he was dragging the chest up the stairs, a clanking sound was heard, and Bess ran to the cellar stairs and Dunninger got to the top and said there's something wrong with this trunk. He tilted it, and there was a metal flap on the bottom of the side of the trunk. One side of it had been loose, but it had identified the owner on the side of the chest. It was clear that the owner was Blackstone the magician. This was the chest that Blackstone had used before Houdini had ever done the underwater escape. End of story.

McCARTY: Cool. Very creepy, please go on.

KRESKIN: As I have said, in Victorian days there was much greater belief in a person coming back from the dead. One of the ways of fighting vampirism was to bury the body face down in case it came to life and tried to crawl itself out of the grave.

Houdini, of course, was famous for escaping under all conditions, and one of the classic incidents in his life, which is rarely talked about, was in later years he decided to show how he could survive in a coffin with a limited amount of air. In Hollywood he was placed in a coffin, lowered into the ground, some 6 feet of earth was poured over the grave, and there Houdini lay...except he became his own worst enemy.

It gradually hit him that this was the position that his beloved mother, to whom he was immensely close to, was now lying, as were others, and this is where he would be when he finally passed away. This caused Houdini to rapidly lose oxygen. He eventually somehow broke through the lid of the box and crawled through what had to be a mountainous weight of earth. When his hand appeared out of the earth, they pulled him out, literally to save his life. He never again even remotely considered being buried alive for an escape or demonstration.

Indeed, in the famous stunt that he did where he was supposed to be debunking a certain mystic as fraudulent, he showed that he, too, could enter a boxlike coffin where there was limited oxygen and do it without some special mystical state. However, it was not under earth, but in this case it was underwater in a swimming pool of the sports club in New York. Men simply held the coffin underwater until they got a signal from Houdini to bring the coffin back to the surface and open it.

Walter Gibson, the great writer and creator of *The Shadow,* was an authority on magic and mysticism and a very close associate of Houdini. Walter felt he didn't debunk anybody, for in order to maintain the calmness of staying in the coffin until he signaled he needed to get more oxygen, he was doing basically what the mystic did—suspending the speed of the metabolism of his body that would use up energy and oxygen.

McCARTY: Did he make movies, too?

KRESKIN: We hear about Houdini making movies during the silent era and wonder why such movies are not seen from time to time. The answer is very simple. Purchase one of them. They're available. I challenge you to sit through an entire movie. Houdini was not a movie actor. He certainly could not handle himself in front of a camera, and, to put it mildly, the movies were dreadful. He lost a lot of money. He didn't realize that magic and movies simply do not work. This is the danger that the stage illusionist has facing him today, for anytime they use camera trickery, or altering of shooting angles, or editing, and it finally leaks out—as so often it does—it will tend to jeopardize or contaminate whatever they do in public again.

There were two causes for the demise of Houdini's escape act. One, of course, was the death of vaudeville. The other things that helped to kill Houdini's career were Douglas Fairbanks and *The Perils of Pauline.* Every week, someone could go to the movies and watch these devil-may-care adventurers in horrendous conditions where they were tied and trapped on the verge of being blown up, burnt, or being run over by a train, and the next week we saw them escaping. In the early days of movie attendance, the public did not have a true understanding of camera work and movie making, and, in a sense, what they saw Douglas Fairbanks doing was the same thing that Houdini did, except in a dramatic story, so it took the edge off of Houdini's escapery.

So for all people knew, they were seeing the same thing, except not live. It is for this very reason that magic in a movie certainly does not have the mystique, the mystery, the mystification that one can possibly experience seeing an illusionist in person. Closest to that is a television broadcast that is presented live and unedited. We can somehow imagine and feel what it would be like to be there in person. And yet today—and I've said this many times—no matter how skillful an escape artist is, it would be extraordinarily difficult for him to build a full reputation as the master of escapes. Why? Because unlike most other forms of magic, escapery is built on suspense and danger, the danger being that the artist may not release him or herself from the restraints and could be hurt or possibly killed. Well, they have an immense, modern problem facing us, actually two. Much of television is recorded ahead of time, before it's seen by the public. The shows are done as if they were live. Yes, the shows don't have to be edited, and you could be seeing exactly what took place. So, if you see an escape artist on a variety show, yes, you're seeing it just as if you were there in person, but—and listen to me—because even a youngster has an unconscious intuitiveness about this. If the show is not live, but has been taped, you have the interest of seeing it the way the audience saw it, but you haven't the slightest real suspense as to whether he succeeds or not, because had he failed, been injured, or worse than that, we all know it would have been on a television news show or on a cable station within minutes after it took place. Heck, a funny line made by Jay Leno or Jimmy Fallon is often on cable news 2 or 3 hours before the public sees the taped show. So, we intuitively know the escape has to succeed. If there were a tragedy, it would be news, and that's killed the very strongest element, the unknown success or failure of the dangerous stunt.

McCARTY: There have been many escape artists since Houdini. Why do you think there is such a mystique about him even today?

KRESKIN: The answer was given me by Walter B. Gibson, who knew Houdini probably as well as any person related to show business could. I became a close friend of Walter's and have some 20 to

30 hours recorded with him. Much consists of intimate glimpses into the real Houdini.

How did Houdini become such a legend? He wasn't thought of as a magician when alive. Oh, he was referred to by magicians, but if you look at the writings of authors in those days, even magicians, and they rated the top magicians of the period, many of them never even listed Houdini. He was a novelty act, and a very fine novelty act, but after he died, occasionally an author, a writer, or a newspaper man would have to fill space so Houdini's magic would be included.

Once in a while, Walter Gibson would introduce a story about Houdini. After all, he may have written about an evangelist, or a gangster, or a successful golfer, or an inventor, or someone in town, who found a safe haven for a certain kind of animal. Houdini became an interesting subject for a Sunday story. He captured the imagination of the reader. People read newspapers every day and spent hours pouring over them on a Sunday. And, as Walter Gibson admitted to me, "Kreskin, these stories had to be elaborated upon, they needed to be embellished, and to write another story one had to add a little bit more, and add more material than the previous story."

If all the articles of the stunts and the accomplishments of Houdini were put together, Houdini would have had to live 10 lifetimes to have achieved them all. Many of them that were written about never took place or were described in a way other than how he actually accomplished them. This was the literary license that an author uses when he wants to mix fantasy with legend, and even Walter Gibson was a writer of fact and a writer of fiction. After all, he did create *The Shadow*.

So, if another movie were done today on the life of Houdini—and many times it's been promised—it would take extraordinarily skillful writing and skillful acting. It would take ingenuity in the writing to maintain interest, because in truth it may be that the legend of Houdini is far more fascinating than the real story.

McCARTY: Did he really work as a spy for Scotland Yard?

KRESKIN: A book was published which promulgated the idea that Houdini worked for Scotland Yard. It just does not seem to click.

When I think of the multitude of hours I spent with Walter Gibson discussing the behind-the-scenes personal life, whims, and prejudices of Houdini, Walter would have brought this fact up immediately. Do I think Houdini would have kept this information from Gibson? Not on your life! His ego was too big.

McCARTY: In exposing fake mediums was Houdini in the same breath exposing great stage illusions and as a result breaking the golden rule of magic? Or was he doing a public service? Do you think it is ironic that Houdini, while he was debunking mediums, personally felt he could talk to the dead?

KRESKIN: This was not really a major issue in Houdini's attack on spiritualistic mediums. As the vaudeville era began to wane, and vaudeville theatres began to close down, and movie theatres came into the forefront, it became clear that Houdini needed to seek other arenas for his work. His escapes did not fit into much of the current scene. Houdini had lost his mother, with whom he was very close, and in some ways he hoped he could communicate with her. It was pretty clear to him that the mediums who were flourishing were fraudulent, but they had existed for many years.

After a while, he found in attending séances in the dark that ghosts seemed to be appearing and trumpets, which supposedly carried the voices of the spirit, moved around the table. It got him annoyed, because it didn't take much to see through the trickery. In 1920, for about the first 6 months or so, he attended scores of séances. Eventually, in a few years he would set out to appear as a professional ghost breaker. A pivotal point took place in 1922. Houdini and his wife, Bess, were joined in Atlantic City by Lady Conan Doyle and her husband, the legendary Arthur Conan Doyle, who, of course, created the greatest fictional detective of them all, Sherlock Holmes.

The Doyles believed in spirit communication, and Lady Doyle apparently went into a trance while she was sitting holding a pencil over a pad. While she was in the trance, her hand started to move and scribble a message at a high speed. Inevitably, there was a message from Houdini's mother. Bess had met with Lady Doyle the night before and given her some information on how Houdini would lay his head on his mother's breast to hear her heart beat, but she did not tell Lady Doyle two important facts: one, that his mother did not speak English, and the other, that June 18th was her birthday, a day that Houdini kept sacrosanct, literally holy. Hearing these facts in the ramblings that Doyle came through with upset Houdini and gave him cause for strong emotional angst. Eventually, Houdini realized that there was obviously passionate interest and for many a belief in spiritualism. He saw the misinterpretation of a lot that took place, and also he saw through the fakery of many mediums. With this blossomed a new direction for him, the public exposure of fake mediums. No, he was not exposing the stage illusions of the great theatrical performers, but just the maneuvers and tactics that were done in the dark for the gullible sitter. It was a way of attracting great attention, and Houdini was a master of theater.

He had his ear tuned to the media and what would intrigue the public. Indeed, Walter Gibson mentioned to me one particular gathering in Philadelphia at a magician's club. It was a group which included Houdini. The conversations were interrupted when news came of a tragic train accident that had just taken place. Everyone then went on with the meeting. But not too many minutes later, Walter and others saw Houdini get up and then quietly leave. There really was no explanation.

The answer came the next day. Houdini found his way to a location near where the train accident had taken place and proceeded to lie down on the tracks, his head and shoulder on one track, his legs dangling over the other. Since the original accident had resulted in deaths, this dramatic symbolism of the disaster got into some of the newspapers. Such was the way Houdini's mind worked. I could tell you that today he would have a full time job on one of the "reality" shows on television.

By 1923, Houdini was lecturing to students, occasionally at universities, on spirit mediums, etc. The magazine *The Scientific American* had an award for psychic phenomenon if its experts would endorse any such demonstrations as genuine. Houdini took advantage of the trend by posting a $5,000 reward to any psychic who could produce physical phenomena, which Houdini could not duplicate by natural means. Understand that when he says physical phenomena he's not speaking of telepathy, thought transference, or hypnotic demonstrations; he's talking about phenomena such as psychokinetic effects, the breaking of an object, or spirit possession, such as tables moving by apparently a special force, including possibly the spirit world—activity that could be clearly embracing some strange physical phenomena.

If you think about this, this may not even necessitate that the medium was fraudulent, but the fact is that Houdini still could duplicate it. That doesn't mean he'd be doing it the same way as the medium, but that specific was not made clear in Houdini's challenge. After all, he was looking for publicity. Magicians have through the years duplicated mind over matter, especially in the early days by putting a dollar bill on a table and causing the dollar bill to move around the table, when it was clear there were no wires or anything attached to it. God forbid anyone turned over the bill and saw that sticking to the bottom of the bill was a live cockroach, but such was used to duplicate mediumistic phenomena. In time, Houdini became part of the Scientific American Team, although he was not popular with all of its members, because certain ones had embraced spiritualism and believed in spiritualistic phenomenon.

McCARTY: Let's talk about the famous case of Margery the Boston Medium versus Houdini.

KRESKIN: What follows is a true story that could be made into a movie, and I'm prepared to follow through with that conviction, as I think done in the right way it could be a tour de force. The bottom line is that in 1924, just 2 years before Houdini's death, he met probably his greatest competitor. She was from Boston and had become a legend in a short amount of time through the séances that she held. She was known throughout the area as "The Blonde Witch of Boston."

Her séances were held for the elite of Boston. After all, she was not a poor individual, but part of Boston's society. Her name was Mena Crandon, and she was the wife of a very distinguished surgeon. She didn't perform for money. She was an elegant, sensual individual who produced automatic writing in many languages; caused objects to appear in the séance room, including a living pigeon; caused tables to rise and bells to ring; and furniture to move all over the floor. She produced spirit messages and did an unusual test where a bucket of melted paraffin was placed near her, and don't you know when the lights were brought up later the spirits had dipped their hands into the paraffin, leaving paraffin gloves, because after their hands were in the paraffin they then dipped their hands in cold water and then dematerialized, so the spirit left the glove but the glove kept its shape. On and on went her demonstrations. Even in one story, *The New York Times* reported that "Margery, the Boston Medium passes all scientific tests" and that "scientists could find no trickery."

Of course, this upset Houdini immensely, especially when he was informed that the committee was on the verge of giving Margery the prize of legitimacy. Houdini demanded to attend one of her séances. Here was an elegantly styled Canadian woman, an accomplished musician, who had a very beautiful body. When she allowed herself to be searched before a séance for any gimmicks, she had no false modesty. In fact, when she was in the séance room, she wore a very flimsy outfit with nothing under it.

In the 1920s, talk about sensuality, heck there was a lot more aroused than spirits in her séances. When Houdini attended the séance, he found that it was one of her conditions that it be in total darkness. Some mediums were content with dim light; not Margery. There was a very famous bell box that was placed between Houdini's feet. It was a rectangular box made of very thin wood, and it contained an electric bell with dry cell batteries. The top had a wooden flap. When the flap was pressed in slightly, the metal contacts joined and you would hear the bell ring. This box was supposedly placed far enough away from the medium's body that the only thing that could make it ring would be either a spirit force or some special energy that would emanate from her. Houdini was sharp enough to realize that even though people were holding her arms and so forth in position, that she was moving her leg around and that slowly she was gaining enough proximity to the box that she was setting it off.

There were many standard tactics that mediums used to release the grip of people holding their arms in position, to the point that if they released one arm to scratch their head and put that arm back to the person who was supposed to be holding it they could be using the hand of the other arm. In the dark, it would leave the impression that one was holding the hand of one arm and the other person was holding the elbow of the other arm, when it was the same arm, leaving one arm free. In the dark, one's perception is easily tricked. Houdini "exposed" to the officials at follow-up meetings what he thought was the trickery, and a raging controversy ensued as others defended her as legitimate and pointed out that he really had no proof that she was doing what he said in the dark.

The turning point was that Houdini had his assistant, James Collins, design a cabinet or box which would humanely control the medium's hands and feet, and this cabinet was built. It was deep enough so a person could be sitting in a chair, the lid sloped in the front, and there was a circular hole for the neck. On the sides were two openings so the medium could thrust her hands, which were controlled by the sitters. In essence, she was in a makeshift cabinet that was designed to control the position of her hands and her feet.

When they met at the next séance meeting, the bell box was placed on a table in front of the controlled cabinet. Margery was put in the box, and the lights were turned out, and the bell rang. When the lights were turned on again, it was discovered that the cabinet's lid had been moved, some thin strips of brass had been moved, and the lid was loose, and that Margery could have stood up in the cabinet, pushed up the lid, and then simply bent forward knocking the bell box with her forehead, forcing it to ring, never having to use her hands, simply standing leaning forward and using her head to accomplish this.

It's interesting Houdini reported that when the séance was over, he found the medium, Margery, and her husband measuring the diameter of the hole for the neck in the cabinet. Houdini claims that to be the case. There was no one else to back up the statement. The next séance was a critical one, for Houdini's assistant had secured the cabinet and there were no loose parts that could be opened. Margery was encased in the cabinet, and within a short amount of time, a blistering series of shouts took place, and Margery was suddenly taken over by her deceased brother, Walter.

In a trance, the spirit apparently took her over and snarled, "Houdini, you are very clever indeed, but it won't work. I suppose it was an accident those things were left in the cabinet?" What then followed was a screeching argument because Margery explained that in the cabinet was a ruler and she accused Houdini or his people of putting it in there to discredit her. After all, using her mouth the ruler might have been extended out to move objects. In the days of fake mediums extension rods were sometimes used. Walter, her spirit guide, shouted, "Houdini, you god damn son of a bitch, get to hell out of here and never come back. If you don't, I will."

Obviously, in the end, it became a controversy between Margery and Houdini. Houdini denied that he had his assistant or that he himself had dropped this ruler into the cabinet, and intimated that Margery or her people had smuggled it into the box. The controversy continued, and of course the followers of Margery attacked those who sought to expose her, but that is not the real point of the matter. The question that ensues is not whether she was a trickster or legitimate. Most people would assume that she was using some form of trickery. But she had amassed such a following and really had pretty much called Houdini's shots. Would she have been foolish enough to hide a ruler inside a cabinet, since later on such could be easily discovered when her séances were completed? The guessing match continued, even years after they were gone. Certainly the suspicion that Houdini planted this is not hard to believe, because he would do anything to discredit a medium. Had she simply continued with another séance and nothing happened, he would have been left mumbling and rambling, but the finding of a ruler would be, for him, the proof of her dishonesty, her fraudulence.

With the research I've done and my conversations with Walter B. Gibson, and Gibson reflecting on the people he knew, and the person he knew best, Harry Houdini, there's little doubt in my mind that Houdini framed Margery and planted the ruler in the cabinet. He couldn't beat her at her own game. He had to do it on his terms, which was cheating.

Bear in mind that already Houdini had been gaining publicity in different cities by appearing as a lecturer on spiritualism. Walter

Gibson attended a number of his appearances in former vaudeville theatres in Philadelphia, and there were times when members of the audience were standing, shouting accusations about mediums and arguing amongst themselves. The audience didn't realize that these people were hired by Houdini to cause the commotion. Houdini also had an assistant named Rose Mackenberg acting as a detective. Since he was now making a career coming into cities to expose mediums, he had Mackenberg as his advance agent. She would travel ahead of him, sometimes weeks or even and months before, and attend séances in the cities where he would later be playing.

When he came into town, he knew full well that the mediums would attend his shows. He alerted the press, often having an exclusive agreement with one newspaper, which would put him in the position to fan the flames of the story. He knew that the mediums were in the audience; he would be advised that they were and where they were sitting. So, in the middle of his lecture, he would then point to the mediums and make accusations. He made some reprehensible statements about what took place in the séance room and the fact they were using luminous garbs and phosphorescent costumes, etc. Some of the mediums would stand up, shouting back that Houdini was a liar, he was dishonest. That's all he needed.

The press was there waiting for their story, and in many cases out the door went Houdini with the press, along with at least one of the mediums who agreed to lead them through town to the séance room. Houdini would enter the room, and the medium would defy him to show any signs of trickery. And Houdini would wander around the room, finally finding one of the chairs, ripping open some of the covering, and finding costumes or other suspicious material. This made front page stories. Ah yes, Houdini had "exposed" the medium.

McCARTY: How did Houdini do it?

KRESKIN: That needs to be explained. Ernst, his attorney, told Walter many times that had Houdini lived a few more years he could have been in gigantic legal troubles with the likelihood of being imprisoned. You see, Rose Mackenberg, when she attended the séances, would take it upon herself to reach underneath her clothing and remove certain materials and stuff them into areas of the chairs where they could remain until Houdini came into town to discover the trickery. Houdini would enter the room and, much to the delight of the press, walk around, point out a chair, and pull something out of the lining. He would find in the chair strange clothing or phosphorescent gowns that would glow in the dark when worn. The mediums were left in a state of shock. She had set up the exposé to make Houdini look good. I am reminded myself of something that Walter B. Gibson said to me many times, "When will magicians realize that Houdini was often as dishonest as the mediums he purported to expose?"

McCARTY: Let's talk more about Houdini's life. There are many more fascinating details we can explore.

KRESKIN: Indeed. Houdini's brother, Hardeen, had gotten so disgusted in the early 1940s with the God-like image that magicdom was making of Houdini that he decided to collaborate with Walter and do a book telling the truth about his brother. Unfortunately, he went into surgery some weeks later and died soon after.

In the last couple of years of Houdini's life his crusade against the spirit mediums became more heated. Around 1925, he attended hearings in Washington. Believe it or not, Congressional hearings were held seeking to pass a bill, at least in the Washington area, controlling the future of the spirit mediums. The fact that the law did not go through surprised nobody, as at that time there was no question that a number of members of Congress had attended séances, and if they did not, their family and relatives certainly did. Spirit-mediums were popular there as they were in every major city in the United States.

Incidentally, when I was a kid, if you looked up Houdini in the encyclopedia you read about his home town of Appleton, Wisconsin, which Houdini proudly announced through the years and in Congress as well. He perjured himself in Congress, because Houdini was not born in the United States; he came from Hungary. But so be the legend that he created.

As a postscript on all that I've recounted let me raise the question, "Did Houdini believe in spirit communication?" Walter Gibson recounted to me that on many days when Houdini and Bess were home and not on tour she could not find Houdini in the house. She would find him at his mother's grave. There he would be, lying face down on the ground for hours, conversing with his deceased mother!

FINAL CHAPTER 6 THOUGHTS BY KRESKIN

KRESKIN: One of the background factors that has never been written about but was explained to me by a number of people who worked for Houdini, and by Walter Gibson as well, revealed the personality of Houdini and the tough times he came out of. One of the greatest dangers was the mishandling of the locks by people who came forward on stage. The locksmith in town could have offered his own lock that he created, but then again they could be simply regular handcuffs that police used. The problem was that if something like buckshot or tiny BBs were dropped into the lock itself as it was shut and no one noticed this, even a key wouldn't have sprung the lock. It would have been almost impossible to open the lock by normal means, and Houdini would have been seen as a failure. In truth, this happened once or twice. Whether that was the cause or not, he was not able to escape, and he carefully suppressed that information in his career, although I think it would have added further to his credibility.

We understand now that he was creating a legend. However, he had another major safeguard. He did invite people on stage to restrain him. However, on many of these occasions, his people had met with them earlier to check the locks or the equipment. That way they were able to report back to Houdini and figure out how he was going to get out of the locks. However, when you're in a town more than a day or two, and the legend or the reputation has built up, who's to stop others from coming on stage with their own locks?

Houdini tried to have all the locks he knew how to get out of put on his body first. The reason is that tougher locks could be put on the upper part of his arms, which were thicker, and consequently if he got out of the locks that were around his thumbs, wrists, etc., the other locks could then be made to slide down his arms and off his hands. There were times when an unexpected restraint was detected, not always by Houdini, but by his onstage assistants. He usually had at least two of them that would come up on stage with the other people from the audience, so no one knew they were working for him. In this way they could observe the crowd, size up what was going on, and be alert to an impossible restraint. Thus, they were Houdini's protection.

Earlier I mentioned that Houdini could have ended up in prison within a few years of these activities. The reason is not simply because of his framing mediums, but for the following ruse he and his assistants had the audacity to use on stage. At one theater in New York, the management was so concerned when they found out the tactic he was using that they placed an alert on their staff in a warning to Houdini to restrain from such idiotic action. If someone were offering an impossible restraint and his key men saw it, they would slowly force the man to the rear of the stage, away from the audience, and, consequently, the person was lost behind the sea of people, sometimes in the dozens. But if the person seemed uncooperative, the answer was simple: They forced the person against the backdrop, and on the other side of the curtain another assistant with a heavy object would simply whack the volunteer over the head, and the two assistants would quietly, surreptitiously carry the unconscious body out into the wings and throw him in the alley.

Indeed, years ago during a late night radio show on WOR in New York City, a popular gag writer recounted to the host Long John Nebel that his dad had been a victim of Houdini's henchmen years ago when he had volunteered on stage. Today, of course, just one such incident would have resulted in a massive lawsuit and 15 minutes of fame for the victim, but not so in the 1910s and 1920s.

There were a few times when Houdini appeared on stage at the same time another escape artist was appearing across the street. There was such a rage of "Houdiania" that there were Houdini imitators all over the United States and England. This is somewhat similar to the legendary Al Jolson, who had at one time hundreds of people in vaudeville imitating his singing style.

When he could find his way unnoticed into the theatre, Houdini was known to come up with a lock and either he himself or his assistant would inveigle the escape artist into allowing himself to be handcuffed. The escape artist would fail to extract himself, because Houdini and his people would have seen to it that the lock was jammed and could not be opened by anybody—that's right—not even Houdini.

There's even a case of a female "Oudini" in Europe who did a water escape somewhat similar to Houdini's. The story has it that she submerged one day and was brutally harmed, as much of the water had been replaced with acid. Not to say that Houdini himself did it, or his assistants, but let's just say this: Houdini was far more ruthless than the public realized or the writers about him will admit.

In early October of 1926, Houdini was moving boxes and crates from his home to another part of the city and had invited another entertainer to help him. As they packed the car and started to drive away, Houdini said to turn around and take him back to the house. They turned, Houdini got out of the car, stood by it, and kept staring at his home, as the rain cascaded over him. He quietly got back in the car and said to his friend, "I'll never see that house again." A few days later, he left New York and was performing out of the country. In the latter part of October, he received blows to the stomach from a college student. Houdini had claimed to be able to tense his muscles and take such blows. But in this case the student rammed his fist into Houdini's stomach while Houdini was reading mail lying on a couch in his dressing room after a show. His stomach ruptured, peritonitis set in, and Houdini died. Ironically it was on October 31st, Halloween night.

7 | Notable Magicians

Magic and magicians in recent years have played a minor role in Kreskin's life, and he has disassociated himself from magic in general. However, we should not overlook the influence of these figures, and we certainly must not ignore the most influential one of all on Kreskin's career and that is, of course, *Mandrake*. With his impact on Kreskin, the irony is that of all the magicians *Mandrake* was a fictional character. The other notable magicians of the 20th century were those that Kreskin wanted to converse about.

McCARTY: Did you ever see Harry Blackstone perform? What was his show like?

KRESKIN: In my childhood, the first real stage magician or illusionist I saw was Harry Blackstone, the father. His son followed in his footsteps some years later. Harry Blackstone, Jr. was an eloquent speaker. He had been in radio and was very erudite, but he did not have the prestige or the grandeur that his father did. When Blackstone walked on stage, you saw this man with bushy white hair in white tie and tails. There's only one profession you could imagine him having, and that was that of a magician—a magician of the grand school with the stage illusions, the glamorous women subjects, assistants, and men dressed perhaps as bellmen, moving the equipment around.

As a stage illusionist, he sawed a lady in half, but he took it one step further. Instead of having her in a box, he had her simply lie on a table after he had apparently mesmerized her, and her outfit was made with a bare midriff. He used a circular saw, one of those ominous saws that spun and made incredible noise. He sawed a block of wood at first to show how strong the saw was, and then he'd put a block of wood under her, and you'd see the saw slowly lower near to her midriff. Low and behold, the saw slowly cut through her midriff in plain view, with the wood under it, scaling saw dust all over the place. It was a remarkable moment.

Years later, Ricciardi, a South American stage illusionist, presented the same stage illusion, except that as the saw slowly descended and broke into the woman's flesh, blood squirted all over the place. The entire backdrop of the stage was covered with blood, and there she lay helpless. Ropes were put up so you could come onto the stage and walk past her just a few feet away and see the helpless body with blood all about her. It was of course an illusion.

McCARTY: Blackstone was famous for many of his tricks, such as the "Vanishing Bird Cage." Did you see that act?

KRESKIN: I did see that act. Blackstone held in his hands a bird cage and then made it vanish, even though he had people come up on stage and hold the corners. His garden of flowers was a thing of beauty. He took a cloth and shook it all over the place, reached under, and then produced a beautiful bouquet of artificial flowers. It didn't end there. He'd hand that to a woman on stage, and he'd produce a second bouquet, a third bouquet, a fourth bouquet, a fifth bouquet, and on and on it went until finally there was a giant bouquet of flowers.

Some of his greatest magic involved the use of smaller items that riveted the attention of a large theater audience. A woman walked on stage with a lamp that had a light bulb lit in it. He unscrewed the light bulb, and the bulb went out. He'd screw it back on, and it would stay lit. Then, when he proceeded to take the bulb out of the lamp, it remained lit. He held it between his hands, and then it floated about the stage, as he passed a hoop over it. Then, he had the audacity to walk down to the audience. How well I remember that bulb floating about 3 feet in front of his body as he went up and down the aisles, and he sometimes had people reach to touch the bulb.

I saw Harry Blackstone, Jr. do an incredible master version of that trick. He stood on stage, and the bulb floating between his hands suddenly scaled out into the audience, down the aisle, and hovered there before it came back on stage, passing through the hoop he was holding. This was one of the highlights of the Blackstone show.

But my most memorable moment took place with an old illusion called "The Girl Without a Middle." It was the most brilliant rendition I ever saw in my life. A woman entered a cabinet, stood there, they closed the door that covered her face, a door that covered her middle, and a door that covered her legs, proceeded to pass sheets of metal through the part below her head and through the part below her waist, which in essence would sever her. Blackstone, Sr. opened the upper box and saw her face, the lower box her legs; in fact, one of them kept kicking out until he stopped her, and then for a moment you wondered, as I well recall, if you were seeing things. He opened the front door, and there was no body in the middle. There was nothing there. You saw the back door. You thought mirrors, although mirrors never made that much sense in magic. And in a moment that I never saw handled as brilliantly as Blackstone, he walked behind the cabinet, opened the back door to the middle, and you saw him look through to the audience. Where there should have been a middle, there was nothing.

It took him only 5 or 6 seconds to do this. He closed the door, and you were now looking at the inside of the cabinet with no person in the middle, and you wondered, because he did it so fast, did you really see no one there? Did you actually see him looking at you through the rear of the cabinet? I consider it one of the most brilliant magical moments I've ever seen in my life. So, Blackstone looked, acted, and moved like a magician.

Blackstone was greatly influenced by Harry Kellar. Kellar was a magician at the turn of the last century who was often referred to as the "Dean of American Magicians." After he retired, he continued for several years to work on an illusion known as the "Levitation of Princess Karnack." When he was satisfied with it he turned it over to

Blackstone. Many magic authorities consider it the greatest stage illusion ever developed. Walter Gibson pointed out that Blackstone's presentation of the illusion did not quite capture its awesome mystical beauty, because Blackstone, by his very nature, was constantly moving at a high pace. His energy was reflected in this kinesthesia about the stage. The levitation required a calming approach that gave a hypnotic quality of one's viewing a woman rising in midair and floating with no visible means of support.

One of the masterful pieces I saw Blackstone do was with playing cards. Some describe it as a set of passes with five cards. He would take five cards in his left hand, and, one at a time, he would take them with his right hand, and the cards would vanish in front of you. He'd show both sides of his hands, and no card was there. One at a time he'd reproduce the cards. It turns out Thurston had done a similar effect, with a slightly different approach. By the time I was 12 years old, I was doing that particular piece of pure sleight of hand in my programs. Incidentally, there's one carryover piece of magic that remains in my program, which I borrowed from Thurston. I take a card and toss it into the audience. The card, which is a playing card or reasonable facsimile, sometimes can at my decision scale to the third balcony of a theater or to the person in the back of the downstairs orchestra of 1,500 people. Many times, I can cascade the card into the lap of the person I pick out. Thurston made that a famous flourish in his performances, and I've kept that touch in deference to my early influences.

McCARTY: Let's discuss one of the great influences on your life, Howard Thurston. Did you see him perform as well?

KRESKIN: Though I never saw him, Howard Thurston, who preceded Blackstone, was a great influence. He died in 1936. Before Thurston, in the 1800s to 1900s, there were some great magicians, like Alexander Hermann, and then later on, Kellar. Hermann, I suspect, had much of the bravado of Harry Blackstone, Sr. Sometimes he'd walk into the audience and produce a rabbit out of cloth that he was holding right within a few feet of the audience's view.

Thurston had seen Hermann work. Hermann was a magician at all times! It was nothing for him to be offstage and meet someone and find an egg in their clothing. He traveled in a beautiful railroad car. The railroads offered three to four or more cars to the stage illusionist to carry the illusions, the magician paying for the trip, the carting of the equipment, and the people on the staff, who were often a couple of dozen assistants. It paid at that time for the railroads to do this, and it became a very glamorous lifestyle. He was introduced to President Grant at the White House. He produced a handful of cigars from the general's whiskers, and it turns out it was rather appropriate, as they were the favorite cigars of Grant. It was nothing for him when he was finishing a drink at dinner to toss the glass in the air where it would vanish. Well, Thurston was enamored with this brilliant magician.

I never saw Thurston or Hermann, as they were before my time, but as a kid my dad regaled me with stories of the great Howard Thurston and his wonderful stage show, which my dad recalled with awesome vividness. Early in his life, Thurston was torn between going into the ministry and becoming a stage magician. A pivotal moment in his life took place when he was about to take a train to study at a missionary school. The night before he saw an advertisement announcing that the man he admired so much, Hermann, was performing in town. This story in itself has magic to it. Thurston went to see Hermann. Although by now he had studied magic and learned the secrets of the craft, he was mesmerized by Hermann, and he found himself absolutely enchanted. He was charmed the way he had been years before when he first saw the master.

After seeing Hermann the night before, he saw him again the next morning at the railroad station. Thurston was prepared to take a train connecting to New York and then on to Philadelphia. He saw Hermann walking through the station with a soft hat and gold-headed cane, looking like Mephistopheles. He was accompanied by his wife, Madam Hermann, who was classically dignified in his programs. Hermann went over to the ticket window and inquired about the time of the next train trip to Syracuse. The agent responded with a time to Syracuse, which was 8:20, and Thurston immediately followed with cash in his hand to buy a ticket to Philadelphia.

Surprisingly, when he looked at the ticket, it read Syracuse. On an impulse, he followed and boarded the same train. Either the ticket agent misheard Thurston, or Thurston unconsciously gave the city that Hermann was to go on through. At that point Thurston's life changed. He again attended Hermann's performance, this time in Albany, and by then, he had made up his mind that he was going to become a stage magician.

Indeed, sometime later, he was in town, and Hermann was appearing there. But it wasn't Alexander, it was his nephew, Leon, who was not as successful a magician. Thurston somehow got his way into the staging area where Leon was appearing, and he convinced Leon to let him show his sensational "Rising Card Trick." The audience was out front, the curtain was closed, and the orchestra was playing. Leon, somewhat reluctantly at first, agreed to see this effect, in which some cards were called out. Thurston shuffled the cards, held the deck in one hand and his other hand a few feet above, and, suddenly, one at a time, the cards just floated out of the deck into the other hand Thurston was holding above. Leon was stunned and mystified.

There were newspaper articles about the event that were titled "The Man Who Mystified Hermann." It wasn't "The Great Hermann," but the name was so mystical in show business that Thurston was able to gather the attention of agents, and thus began his show business career.

He also inherited some of the illusions of Kellar, including the "Levitation of Princess Karnac." On a bare stage, a glamorous woman stood there for Thurston to hypnotize. She slowly drifted into an apparent trance and started to become rigid and topple over. Thurston's assistants caught her up and laid her across a couch. Then he gestured with magnetic hypnotic passes above her body. Slowly she began to float, inches, a foot, 2 feet, 4 feet, 5 feet into the air. When she was in midair, Thurston would take a solid steel hoop and pass it completely around her, to prove there were no supports. The grand touch was that he would bring a young man up from the audience to stand within a foot or two of her, and Thurston proceeded to then walk the young man around this floating figure. The young man would finally be allowed to go back to his seat, and the subject would slowly float back to the couch, be picked up, and awakened. It was an illusion of pure hypnotic impact. A friend of mine, Al Flosso, a real authority on magic, who knew all the greats of that era, would walk me through the Thurston illusion, explaining step by step this incredible piece of stage magic.

A doctor friend, Robert Stein, told me of the day that he was brought up on stage and touched this floating form in front of him, seeing nothing that could be holding her up, no wires or what have you. Lee Falk, who created *Mandrake the Magician*, related to me one of the most memorable experiences in his life when he walked onto the stage by Thurston's invitation. He said, "Kreskin, I walked around her, I touched her, there was nothing holding her up." Yes, Thurston had an incredible charisma.

Years later when magic had become a lesser part of my career as far as public performances were concerned, I met a gentleman who booked me for two seasons touring Florida. He was in the real estate business, and I asked him during the second year why he was spending time booking entertainment. His answer was, "Kreskin, the only entertainment I'm booking is you." I said, "I'm very flattered. You've watched me on television?" He proceeded to tell me that this was not the whole picture. He recounted how when he was going to college he told his dad he was going to work for Houdini. His dad, who was of comfortable means, knew show people and didn't know how to react to that remark. He wanted his son to take up a "legitimate" business. But since he knew show people and he thought he couldn't stop his son, he met with Houdini and his wife when Houdini was in the area and said, "Listen, my son wants to work for you." And Bess, who was an extraordinarily kind human being, said, "Don't worry, we'll look after your son and take care of him." Well, that was this man that I had now been working with for a second year.

He described that the second year he worked for Houdini the show would last about 2 hours. There was a magic part, there was an escape act, and then he lectured on fake mediums. The show included an illusion he had created, where he would stand on a trunk after his wife was locked inside, pick up a cloth, drop it, and, surprise, she was standing there, not him. He was found locked in the trunk.

His best memories of Houdini were after the show. He said many a night at the end of the show he would see Harry sitting on the substitution trunk. There Harry sat with his legs dangling over the side, clearly exhausted. He was not used to maintaining a full, evening concert, which no matter how many assistants you have, centers around one person, the magician. He was used to vaudeville.

But he said when Houdini died, he ended up working for Thurston, and he said it was the dream of his life. I interrupted and said, "I can understand your feelings, but why are you bringing this up to me?"

His answer was, "Thurston often said to me and other members of his staff that in years to come the great mystery on the stage and in show business will not be the stage illusionist, but a person who deals with the mind." Then he said, "Kreskin, that's what you're doing. Another thing, Kreskin, you have the same remarkable mannerisms that Thurston had, and often walk the way he did. You gesture the way he did, and your outlook on things is so similar to things I've heard him say." This left me stunned, because I have never seen a film of Thurston, nor heard his voice, nor really knew what he said on the stage, except in the reports of others.

Years later I brought this up to Walter Gibson. Walter asked, "Kreskin, has anyone ever called your attention to this?" I said yes, and I mentioned the person, whose name Walter recognized.

He said, "You have some of the makeup, almost as if you've inherited some of the genes of Thurston. I know you never saw him, because you were born just a few months before Thurston died."

I said, "Yes, Walter, and what is equally haunting is that you know about Thurston's religious plans." I told him that much of my family, for the first 10 to 12 years of my life, was convinced I was going to become a Catholic priest. I did minor in Catholic philosophy when I studied psychology at Seton Hall, but the truth of the matter is that I knew from age 5 what my calling in life would be.

Clearly, Thurston, with his background, had a wonderful spiritual outlook on life, and it is to be expected that he would be referred to, even in books like Dale Carnegie's *How to Win Friends and Influence People.*

McCARTY: I don't know much about John Scarne, except that he was a technical advisor for the movie The Sting *and that he doubled for Paul Newman's card tricks in that movie. Why is he a noteworthy magician?*

KRESKIN: John Scarne was a legendary card expert, who really came into his own during the Second World War. Growing up in New Jersey, he became enamored with sleight of hand and decided he wanted to become a magician, but he never quite succeeded as a performer on stage in front of an audience because his magic just did not come across. In his developing days, his passion in all the areas of magic embraced the 52 Devil's Paste Boards; that is, playing cards. He spent hours manipulating cards, and while he could handle dice in a gambling situation, it was playing cards that obsessed and possessed him.

As he became more skillful, he was hired to do close-up performances before, of all people, members of the underworld, because he was able to stack a deck of cards while shuffling them face down so he could deal himself four aces. He showed this hundreds of times on television. He was able to deal cards from the bottom of the deck and make it look like they were coming from the top. He was a remarkable second dealer. By that I mean he could appear to be dealing cards off the top of the deck when they were actually coming second from the top. This is a cherished skill of card cheats. It was mainly second dealing and bottom dealing that caused him to be embraced by the underworld. Indeed, when he performed for some of them they told him to cast away card tricks that evening and show them his skill with playing cards.

As the Second World War approached, Scarne found an outlet for his skills. He appeared before various military groups and explained to them how to protect themselves while they were gambling. With cards, he showed how readily they could be cheated. The truth of the matter was that if the players were as skillful with their hands as Scarne, they couldn't be detected cheating. He wrote a monthly column for a military magazine that was read by servicemen all over the world. Thus, he came into his own as he self-styled himself as the greatest expert of card chicanery.

After the war, the setting started to change. The need to expose how people could be cheated by card sharks seemed to lessen. He was hired by some casinos to advise them on how to deal with and protect themselves from cheaters. He had written books, and in the latter years wrote how to win playing various gambling games. His advice included blackjack, but his credibility was seriously threatened by the work of Edward O. Thorp, author of *Beat the Dealer*. Thorp was a prominent mathematician who had reexamined blackjack. Indeed, his writings influenced how blackjack cards are now dealt, not from a single deck, but with as many as eight decks in a shoe.

In his writings, he advised when to bid, depending on the dealer's up card and the two cards the players possessed. Many of his tips were in complete contradiction to what Scarne had been advising on how to play blackjack. Scarne was infuriated, but he never was able to prove Thorp wrong.

Finally, John Scarne tried to throw a monkey wrench at Thorp's credibility. He wrote a book, *The Mafia Conspiracy*, but he could not get a publisher after trying many. He went to Walter Gibson, but he could not help him. He even asked if I could help him get a publisher. I read the book, but I wouldn't touch it. First of all, the book was poorly written. People who had written for Scarne in the past were not available for various reasons to write the book, and I suspected it was largely written by John Scarne himself, although I'm not sure.

Much of the premise of the book is that the Mafia does not exist. He said it was created for many reasons, including perhaps prejudice against the Italians by various major newspapers and communication groups. The book was a fiasco. Scarne could not get much exposure. He did go on the air with Barry Farber, a gentleman I've admired for years, who is a friend in broadcasting. Within minutes, Barry tore him to shreds, and Scarne almost got into a fistfight with him. To suggest that there was no Mafia and that there was a conspiracy for various reasons just made no sense. Unfortunately, in later years Scarne became a forgotten giant, but he will always be remembered as one of the greatest sleight-of-hand artists with playing cards.

McCARTY: Why did Harry Houdini take his name from Robert-Houdin?

KRESKIN: When Houdini was a youngster, he tried to get his hands on anything associated with magic, and he found a book that enchanted him that was translated into English, *Recollections of Robert-Houdin*. Jean Eugene Robert-Houdin was a legendary French magician who lived in the 1800s and was rather innovative with his magic, since he didn't use suspicious materials on stage and dressed like an elegant man of society in white tie and tails. It was a far cry from magicians before that, who seemed to have suspicious, bulky equipment that didn't often make sense with the illusion they were trying to present. So, he was the innovator, and he was accomplished in sleight of hand as well.

Houdini, born as Ehrich Weiss, was so enchanted with Robert-Houdin that he changed his name and made a stage name by taking Houdin and adding an "i" so as to create the name Houdini. In later years, Houdini wrote a scathing book about Robert-Houdin, showing that the illusions Robert-Houdin employed were created before him. It was more of a sour grape-type book, because the bottom line was that Robert-Houdin was an inspiration to many magicians of that century, and obviously initially to Houdini.

Certainly, he had to credit an accomplishment that Houdini never achieved, and that is working for the French government. It seemed that one of the islands owned by the French was having uprisings that were of an anti-French nature, and Robert-Houdin was asked by the government if he could do something as a great performer to quell the anti-French uprising. Therefore, Robert-Houdin was taken to the location and impressed the Arab chieftains in Algiers with his magic.

There was a group called the Marabouts that were trying to arouse Algerian tribes to revolt against the French. The French government felt that by having the French magician perform before this group it would suggest that the French were superior, perhaps even having some power. The key illusion that he had created was called "The Light and Heavy Chest." He placed on the stage or runway a small chest that was solidly constructed. While it was sitting on the stage he would simply have people come up and lift it. After they put it down, he caused it to become heavy whenever he willed it, and they could not lift it. The French audiences found this very amusing.

However, in the case of Algiers, what he needed to win was their awe. So rather than calling the illusion "The Light and Heavy Chest," he stated that he was going to take the strongest man and turn him into a helpless weakling on command. Almost a dozen men came up on stage, and by using an interpreter he suggested that one of them lift the chest. The Arab understood and lifted it. Then, through the interpreter, he told the audience he was depriving the volunteer of all his strength. He would make mesmeric or hypnotic gestures in front of the person, and then he suggested that the Arab again lift the chest. The man became disgustedly disdainful and exclaimed how easily by gripping the handle he could lift the chest high in the air. He could not budge the object. He tried and struggled, and when Robert-Houdin waved his hands again, the subject started shaking. Moments later, Robert-Houdin gestured again, and the Arab suddenly let go of the handle, jumped to the aisle off the stage, and ran from the theater. By the end of the demonstration, Robert-Houdin had, in the minds of the Arabs, demonstrated his incredible powers.

What was behind that illusion was later exposed in a silent movie in the United States. Robert-Houdin had tapped into the use of electricity. Beneath the stage was an electromagnetic setup, and the conducting wires ran to a switch off stage. The chest had an iron plate on the bottom, and when an assistant pressed the switch the magnet took hold and it was impossible to lift until the current was shut off. Robert-Houdin had also wired the handle so that another switch caused the person participating to get an electric shock. Electricity was not well understood in those days, so the stunt intrigued audiences both in the civilized world and on the islands.

More than a century later, I presented the effect in public on a number of occasions on my own television series, as well as a guest on various shows including *The Mike Douglas Show*. There was one difference: I was not doing what Robert-Houdin did.

He used trickery, but implied that his will could paralyze the subject. In my case, there was neither trickery nor gimmicks. I did the stunt legitimately by using my abilities and the power of suggestion. In some shows, I made it impossible for weightlifters to lift an object as small as a tiny stool. At universities, it was nothing for me to have a group of four or five athletes attempting to lift a tiny stool. But my final touch was when I had a 5-, 6-, or 7-year old youngster come up and using just one hand lift the same object with the greatest of ease. The crew onstage was stunned.

McCARTY: And you borrowed the latter part of Kellar's name to create Kreskin. Why?

KRESKIN: When I was in the tenth grade, I decided to be successful as a mentalist with hypnotic abilities, rather than a magician or an illusionist. My professional name is an original. My given name was George J. Kresge, and before that the family name was Gorczyca, which is of Polish extraction. Just as Houdini added "i" to Houdin, I did two things with Kresge: I dropped the "ge" and added the letter "k," which stood for Kellar. In his later years, he felt strongly that the greatest and most successful illusionists had almost hypnotic abilities to mesmerize their audiences. That was years before Thurston's prediction of the mind being the great mystery of theater in years to come. So, in respect for Kellar, I added "k" to the Kres, and then I decided why not borrow from Houdin and take the last two letters of his name and create Kreskin, an original name.

"The Amazing" was never intended as part of my public name. The man who created it was Johnny Carson. On shows that I wasn't even on, he used the name Kreskin and coupled it with the word "Amazing." In a bantering discussion with Ed McMahon on the day before my appearance, Johnny said something to the effect that, "You know, Kreskin was on a few weeks ago. He was 90 percent amazing." Then, Ed McMahon said, "No Johnny, he was 95 percent amazing." And then another time, Carson said, "We're going to have Kreskin on Monday, but Ed, last time he was on, he was only 95 percent amazing." Ed said, "Johnny, he was 98 percent amazing."

FINAL CHAPTER 7 THOUGHTS BY KRESKIN

KRESKIN: While walking through airports, I heard people shout across, "Hi Amazing!" Not "Hello, Kreskin," but "Hello, Amazing." Carson had caused the prefix to stick, and I decided heck, why fight it? So, even my business cards and credit cards have on them T. A. Kreskin, since the name Kreskin is my legal name. A lot of people that look at the credit card don't realize what the T. A. stands for (The Amazing).

In spite of retaining my name Kreskin, by my mid-to-late teens I was already strongly veering away from magic. Indeed, by the time I entered my twenties I was even dropping the tricks, etc., involved in fake mind-reading acts, as I was seeking more and more legitimate ties. I wanted to create phenomena on the stage as much as possible without the use of sleight of hand and other devices of the magician. While I've separated myself from the so-called mind readers of today and the occultists, I have never lost my love for the fine art of magic. Mankind is an incurably mystical race.

8 | *The Great Buck Howard* and Movies

Hooray for Hollywood. I think everyone has fantasized about being in a movie or having a movie made about them at one time or another. Kreskin has done both. He was the inspiration for the mentalist Buck Howard in *The Great Buck Howard* and also appeared in such movies as *Horror* and *Wake-Up Callz*.

The Great Buck Howard is about Troy Gable (Colin Hanks). A recent law school dropout in Los Angeles is searching for a job when he comes across a personal assistant position advertised in the local paper. He attends the interview for the position at a local restaurant, where he meets and is struck by the Great Buck Howard (John Malkovich) a tuxedo-donning mentalist. Although skeptical of Buck, Troy is convinced the job will be an exciting change from his ordinarily mundane life. He goes on the road with Buck playing in small towns and cities across the country.

My personal opinion is that *The Great Buck Howard,* produced by Tom Hanks, may not be the "greatest" movie ever made, but it sure is an entertaining one. The film really gets cooking with all the Hollywood cameos: Tom Hanks, George Takei, Jay Leno, Tom Arnold, Regis Philbin, Kelly Ripa, Jon Stewart, Conan O'Brien, and Martha Stewart.

McCARTY: The Great Buck Howard was written and directed by Sean McGinley. Was he a former road manager of yours?

KRESKIN: Sean McGinley was indeed a former road manager of mine in the mid 1990s. The storyline of the movie has nothing to do with me. It is not biographical, and the persona of Buck Howard offstage is not me in any way, shape, or form. It is a character that is embellished in that movie, along with a love interest, which is not a portrayal of my private life. But what is significant is that every single incident that happens on stage or other performing times took place in my career during the period of time that Sean McGinley was working for me.

An example of one such incident is one that took place in a Mid-western town while I was appearing on a local TV broadcast. I was going to demonstrate how I could influence a person's muscular reactions and cause a coin to drop that the news anchorwoman was holding between her fingers. It did not happen, and it wasn't because she not was receptive. She was a news reporter, and she was too preoccupied with a breaking story to be influenced by me.

Another incident in the movie was based upon an incident where I had been conducting a demonstration of mass suggestion in which I caused scores of people to respond to my suggestions. It was so effective that they ended up lying on the floor and were unable to move, let alone get up. Unfortunately, not long before the demonstration, a major political story broke out, which took the attention of the press off my publicity stunt and it was never covered.

There's an old saying that when one is involved in any publicity release, whether it be a demonstration, a new book, etc., one prays that God forbid a new World War doesn't break to take everything off the front page.

Let's go back to the beginning. The way I learned of the *Buck Howard* movie was in a rather circuitous series of events that I could only describe as synchronicity. A year and a half before there was any *Buck Howard* movie, I had an appearance in Atlantic City. It was a private affair. After the event I was sitting at a blackjack table just relaxing my mind. (I am permitted to play in most casinos, since my ability as a thought reader has no advantage there. The dealer has no idea what cards are coming up.) While playing, a man came up to me and said he was a very good friend of Sean McGinley's. I hadn't seen Sean in over a decade.

Years ago Milt Suchin, a very fine manager in LA, had put me in contact with Sean for the position of road manager. Our interview went well, and Sean moved east to New Jersey even though his father did not want him to take on such a job. Sean had revealed to me that he had his heart set on sometime becoming a writer. During the time he worked for me as my road manager, I assured him that if he really wanted to be a writer he could write anywhere, just as writers in the past wrote on trains or in idle hours on workdays. He should pursue his passion. While Sean's friend was placing his bets at the card table, he said that Sean talked about me all the time at private parties and elsewhere. He was seriously thinking about writing a movie in which I would be the inspiration for the key character. He had by that time already worked on other movies. The friend then gave me McGinley's parents' phone number in the Virginia area.

Not too long after that, the second event took place. When my current tour ended I called his folks' house and spoke to his mother. Sean's mother, I believe, is a teacher and his father works in some other area of education as well. They are wonderful, down-to-earth, friendly people. She said of course she knew who I was and that Sean had talked about me frequently. He had many reflections about me from the time he was working for me and she added, yes, he was thinking about working on a movie built on a character whose professional career was like mine. Sean was in the process of moving so she couldn't give me a phone number, but she made me aware of his activities.

Now passes a few months, and I'm in New York City at a nightclub for an opening of a singer. I was invited to sit at the table with Bette Midler, who of course was with me years ago on the *Johnny Carson Show* when I stretched the host between two chairs, as I made him rigid like a bar of steel. It was Midler who ended up sitting on him.

Bette and I were sitting there talking when a gal at the table who had been considered for a role in a movie, said, "Kreskin, you must pursue something; this movie is built around you." She continued, "Kreskin, you've been mentioned frequently during the production of the film." As a result of that conversation I had my people contact Tom Hanks' people. Soon afterwards a couple of Hanks' representatives were sent to New York to discuss the project with me. I have never worked with a finer group of people. It reflects (and I said this to Tom himself when I finally met him) that the man that the public knows and his persona fit him ideally. The public persona is the true Tom Hanks, offstage as well as on. I think he is a rare figure in the tough business of show business.

In the discussion with Hanks' representatives, it became clear to them that much of the movie story was reflecting Yours Truly. There are approximately four dozen incidents in the movie that happened to me all during the time that Sean McGinley was traveling with me as a road manager.

For me, the exciting thing about the movie is the comments that appear on the screen at its conclusion. It was an on-screen statement that said I was the inspiration for the movie, thanked me, and spoke complimentarily about my life's work. I'm very pleased that the Tom Hanks' people, for whom I have a tremendous regard, gave me that special recognition at the end of the film.

McCARTY: John Malkovich portrayed Buck Howard, who is inspired by you. How would you rate Malkovich's portrayal of you? What did he do right? What did he do wrong?

KRESKIN: John Malkovich, who is the star of the movie, does indeed portray a character named Buck Howard. That's true, but in doing so he is also portraying me. In a conversation with Tom Hanks at the Broadway opening of the film, he related to me an anecdote that Regis Philbin got a kick out of because Regis is in the movie. Hanks reminded me that Malkovich studied video after video of me over a period of 3 days. Hanks said that was okay. The down side is for 3 days after he had studied these videos he went around shaking hands with often 30 people in a day and did it with the same vigor with which I shake hands. As Regis says, "shaking hands with Kreskin is the dream of every chiropractor, because they will have more business."

Incidentally, the first time the prominent physician Dr. Oz came on the *David Letterman Show*, Letterman stopped him and immediately talked about his handshake, saying it was as close to Kreskin's as anybody. It was an energetic one. Malkovich got it right. It is one of my trademarks. He really captured my mannerisms in the movie. He even uses the phrase, "Isn't that wild?" which I have said thousands of times in my career both on and off of television.

During the nonpublic scenes in the movie, the offstage moodiness is really not me. People who know me have pointed out that my energy carries itself off stage. It is not as high, but it is still there because I do not become a different person offstage. So the movie offstage persona is not really the way that I am offstage. It is just part of the script. I think Malkovich did a brilliant job. Meeting him in person was quite an experience. He is a quiet, gentle man, and of course an accomplished actor.

McCARTY: Colin Hanks, Tom Hanks' son, is in the movie. Did you get a chance to meet Colin Hanks, and, if so, what was he like?

KRESKIN: Yes, I did meet Colin Hanks. I also attended a Broadway show he was doing. He is a fine young man. He is modest in his way and is clearly conscious of the footsteps and the shoes that have been shared with him by the giant icon of his dad. He is obviously very proud of his dad but determined to make it on his own, which he will do. Recently, on the *Letterman Show*, he came on to discuss the television crime series he is on, and don't you know halfway through the interview Letterman asked him about his experience with me, meeting me, coming to know me, etc. He related something which I thought was a rather poignant remark. He said, "You know, after I met Kreskin for the first time, I received a letter from him. On his stationery as part of the embossment on the letterhead it says, 'Even now, I know what you're thinking.'"

McCARTY: What are your overall thoughts about The Great Buck Howard *film?*

KRESKIN: It is a quality film, no question about it. Who would have ever dreamt that just before the television showing of the 2009 Academy Awards, Michael Moore, the controversial movie producer, decided to announce on the Internet for everyone to see worldwide his picks of the top movies of the year. One of them, he said, was a movie based on The Amazing Kreskin called *The Great Buck Howard*. He put that as number six of his favorite movies of the year. It's all the more interesting because when David Letterman was interviewing Colin Hanks, David brought up that one of his favorite movies of the past year, one he really loved, was *The Great Buck Howard*.

Some people had concerns about how I felt about a movie character that had a rather negative offstage personality, difficult to get along with, disagreeable, perhaps not that loyal, and not especially successful when he was performing, and so forth. Clearly, as those who knew me understood, this did not reflect me.

Former managers of mine were not so forgiving. They felt it just didn't do justice to me. But I can't think of it that way. To have a movie whose principal character is based upon you during your lifetime is a rare phenomenon. Beyond that, I appreciate the class with which Tom Hanks and his people handled the publicity built around me.

McCARTY: At about the same time that The Great Buck Howard *came out, you were in the horror movie* Wake-Up Callz. *What was that like?*

KRESKIN: Before *The Great Buck Howard* was released in January 2008, I was involved in another movie called *Wake-Up Callz,* also released in 2008. It didn't get much attention and acclaim, but I loved the opportunity to play a "villain" in a horror story. All the hypnotic scenes involving me were done legitimately. The actors were truly responding.

I play Dr. Dream. He was not a pleasant character, an individual with strange hypnotic powers. While I don't wish to leave the impression it is one of the greatest movies ever made, it was a challenge for me and I think brilliantly done by its producer and screenwriter Adrian Horodecky. Adrian did it on a shoestring, but you've got to know that he put his heart and soul into it.

What made me agree to work in the film was that I was just playing an evil version of myself. The hairpiece I wore helped to alter my persona. And what made the movie most intriguing, and certainly causes it to stand out, is that all of the hypnotic phenomena I demonstrated in the movie were being done legitimately.

The movie required a number of bit players for some of the larger scenes. They were auditioned outdoors in a location here in New Jersey. They all wanted to be in the movie, but they didn't understand what it was all about. They certainly had an idea when 10 minutes after they met me a number of them were lying prostrate on the grass and could not move. I had paralyzed them through the power of mental suggestion.

I had a lot of fun with the movie and would love to do a similar project in time to come. Not being an actor, I would just in essence have to play myself but somehow incorporate what I do within the framework of the movie. Parenthetically, I know Orson Welles would have loved this scenario and probably with his outrageously outside-the-box way of thinking would have considered a similar project. He had done a movie years ago called *Cagliostro*, which in the United States was called *Black Magic*. In that movie he played an evil hypnotist in the 18th century who had actually lived. Welles was absolutely fascinated playing the role of a hypnotist.

McCARTY: You starred in the movie Horror. *Can you tell us about that film?*

KRESKIN: *Horror* focused on an evil character, who was a healer with hypnotic and, yes, even demonic, powers. I welcomed that opportunity to analyze the structuring of the character and present my suggestions to the director. Meeting writer/director Dante Tomaselli was an extraordinary experience, as we shared a tremendous enthusiasm for horror movies. Before we even got to his script, we discussed, at some length, scores of horror movies. I went on to recount movies that had influenced me.

Our conversation created a bond, and when we finally got to the movie, and the structure of the movie, I made my comments, and Dante asked if I might read two of the pages of dialogue. I was not enthusiastic with the idea. I am not an actor—I consider what I do as an entertainer and mentalist to be legitimate. I have never sought to take on a role of playing someone else. Nonetheless, I read the two pages and that was it. By the time I got home, the decision was made to give me the starring role of the movie!

In a sense, as all of this was unfolding, I recalled my first meeting with Orson Welles. It became a compelling, almost haunting memory, one that I relived day after day from the moment I saw Tomaselli.

Welles and I had discussed his role in *Black Magic* (1949). The entire theme of the movie was built around hypnosis in the Middle Ages. I suggested that someday, within the framework of the effects, hypnotic influence could be done legitimately. Welles turned to me and said, "Yes, Kreskin, and you are the one person who could really do it." I will never forget those words. There were certain scenarios that Welles discussed, and, in both cases, Welles repeated, "But you are the one person who can do it."

I came back to Dante with a premise—I wanted to add three or four scenes that would capture the essence of what I do, while keeping within the framework of the character. In the scenes I exert my influence legitimately, and so unfolded the movie. It is a first in movie history. All hypnotic effects that I performed in the movie were done legitimately. The actors were playing a role, but their responses were authentic. Later a mini-documentary was done where the actors were interviewed. They recounted how powerless they had become when I either paralyzed them or influenced them in ways that were exhibiting hypnotic power.

McCARTY: You were involved with the 1994 movie Mesmer?

KRESKIN: *Mesmer* was a biographical movie about the 18th-century physician France Anton Mesmer played by Alan Rickman. *Mesmer* is the root for the words *mesmerize* and *mesmerism*. Dr. Mesmer believed that magnetic powers were involved between the patient and the mesmerist. I had not been an advisor on the making of the film but I had been engaged to publicize its debut.

McCARTY: What is the difference between mesmerizing and hypnotizing?

KRESKIN: There is a difference in the techniques of the mesmerist and the hypnotist. Mesmerism is based in a belief that a force of a magnetic quality emanates from the mesmerist. Sometimes the mesmerist held magnets and moved over the body of afflicted individuals as a healing technique. Mesmer thought that certain individuals had this inherent power, similar to the magnets. Even today, people have been known to wear magnets and even have them embedded in some parts of their clothing or shoes in order to alleviate pain.

Mesmer finally decided that the force could just as easily and effectively emanate from an individual himself. One who had a powerful force field in his own body. The mesmerist often held his hands over the body of the subject and, without touching any part of the body, would slowly begin to move them around the subject while making gestures in front of the subject's face and the afflicted areas.

The traditional, old-time mesmerist used fewer verbal suggestions. Today's hypnotist uses mainly verbal suggestions. Indeed, most have dropped the physical actions altogether. Hypnosis has become a kind of verbal diarrhea, and in some respects I think it has lost some of its effectiveness. There is something to be said about the unspoken word, like the movements and the gestures which I have incorporated into my work on the stage. I find that such gestures, if they are done in a natural but compelling way, can be even more effective than the verbal suggestion.

Regarding the *Mesmer* movie, Dennis Potter's screenplay was more accurate than so many in that it encompassed an incident in Mesmer's life where he treated a pianist who was obviously functionally blind. She regained her sight as a result of treatments by Mesmer. Within a short time after leaving Mesmer's treatment, her "blindness" returned. In a bygone era, this was described as a form of "conversion" hysteria, since the affliction was more mental than physical. I have to say that in *Mesmer* Alan Rickman's persona and actions as a mesmerist were extremely effective.

McCARTY: You also were involved with helping out with the publicity for the play on Mesmer by Jerome Lawrence and Robert E. Lee called Whisper in the Mind. *What can you tell us about that play?*

KRESKIN: It is ironic that just a few weeks after finishing my involvement in the *Mesmer* movie I received a call for the debut of the play.

The movie people didn't know about the play, and the play people didn't know about the movie.

The bizarre thing is—it hit me with almost a shudder of synchronicity—the play starts where the movie left off. When you realize that neither party had anything to do with each other—I find that rather fascinating.

McCARTY: Any more thoughts on the Mesmer *movie or the play* Whisper in the Mind?

KRESKIN: The movie had been made in Europe, and unfortunately received very limited viewership here in the United States. Some legal situation had the movie tied up in the courts. As it was being released the publicity department wanted me to showcase that release with demonstrations. I was going to demonstrate the kind of techniques that Mesmer (Alan Rickman) had used to influence people. Mesmer's theory was built on the idea that our bodies and our hands when we gestured gave off highly magnetic forces. Actually, in the days before hypnosis was used, mesmerists were often called *magnetists*. Unfortunately, my demonstrations never took place, as the legal complications thwarted the publicity plans. Much later, when the movie was released, it received negligible attention. The dramatic demonstration for the opening, which was to take place in France during a film festival, and the way we had planned it, which would have tied up traffic, was never to be.

Mesmer, the movie, was not my only theatrical connection with Dr. Mesmer. In the early 1990s, the authors Jerome Lawrence and Robert Edwin Lee, who were outstanding playwrights known for *Auntie Mame* and the legendary *Inherit the Wind*, approached me with a fascinating concept. They had written a play called *Whisper in the Mind*. It was about an imaginary meeting between Benjamin Franklin and Franz Anton Mesmer. The play was about a period when Mesmer and his work were all the rage in Paris. He was "healing" wraths experienced by the wealthy, often in groups, and had become highly controversial. There was tremendous jealousy on the part of the physicians who were always seeking favor of the heads of state. At that time,

Ben Franklin was living in France as an ambassador from the United States. He ended up investigating mesmerism, which historically truly happened, and is the pivotal point in the history of Mesmer and mesmerism. Franklin made an oversimplified judgment of the Mesmer phenomena, which was deadly at the time. His conclusion was that it was all in "the imagination."

I attended opening night, May 7, 1994, in Kansas City, Missouri. At the end of the play, a few dozen members of the audience joined me in the lobby. I proceeded to use the classic mesmerists' techniques, which are not seen today. (We see in pictures today, whether it be *Mandrake the Magician* or cartoons, magnetic forces or electricity coming from the hypnotist's hands and eyes.) It was Mesmer's theory that the magnetist or mesmerist was influencing his subjects with a magnetic force. Thus, in the days of this mesmeric phenomena large gestures and passes with the hands were made, which in their own way visually influenced the subjects. I ended up mesmerizing a couple of dozen people, who within minutes were lying prostrate on the floor of the lobby. Needless to say, the opening was in the news all over the area and became much more than simply the opening of a play. The two authors decided that when the play opened on Broadway I would do the same demonstration, not only on opening night but for the first month or so. Unfortunately, the money was never raised to bring it to Broadway, and Mesmer remained quietly in a dormant-like state.

McCARTY: Why did they call old horror movies "chillers"?

KRESKIN: Years ago, the old-fashioned horror movies were called "chillers" for obvious reasons. You could be watching them in a theater, dimly lit, perhaps heated because it was wintertime, and yet become so frightened by some scenes that you had goose bumps. It doesn't surprise anybody. It doesn't seem particularly supernatural, and yet it is a demonstration of how just ideas are capable of influencing the human body.

McCARTY: You are a big fan of Sherlock Holmes films; why?

KRESKIN: Sherlock Holmes has intrigued me for many reasons, aside from the fact that Arthur Conan Doyle seems to have created the most venerable detective in literary history. There seems to be little doubt that Doyle based Holmes on a doctor/professor whom he had in medical school. Doyle had been out of town for a weekend, and when he returned to class the doctor proceeded to tell Doyle in some detail where he had been for that weekend. Doyle was absolutely stunned, and it was the beginning of many conversations. It turns out that the doctor had seen a certain type of clay on the shoes of Doyle and knew that this particular type was found in another part of England. This played on Doyle's mind and obviously helped to influence the formation of a mastermind of deduction who could by observing an incredible amount of details come to some sage and wise conclusions. While this is a far cry from telepathic and hypnotic phenomena, it does show that by sensitizing oneself to our environment, we can pick up ideas, details, and information that are often ignored in everyday life.

McCARTY: What is your favorite Sherlock Holmes *film?*

KRESKIN: My favorite Holmes movie is *The Woman in Green* (1945) for a number of reasons. Of course, Basil Rathbone and Nigel Bruce play Holmes and Watson. Critics and aficionados of Doyle's writings have been less than enthusiastic of Nigel Bruce often playing a bumbling assistant to Holmes. In truth, Basil Rathbone and Nigel Bruce were very close friends and shared a great affection and respect for one another. It was, however, decided by the director and movie people at the time that Nigel Bruce could naturally give a humorous contrast to Holmes' often austere and very serious pontificating. It played well. There were times when they had Watson more frivolous than in other movies, but you could sense, even in the structure of such scripts, the great rapport they had for each other. It worked.

In *The Woman in Green*, Hilary Brook, a very attractive actress, became the pivotal point of the story. People were murdered, and one of their fingers was missing. Men were awakening in strange hotel rooms finding a finger on their person and not remembering what they had done. It was suspected that this was a maniacal Jack the Ripper–like individual.

The story was ingenious in that it turns out that Hilary Brook's character was a member of the Mesmer Club in London, as well as being an accomplished hypnotist. She was hypnotizing these men after luring them to her apartment, and she then planted a finger on their clothing, apparently that of a person who had been murdered in the city, and then sent them back to some hotel to sleep off the night. They awakened to a situation that put them in the position of being blackmailed. Behind the scenes loomed the genius of crime, one of the truly unforgettable figures that Doyle had concocted and that is, of course, Professor Moriarty, whose genius was equal to Holmes'. He was controlling and overseeing the plot to blackmail these wealthy men.

In *The Woman in Green,* Moriarty is played by the great British actor Henry Danielle. There is a scene in which Watson is lured from the quarters that he and Holmes shared. Then in walks Professor Moriarty. Holmes had been playing the violin, and the two meet and sit together and carry out one of the most violently compelling conversations I've ever seen in a movie. Bear in mind this was a movie that was relatively without violence, as is true of most of Doyle's writings. In their conversation, we see two geniuses who have a measurable respect for one another; this is equaled only by their contempt for one another.

Although despising one another, they discuss how each inevitably will destroy the other. There is a line, if I can paraphrase, in which Moriarty says, "Everything I have said or planned to say has already entered your mind, my dear Holmes." In essence, it was showing the genius of both. It was borrowed from a play about Sherlock Holmes that toured throughout America in the 1920s and 1930s. Basil Rathbone in his autobiography states that this was a remarkable scene, and, in his opinion, Danielle played the ideal Moriarty. It was a shame that he was not cast for the role of Moriarty more often, as he was perfect, brilliant looking, distinguished, businesslike, and yet with an aura of evil. I can imagine today Anthony Hopkins in the role of Professor Moriarty with incredible effectiveness. Of course, the hypnotism movie scenes made it all the more memorable for me.

McCARTY: In 2009, Robert Downey, Jr. starred in an action adventure simply called Sherlock Holmes. *I was wondering if you saw the movie and if you had any thoughts on it?*

KRESKIN: I saw the 2009 Robert Downey, Jr. movie *Sherlock Holmes* and enjoyed it. It was fast moving, colorful, and the characters Holmes (Downey) and Watson (Jude Law) related very well. But as far as the classic Sherlock Holmes, the movie was a giant disappointment. Having read all of the Doyle writings of Holmes and seeing the classic movies, this had for me more of a sci-fi flavor. It was fast moving. Situations kept changing. At times I almost expected a spaceship to land. It wasn't really Holmes. Perhaps the greatest disappointment is that it really didn't capture or hint adequately the reason Sherlock Holmes became the definitive, singularly unique detective in all of crime fiction. He is revered as if he had actually lived. He stood out from anyone else because of his giant intellect and his ability to think along the lines of the criminal mind.

Today, there are endless, fast-moving crime-adventure solvers. While there was action in Holmes' life that was captured in his films, it was never at the expense of this remarkable man and his persona. Bear in mind that there were quiet moments in the Sherlock Holmes movies. There were scenes that moved slowly, but they reflected the true Holmes. Obviously, the writers and the actors were never afraid of losing their audience. But does the Downey movie capture the essence of Holmes? I would say largely, no.

Of course with the success of the movie there is a sequel, and who is coming into the picture but the Napoleon of evil, Professor Moriarty. My concern is that he will be portrayed with a wand that exudes electrical forces of evil or somehow be turned into some outer space element or UFO. I can almost predict that in the next movie there will be a point where Sherlock Holmes simply says "shazam" and suddenly he'll be able to gymnastically go beyond physical jumps, being helped by the cape that would suddenly appear hanging over his shoulders.

Oh, there will be a number of subplots. Sometimes it will get confusing. But that's okay. Some great movies and stories have been filled with numerous conflicting directions that somehow all come together, and, of course, this will be necessary. After all, we're thinking in terms of a movie of 2 hours or more, and it can't be filled with car chases because of the period of history. We should bear in mind, though, that some of the finest Sherlock Holmes movies were only an hour and 15 or 20 minutes in length. But the stories, so direct and complete, captured the "real" Sherlock Holmes.

McCARTY: Let's talk about some other movies involving hypnosis. I know one of your favorites is Svengali *(1931).*

KRESKIN: During the 19th century, mesmerism and hypnosis were frequent tools in fiction. Whenever there were allusions to an influence someone had over another, it was understood to be of a mesmeric effect. Naturally, it found its way into movies such as *The Cabinet of Dr. Calgari* (1921).

Another early favorite is John Barrymore's highly successful role in *Svengali*. Svengali—a character from *Trilby* by George DuMaurier—is a hypnotist who meets an innocent, uneducated girl in Paris. The girl suffers from headaches. Svengali proceeds to hypnotize her to relieve the headache, much to the amazement of her friends and suitors. Svengali, who is a pianist/teacher, proceeds to cause her to sing in a way that leaves everyone in total awe, since she is actually tone-deaf. Inevitably, she tours the world as one of the great singers, with Svengali conducting and always under his control. When she is not in the so-called "trance," the girl has no voice at all. The term *Svengali* of course has found its way into everyday conversation referring to a special control over someone.

There was an ingenious incident that happened when the movie opened in New York. At the end of the movie when the houselights in the theater went up and the people in the audience got up to leave, panic ensued. A very attractive woman remained sitting in the audience, glassy-eyed and spellbound. The people nearby her started calling her, and she didn't respond. Initially, they thought she may have died, but her eyes were open and she was breathing. They concluded that she had been hypnotized watching the movie. Some nurses and other help were brought in, and she was released from the trance. What wasn't explained, and I think that this is a devilish touch, is that the PR people for the movie had set this up. She wasn't hypnotized; she was an actress and model. Talk about a publicity stunt!

McCARTY: This is fun. There are so many movies we could talk about, such as The She-Creature, *a 1956 horror flick that had the tagline: "Hypnotized! Reincarnated as a monster from hell!" Are there any other movies we should mention?*

KRESKIN: In *The Mask of Dijon* (1946), the great German director/actor Erich Von Stroheim plays a maniacal, magical stage hypnotist causing individuals to commit murder or accede in other ways to his will. In *The Woman in Green* (1945), Hilary Brook puts a flower in a bowl of water and it starts to spin and move around and around. Of course, in *Dracula* (1931), Bela Lugosi's eyes as the magnetist became the focal point, since it was believed that the eyes had hypnotic or magnetic powers; this was done in several other movies, too.

McCARTY: You were in a TV movie, a cartoon called The Misadventures of Ichabod Crane. *You did the voice for the lead character. What was that like?*

KRESKIN: That television cartoon movie I believe was originally carried on the ABC network. I was asked to be the voice of the key figure in the story. You can quote me as saying "I had a hell of a time" taking on my voice with a slightly different cast and synchronizing it with the cartoon character on the screen. I had a voice coach who had worked in movies who was patient with a novice performer such as myself. I was not an actor and was not used to reading lines, let alone synchronizing them with a character on the screen. I loved the cartoon movie.

FINAL CHAPTER 8 THOUGHTS BY KRESKIN

KRESKIN: Michael, in *The Great Buck Howard* the climax is based on my signature demonstration, the check test. In the movie, there is a rumor that I am using electronic devices of some kind. Indeed, it is stated by a former manager whom Colin Hanks' character meets that I have an assistant in the audience signaling me.

I don't want to ruin the climax of the movie, but it is very clear that I have never used electronic devices, and in the close of the movie the commentary addresses that very strongly. I appreciate that that disclaimer is made in such an authoritative way. Not only do I not use any devices, but there are no stooges or confederates. It is a very important statement so let me restate it. I do not use artifices of any kind.

By the way, some magicians have been trying to fake what I do. They buy sophisticated electronic devices that can be worn by both the performer and a stooge hidden in the audience. For years I have offered $50,000 to anyone who can prove that I employ secret assistants or confederates in any phase of my performance. In response to the wide distribution of the Tom Hanks' movie that offer has now been updated. I now offer $1,000,000 to anyone who can prove I employ confederates or use electronic devices to aid in the accomplishment of my telepathic abilities,

This Million Dollar challenge and assurance of integrity will be valid throughout the continuance of my professional career.

9 | The "Other" Piano Man: Kreskin

Wʜᴇɴ Kʀᴇꜱᴋɪɴ ᴘʟᴀʏꜱ ᴄᴏɴᴄᴇʀᴛꜱ, ʜᴇ'ʟʟ ꜱᴏᴍᴇᴛɪᴍᴇꜱ ᴘʟᴀʏ ᴀ ᴘɪᴀɴᴏ ᴅᴜʀɪɴɢ his shows, which in itself is spellbinding—it has a hypnotic quality to it. A very talented pianist, I thought it would be interesting to explore the musical side of the mentalist. A band even wrote a song about the world famous mentalist, which they titled "The Amazing Kreskin."

McCARTY: Kreskin, tell us the story about the song you wrote called "The Kreskin Theme."

KRESKIN: In the latter years of *The Tonight Show with Johnny Carson* when the orchestra introduced me, the play-on was a song that I had written years before. As a matter of fact, I had titled it "The Kreskin Theme." There were no words to it, but there are a number of reasons why I was able to place the song in the hands of the orchestra.

Some years before that I had been in a restaurant in South Jersey where I had done a show that evening. I looked over, and who was sitting at another table, but the late Skitch Henderson, the fine pianist and orchestra leader. Early in his career he had worked for Bing Crosby. He advised Henderson that people easily remember a nickname of a performer; Crosby of course being remembered for the name Bing, and he suggested Henderson use the name Skitch. Sometime later I had worked with Skitch Henderson on television shows in New York.

In fact, for a while he had a daily talk show series. Here we were at the table. I hadn't seen him for a while, and we got to talking.

In recent years he had left the *Johnny Carson Show* and was pretty much on his own conducting orchestras around the country. He suggested that I appear at Carnegie Hall. When in our conversation he found out that I played the piano, he was surprised and said that nobody ever told him this. So I said, "Well Skitch, I do play piano at my full-evening concerts, the 2½-hour shows." Within minutes he expressed the desire for me to come and appear with the New York Pops at Carnegie Hall, an orchestra he conducted, and what better time to do it than during the time of Halloween. So I agreed to appear around Halloween.

In our conversation, somehow I had let it slip that I had written a song some years before. It never had words to it. I was around 14 years old when I first wrote the song. I had played it a few times publicly, and he asked me to give him a copy of the music. A month or two later was the night I was appearing at Carnegie Hall. I had appeared at Carnegie Hall some years before in a one-man show, my own full-evening show.

The first half of the show was music that Skitch conducted with the orchestra. The second half of the show was built around me. Not only would I play the piano with the orchestra, but I would demonstrate my abilities with members of the audience who volunteered on stage. When I arrived at the theater in the afternoon the orchestra was rehearsing. I got a message that Mr. Henderson wanted me to come downstairs to the orchestra. This is interesting, because he didn't want me to rehearse. He had me sit in the fourth or fifth row, whatever the row is traditionally used by critics and reviewers of programs.

There was the orchestra on stage in short sleeves, and he tapped his baton and started to conduct. I was overwhelmed. I was hearing the song that I had written, but I was hearing it played by a full orchestra. It was an unbelievable sound experience, one of the special moments that I will cherish for the rest of my life. When it ended, I rushed forward on stage to thank him. He said to me, "Kreskin, when this concert tonight is completed, I'm going to turn over to you all of the charts of this orchestra arrangement." One can only estimate that such a unique collection would be valued at thousands of dollars.

One of the people who represented Skitch later explained to me that he had left his farm in Connecticut and taken off to an apartment he had that had no telephones. He had stayed away the entire weekend to arrange that piece for me. I was given permission by him to give it to any orchestra wherever I appeared in the world. Since that night, whenever I appear with an orchestra they play the arrangement put together by Skitch Henderson. You can understand why I have dedicated my song to him in his memory.

Time went by, and about a dozen years ago I met a songwriter, Leigh Madison. She found out that I had composed a song. I turned the music over to her and she added words. The song, which I wrote at age 14 and which was somewhat slightly arranged some years later by a musician and then adapted for a full orchestra by Skitch Henderson now had words to it. The title of the song is "I Can Read Your Mind," with the subtitle "Kreskin's Theme."

McCARTY: You have appeared with orchestras and symphonies. Is this because you are a music lover or were there other reasons?

KRESKIN: Over a decade ago, there was a story in *The New York Times* and some other newspapers about how orchestras and symphonies in the United States were in financial trouble. Even today some have had to close down. I had at that time decided to appear with some symphonies in support of them, so the *Time*'s theme was that I was being brought forward to save the symphonies. I've appeared with the New London Philharmonic in Canada and with the San Antonio Symphony in Texas in 1991, and of course the New York Pops orchestra, etc. It's always been a joy, and I would like to do this again in the near future, since now I can add Skitch's full orchestration of "I Can Read Your Mind."

McCARTY: How old were you when you started playing the piano?

KRESKIN: I started playing the piano when I was 4½. I was very close to my grandparents here in New Jersey. They were from Sicily and did not speak English. They lived about 8 or 9 minutes from where I was growing up with my parents and brother, which was a three-room apartment in Essex County. I would often walk over to my grandparents' house, which was literally six or seven blocks away. On Italian American Day, there was a band and a small parade, and my grandfather had me march with him in the parade, which I loved. At that time, one of my aunts was not married and was still living with my grandparents.

They had an upright piano which she played once in a while. I used to hear her play old tunes from the 1920s, 1930s, and then, yes, the 1940s. I sat down at the piano and in a few minutes my grandparents, my aunt, others who were visiting rushed into the living room as I was playing the march I had heard in the parade. I had never before played piano. A few years later at the age of 9 or 10, I began taking music lessons with a Mrs. Gieb in town. Each year there was a recital, and I became the final performer to play before the families who attended to hear their children. She inquired many times if I would like to consider becoming a concert pianist, but I had known by age 5 what I really wanted to do, and that was not the area that was to be the main focus of my life.

Parenthetically, I've always enjoyed great music. I will have to say that to this day my all-time favorite singer is Bing Crosby. So many famous singers, from Sinatra to Perry Como, had him as their model. He had an incredible grasp on all kinds of music, from religious to jazz to pop, and you name it. I would say, though, that one of the great performers that I enjoyed seeing work on television when I was a young man and then later in person was Liberace.

McCARTY: You knew Liberace pretty well. What was he like?

KRESKIN: I got to know him later on in years. He was a very kind person, very much liked by all who worked around him, and certainly one of the greatest pianists that I've ever seen or heard. Beyond that, he was an incredible showman. We used to kid about it, because if you look at the history of classical musicians, and Liberace began as a classical musician, his showmanship had him stand out. A man who sat with his side to the audience, looked at them, winked at them, flirted with them, smiled at them, and so forth. Oh yes...I'm not talking about Liberace, I'm talking about Franz Liszt, who over 100 years before was flirting with his audience and turning the whole nature of concert piano music into great showmanship as well. People don't realize that during the time of Chopin and Franz Liszt the great matinee idols for the public to see were the likes of these pianists.

Liberace was from Milwaukee, Wisconsin. When he was kid, because both his parents were musicians, a great musician came to his home by the name of Paderewski. Like Liberace, who was Polish/Italian, Paderewski was Polish. Liberace's mother had him play for this great classical pianist, and Paderewski predicted he would become a world famous pianist, but suggested that he use one name, not his lengthy full name, Wladziu Valentino Liberace. They narrowed it down to just Liberace.

Another person who I used to hear on the radio and was popular in nightclubs when I was a kid was Hildegarde. Hildegarde Loretta Sell was also from Milwaukee. She too narrowed her name down to just one word, Hildegarde. When I play the piano in public, I'll occasionally play one of Liberace's theme songs, "I'll Be Seeing You." It was also the theme song of Hildegard's. She introduced that song when it was first written. It is ironic that they were both from Milwaukee and both used one name in their professional title. So when I play it, I think that I am continuing the legacy—one name playing "I'll Be Seeing You." By the way, talk about a Polish musical background: In the 1930s a pianist that Liberace admired by the name of Eddie Duchin used as his theme song a popularized version of the Chopin Nocturne No. 2 in E flat and it became a beautiful love theme all over the world.

I cannot fail to mention Merv Griffin, with whom I did 101 television shows. His orchestra would come up with different songs that reflected my work, songs they would play right after he introduced me. They included songs like "The Very Thought of You" or "I Concentrate on You."

McCARTY: The popular metal band Clutch from Maryland wrote a song reflecting you which they called "The Amazing Kreskin" on their

CD entitled Strange Cousins from the West. *What was your reaction to having a song written about you? How did this come about?*

KRESKIN: "The Amazing Kreskin," was originally presented and billed as an instrumental, and as such I find it haunting. I honestly think I could read thoughts while the music was heard in the background.

By the time it was introduced in the new CD, it became a song with lyrics. While it has no reference to me, I have to say it contains an excellent social commentary. It is so well written and provocative that it will inevitably lend itself to the listeners analyzing the messages and giving their own take on them. It's rare for a song to have life after it's heard, but I predict that this one will.

FINAL CHAPTER 9 THOUGHTS BY KRESKIN

KRESKIN: I continue to play the piano, and to this day will sometimes sit 3 or 4 or 5 hours through the night and play. With my Polish background, of course, I love Frederic Chopin. I also love the great song book of the 1930s, 1940s, and 1950s and the melodious music that appeared during that time. I will sometimes have friends over who will sit around the piano as I play for a couple of hours. We do songs like "The Shadow of Your Smile" and then a haunting song from a movie that was a great ghost story called *The Uninvited*, which came out in the 1940s. I remember seeing that as a kid.

The theme music became so riveting to audiences that words were added. The song, "Stella by Starlight," was recorded by many fine singers of the past. It really was a love song involving a ghost. I will sometimes play that in my program. I also love the music of Hoagy Carmichael. I would agree with many musicians who consider his "Stardust" to be one of the finest American pieces ever written.

There are certain songs, which if I play them in my program, have significance. When the Warner Brothers movie *Superman* came out, the producers sent me the theme song of the movie, which they thought I might enjoy playing in my performances. The music was written by John Williams, and of course the song is "Can You Read My Mind."

Then again, there are times I'll play Bob Hope's theme song, "Thanks for the Memory," because of the significance of the title and the concept of the mind. On my own half-hour TV series, *The Amazing World of Kreskin*, some years ago, a singer, Julie Dejong, appeared, and one of the associate producers, much to my surprise, suggested that she sing a song to me on the air. This was never done before, and it was a touch of brilliance on his part. The song was written by Cole Porter, a haunting Cole Porter melody entitled "You Do Something to Me." There is a significant phrase in the lyrics that goes, "You have the power to hypnotize me."

For many years in my nightclub appearances while a person sat next to me shuffling and handling playing cards, I would talk to the person as they shuffled the cards and enact a scenario, all the time playing the song "Feeling." I still will do that often in my performances.

But it is the second half of my program that has surprised audiences, including music critics. In Ottawa, Canada, a prominent music reviewer came backstage after I had appeared with the orchestra. He said to me, "Kreskin, I have reviewed hundreds and hundreds of pianists in my life. I never saw anything done like this." It was a night reminiscent of Carnegie Hall when Skitch Henderson was there. I sat on stage with this group of people who had volunteered, playing a very melodious, soothing, quiet ballad, and during that period my subjects on stage were collapsing on top of each other or sliding off their chairs on the floor in slumber. One of my favorite songs that I play to accomplish this was popularized by the great orchestra and choir conductor Fred Waring, who opened and closed all his television and theatrical concerts with a fascinatingly beautiful song called "Sleep." You can imagine what happens to my subjects on stage when I play it.

10 | Kreskin's Hundreds of TV and Radio Appearances

LATE NIGHT TV TALK SHOWS—WHO DOESN'T LOVE 'EM? THEY HAVE BEEN popular for over five decades, and for good reason. They are fun: the comedy monologues, the goofy sketches, celebrity interviews, musical performances by new groups and veterans, making fun of the daily news, and comedy performances.

Johnny Carson didn't invent the late night show, but he remains the "King of Late Night Television." His show ran for almost three decades. The early pioneers of late night include Steve Allen with *Tonight Starring Steve Allen*, which ran from 1954–1957, and *The Jack Paar Tonight Show*, which ran from 1957–1962, which Johnny Carson continued after 1962, becoming *The Tonight Show Starring Johnny Carson* from 1962–1991.

The reason Americans don't get 8 hours of sleep? The popularity of late night talk shows is often cited. The hosts are so well known. I can say just their first name and you'll know who I am talking about: Johnny, David, Jay, Conan, Arsenio, and Jimmy.

In this chapter, we will talk about late night TV but also late night radio shows, too. Kreskin's early career was heavily influenced by his first appearances on Steve Allen, Johnny Carson, and as a regular on *The Joey Bishop Show*, which also featured a very young announcer named Regis Philbin.

Kreskin's First Communion. Pictured with younger brother Joe.

Teenage Kreskin in performance.

Kreskin with his parents.

Kreskin has been privileged to perform concerts with many leading orchestras. He often uses the piano in his shows.

Kreskin has had a great love for animals all his life. He currently shares his home with four beautiful cats. Lest they become jealous, he is here pictured with Miss Kitty, who has passed away.

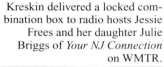

Kreskin delivered a locked combination box to radio hosts Jessie Frees and her daughter Julie Briggs of *Your NJ Connection* on WMTR.

On July 25, 2011, Kreskin delivered his sealed prediction to Jimmy Fallon on NBC TV, not only for the results of the 2012 presidential election, but also who he believed would be running on the Republican ticket. At the time of his prediction, over a dozen people were possible contenders. In addition to Jimmy Fallon, three others were given sealed packages to be opened on *Late Night With Jimmy Fallon* 2 days after the presidential election to corroborate Kreskin's prediction.

Robin Leach, former host of the *Lifestyles of the Rich and Famous* and now a *Las Vegas Sun* columnist, has one of the sealed predictions.

Kreskin gave another copy in a locked safe to be displayed over the bar at Patsy's Restaurant in New York City, which was made famous through the years by Frank Sinatra. Here Executive Chef and co-owner of Patsy's, Sal Scognamillo, is pictured with Kreskin.

Kreskin predicts 2012 Presidential Elections.
Kreskin is shown with the four guardians of his prediction.

In an unparalleled prediction in 2005, Kreskin submitted a sealed package at the beginning of basketball's March Madness. When the games were completed, Kreskin had not only named the winning team, but also the name of the last team to lose.

February 1, 2008: On Fox Business News with David Asman, Kreskin predicted that the Giants would win the Super Bowl by 3. The final score was 17–14.

Kreskin's friend of over 50 years Roger Ailes, Chairman and CEO of Fox News Channel & TV Stations. He played a key role in Kreskin's career as the producer of *The Mike Douglas Show*. Kreskin felt honored to have him write the Special Foreword to this book.

Kreskin does Carnac.

Kreskin befriended the late musician/pianist Skitch Henderson early in his career. Skitch was the orchestra leader on Johnny Carson's show for a number of years and later had his own television talk show. Skitch hired Kreskin to appear at Carnegie Hall with the New York Pops Orchestra, and from there Kreskin proceeded to appear with orchestras and symphonies in the United States and Canada.

Johnny Carson vertical.

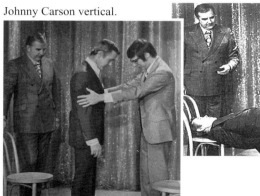

Carson horizontal.

Carson as a seat
for Bette Midler.

Kreskin standing on Jimmy Fallon.

Kreskin standing on Merv Griffin.

Making a famous TV host as rigid as a board through the power of suggestion is a Kreskin signature effect. It started with Johnny Carson and years later progressed to Merv Griffin and then to Jimmy Fallon.

Kreskin's television interview with his friend the writer Walter Gibson, who created *The Shadow*. Gibson was very close to Houdini and other famous magicians.

Kreskin finds his check in the audience. He has amazed audiences with this signature test thousands of times.

Kreskin played chess while blindfolded simultaneously against the International Chess Champion Viktor Korchnoi and the *NY Times* chess expert/editor.

Kreskin with Donald Trump.

Kreskin with Lee Falk, the creator of *Mandrake the Magician* and *The Phantom*. He called Kreskin the one real-life person who comes closest to being a living Mandrake.

Kreskin with William Shatner at his Broadway show. They first met on Kreskin's TV show.

David Letterman watches Kreskin in action.

Kreskin with the pioneer television comedian Milton Berle. Kreskin revealed on the air exactly what NBC paid Milton for his first show.

George Stroumboulopoulos, popular host of the Canadian hit CBC TV night show *The Hour*, interviews Kreskin.

Mike Douglas was a genial host who invited Kreskin back time after time.

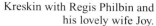
Kreskin with Regis Philbin and his lovely wife Joy.

Howard Stern is a giant of TV and radio. Here he is with his partner Robin Quivers between Kreskin and Dr. Joyce Brothers.

The Amazing Kreskin guesting on ABC TV's *The Joey Bishop Show*. Regis Philbin was Joey's announcer.

Kreskin with his friend Joey Reynolds. Joey's 5-hour late night talk show on WOR Radio from New York City lasted 15 years. Kreskin spent more than 320 hours on the air with Reynolds.

Kreskin tapping into the political thoughts of Gov. Mike Huckabee on his Fox News TV show.

Kreskin with his fictional alter ego the Great
Buck Howard, played by John Malkovich.

Kreskin superimposed
over the movie poster for
The Great Buck Howard.

Colin Hanks did a fine job portraying the
road manager in *The Great Buck Howard*.

Tom Hanks at the opening of *The Great
Buck Howard*, which was loosely based
on The Amazing Kreskin. The movie was
written and directed by Sean McGinley,
Kreskin's former road manager.

Dinner for Schmucks is a comedy starring Steve Carell and Zach Galifi-
anakis. Kreskin's portrait is prominent, because he is the role model for
Zach's mind power.

Movies with Kreskin as role model.

McCARTY: Let's start out with the "King of Late Night," Johnny Carson. His show was originally in New York and then moved to Los Angeles. Do you know how Johnny Carson felt about this?

KRESKIN: First of all, one of the bitter experiences for Carson was that when he moved to Los Angeles after doing so many years of his show in New York he found out that NBC had discarded, destroyed, or taped over many of his early shows. There are many shows that I did with him that are lost for good, and it infuriated Johnny to the point that his shows after that were protectively put in special containers and buried under the earth somewhere, I believe in the Midwest. He never forgave them. But we have to understand that this happened with Mike Douglas as well, and I did 118 shows with Mike. In the early days, the broadcasting industry did not realize the value of these legendary shows and consequently often just simply discarded them.

McCARTY: You appeared on The Tonight Show with Johnny Carson *88 times. Which is your most memorable appearance and why?*

KRESKIN: Needless to say, there were many experiences with Carson, but one haunts me to this day. It showed his concern to have a guest seen in the best light. I was about to go on the air, and a couple of the guests before me were talking back and forth and bantering with Carson. As they always did before every show, one of Carson's talent coordinators came back to me and asked, "Kreskin, is everything all right? Are you ready to go on?" My usual answer was, "Yes, of course." This time I said, "I'm ready to go on, but I've got to tell you something. I can't do what I intended to do."

He said, "What do you mean?" He didn't get upset. He trusted me enough to go out and be able to handle myself under most any condition. I said, "I can't work with the other guests because they are both drunk." It was obvious, especially during the commercials, that these two guys were not with it, and it was remarkable that Carson was able to handle them. As Johnny introduced me, I walked towards him, as I had done scores of times, but this time I was trying to figure out, what am I going to do?

I could do something with cards, something that doesn't require a lot of concentration. And I sat down at the main chair right next to Johnny's desk, the other two men had moved over. There was a glass of water on the table, which had been put there by the prop artist, because I had planned to have someone gaze into the glass of water and require them to see in their mind something that someone else was concentrating upon. There were pads and pencils on the table. Well, suddenly the guest next to me moved his knee forward inadvertently, banging into the table, and the glass of water just poured on the pad. Everything was just made worthless. There was a moan in the audience that I'll never forget to this day. Johnny turned to the guest and said, "I see you're doing your best material." Talk about a retort that was like an uppercut to his chin. He had hit him hard.

Then Johnny looked at me and said in so many words, "Kreskin, you know I'm a little bit fed up with you. Every time you're on you work with the guests and people from the audience. Why don't you do something with me?" The right side of his face was away from the audience and the camera, the left side of my face was away, so both our eyes were not seen. Carson was winking at me, saying we'll make things work. That night I worked only with Carson. Talk about saving the day.

I still consider Johnny Carson the "King of The Late Night Show," and I'm sure if I got to David Letterman he would agree with me, because after Carson retired he often suggested jokes for Letterman, and Letterman had an open line for him to call in. David Letterman had tremendous respect for the gentleman. Johnny knew everything that was happening on his own show. He could hear the camera directions, he could see around him what was taking place. Truly, the show was his life when he was working. His passion was the monologue, which he started working on in the morning, seeing what was in the national newspapers, such as *USA Today*, and letting his comedy writers know which topics he was interested in. He had a handle on everything that was going on with his show, he didn't miss a trick. That is a rare quality for anyone in the talk show industry.

McCARTY: Was Johnny Carson's skit "The Great Carnac" inspired by you?

KRESKIN: I've told the story before, but yes, it was. My first break was on Steve Allen's show. As I walked on cold, with no experience before on major television, I walked to the desk that Steve Allen was standing at, tripped over the edge, and practically fell on my face. Carson happened to be watching that show, saw the incident, and some weeks later created Carnac, who fell over the desk. The full dimension of the Carnac character, and the way he answered a remark by coming up with a question was based on an old vaudeville routine. Long before Carson this was done by Steve Allen. He just sat at his desk as a kind of wacked out newspaper guy who was talking about newspapers and their headlines. Steve Allen's mom was a comedian in vaudeville, so this type of routine had a longer history behind it. But as Carson said to me on his show, my initial break and action of almost falling over something was something he would never forget.

McCARTY: You have an interesting story about Sandy Hackett and Johnny Carson. Please share it.

KRESKIN: While headlining in Las Vegas, I was approached by a gentleman I hadn't seen for probably more than 17 years. It was Sandy Hackett. He couldn't wait to speak with me, reminding me that we had met years ago.

Before we get to Sandy's story let's talk about his dad. Sandy Hackett is the son of the late legendary comedian Buddy Hackett. Whole families would recognize Buddy. He had been in a movie that endeared him to everyone, including children. It was *The Love Bug* about a Volkswagen with which Hackett had formed a bond. Following that movie, Buddy was appearing all over the place, not only on late night television talk shows but also in nightclubs.

It was a rather shocking surprise to some families who took their children to see the stage performances. His personal appearances were hilarious, but outrageous, using language you wouldn't use in a family situation. There were times when the parents of kids left in a state of shock. Eventually, Hackett headlined on late night shows with the warning that the show was not for children.

He was a brilliant comedian, and at the same time a fabulous character actor. Seeing him in movies, you just had to love the man.

Over the years he appeared on all kinds of television shows, including Johnny Carson's. At times Johnny would laugh as loud as any member of the audience at Hackett's outrageous outlook on life.

Many years ago while I was appearing in Vegas I walked into casino, and who did I see there but Buddy Hackett. Immediately, he pulled me over to a blackjack table and told everyone to move away, he wanted the dealer to deal only to me. The dealer was his son, Sandy Hackett.

In reminiscing about all of the appearances that his father, as well as I, made with Johnny Carson, Sandy Hackett told me a story that is poignant and has a real serious quality of "flash" or "crisis" telepathy to it. Sandy himself had appeared only once on the *Johnny Carson Show* and that was when he was around 5 years old. Buddy Hackett mentioned during an appearance that his son Sandy was in the audience and Johnny had him brought him up on stage to sit next to this giant of television.

Now let's move forward to January 23, 2005. Sandy went to bed, and in the middle of the night had a dream, not a common dream, and not one he'd had before. He said it was almost as if Johnny Carson was coming into his bedroom to express a kind of farewell. He said Johnny never seemed to stop moving. He was alert and bright and fidgety, but he spoke in very short sentences and thoughts.

Sandy recounted to me, "I wanted to thank him for being a friend to my dad. I started to say something about how I knew what it was like to lose someone close, for Johnny had lost his son. There evidently was visible pain in Johnny as a reaction to that remark, and Johnny said it was not the same, and that I didn't know what I was talking about." Sandy went on to say, "I wanted to hug him, but he didn't seem approachable. We never touched. When I finally went to say good-bye, we didn't shake hands." Sandy said, "I just woke up, and I felt compelled to write my dream down before it disappeared altogether. I went to the computer and proceeded to type the details of what was an incredible experience." Sandy was typing this in the middle of the night and then went back to bed.

The next morning, around 5 or 6 hours later, Sandy received a phone call from his manager, who was a big Carson fan. He simply said, "Sandy, did you hear Johnny Carson passed away?" Sandy had not heard the news. Sandy told me, "My gut feeling is that Johnny came to say goodbye. Right now in Heaven someone's saying "Here's Johnny...""

McCARTY: How about Regis Philbin? I know the two of you have known each other for a very long time.

KRESKIN: Regis Philbin and I go back to the Joey Bishop days when we were both regulars on his ABC network show. Joey Bishop had his own version of *The Tonight Show*; however, it was opposite Johnny Carson, so its viewership was limited. His announcer, a very loyal man, was Regis Philbin. I appeared on the show a number of times and soon became a regular on the show.

There was a memorable incident when I was doing an appearance with Joey and then proceeding to go on a long tour. On the air, Bishop asked me when I was returning home. I gave him an approximate date, and he said, "Kreskin, that will be the Monday that you will appear on the show. You're going to be my co-host for one week." My jaw dropped. I was, of course, thrilled for the opportunity.

One of my favorite stories of the show involved Regis. Joey and he always bantered at the beginning of the show. Usually before there was any bantering, Joey would walk out on stage and do his monologue. But this particular night, for reasons I couldn't figure out, Regis walked out behind him and was standing there kind of crestfallen. It was very distracting to Joey Bishop's monologue. It didn't make any sense. It would have been like Ed McMahon wandering around Carson during Johnny's monologue. Joey finally stopped his monologue and said, "Regis, is something wrong?" Regis stepped over to him and said, "Yes, Joey, I'm leaving the show."

What I'm about to detail for you now has not been known by many people. Joey seemed stunned, and said, "Regis, can I help you with this problem?" And Regis just continued to say, "I'm leaving the show. I'm leaving the show." Joey seemed perplexed. Where was he to turn? And he kept implying, "Regis, if I can do something, let me know." Finally, Regis walked off the show. Can you imagine that as the opening of a television hour? What else was on people's minds for the rest of the program, no matter who Joey's guests were, who he was interviewing, but that Regis had walked off the program?

By the way, a few days after that incident, I started being called by the Carson people. It turns out that Johnny had seen many of my appearances on *Joey Bishop* and decided that when my run with Bishop ended I would come to his program.

There is more to this incident of Regis walking off the show with no explanation given. It wasn't until years later, after *The Joey Bishop Show* had ended, that I asked Regis over lunch, "What really happened?" The explanation was finally exposed to me. Joey and Regis would take walks at night outside the ABC studio, sometimes lasting a half an hour or longer. They'd talk about anything, just reflect on things, and finally they would turn around and come back to the studio. One night, Joey was bemoaning the fact that they didn't have the best ratings. Johnny had all the ratings. Regis was trying to console him in a supporting way saying, "But Joey, you do a darn good job. Your audience loves you." And Joey kept saying, "Yeah, but we don't have the viewers. I wish we could spark a strong attention to the show."

As they approached the studio Joey turned to Regis and said, "Wait a minute. I've got an idea. Why don't you walk off the show tonight?" Oh, yes, it took me a couple of decades later to find out that the whole thing had been planned, collaborated between Joey Bishop and Regis. It had become the talk of television, until some weeks later Regis came back, and for some reason, all was made up.

McCARTY: How did Regis Philbin and his show save you from major surgery?

KRESKIN: More than a decade ago, I had for a number of years suffered from what has been described by many as the most severe and incredible pain as one could imagine, and that is the experience of kidney stones. One time while on tour appearing in Florida, a business associate assured me that he knew one of the best doctors in the area, and he would come over to ease the pain.

When he arrived at my hotel room after one particular night's show, as I sat there in agony, he pointed out he always wanted to meet me and had been a fan of mine. He couldn't really administer anything to me without putting me through a tremendous amount of tests because of restrictions in Florida in attending to people from out of state. This angered my doctor back home, Dr. Alterbaum, who is no longer with us. He said he would have given the doctor in Florida his code over the phone to prescribe drugs, but the doctor would not contact him, so I went on suffering. Fortunately I passed the stones some days later.

There was another occasion when I was flying home after a television show in Los Angeles. When I got on the plane that day, I experienced another kidney stone attack. I was in tremendous agony and given permission by the crew to lie down on the floor of the plane. A doctor was also on the flight and took a risk, a risk that I will respect for the rest of my life. He got on the intercom and asked if anybody had pain killers. A lady showed him some pills. He gave me one of them, and I was able to sit back in my seat and fly home in reasonable comfort. I remember getting off the plane with a wheelchair available, which I never thought would be necessary.

Fortunately, I have not experienced kidney stones for over two decades, but can remember some years ago, when on the third bout with that malady, that it was decided that surgery would be the route to go instead of the electronic techniques that could be used to shatter the kidney stones. I knew that Regis had been able to be relieved of kidney stones in that matter without intrusive surgery.

The day I entered the hospital a call came to my room from my secretary. Regis by now was doing his tremendously successful morning television show. One of his booking people called my office and asked if they could fly me out that evening as they wanted me to appear on his show the next morning. The show was not in their studio, but at a resort area, and it was going to be outdoors. They wanted me to consider doing it. Don't you know, I proceeded to get dressed and told them to have the ticket ready so when I got home I could head straight to the airport. The Regis people did not know I was in the hospital. I was relaying my messages to my secretary.

A nurse and then a second nurse walked in, asking me what the hell was going on. I said, "I have to leave. I'm going to be on Regis Philbin tomorrow morning." They said, "Kreskin, you're out of your mind." I hurried out of the hospital to my car, went home, got my change of clothes for the show, and went to the airport. Believe it or not, traveling by plane for this trip was the worst agony I had experienced on the three occasions I suffered from this ailment, but my commitment solidly was to do the Regis show. I felt a tremendous loyalty to him. Arriving the next morning, I went into makeup briefly. I was not in a good frame of mind. It was perhaps one of the few times television crews ever saw me disagreeable. I was not quite hearing what was being said around me. This was, I'm sure, foreign to them. But I couldn't tell them why, namely that I was in absolute agony.

I finally made up my mind that I would make my appearance and let no viewer sense a problem. It's interesting what the mind can do when we need to rise above the pressures in our lives. When I was announced and walked out on camera, I sat with Regis and proceeded to do a thought-reading involving a couple of people who were outdoors attending. Both segments went extremely well. I don't think Regis or Kathie Lee had any idea I was in discomfort, and I really did not notice any discomfort until I walked off and saw the production people. They handed me an envelope. My hotel was on the same grounds where the show was taking place. They told me I could enjoy any meals that day or evening at the resort, I could relax all day, and would be able to fly home either that night or the next morning. The truth of the matter is I never did use the passes to see shows or have meals. Instead I just lay on the hotel floor the entire day. Eventually, I flew back to New Jersey. The next morning, I contacted the hospital, and it was decided the surgery would take place the following day.

The surgery was scheduled for about 10 or 11 in the morning, but before that they took x-rays. Sometime later the surgeon walked into my room with the x-rays in his hand. He held them up to the light, threw them on the floor, stomped on them, and cursed me. I said, "What's the matter, doctor?" He said, "Kreskin, since you were last here, probably since you came in last night, you have passed the kidney stones, and you can go home." To this day, no one has known this, not even from Regis' people. I never made it public. The call to do the show and the postponement saved me from surgery. Thank you, Regis.

Regis is one of the most natural people in the business. What you see on television and what you see off camera; that is the real Philbin. I can say, after doing over 100 shows with him, that success really has not changed him. He is the same personality, very expressive; talks off the top of his head. Indeed he never felt he could do a monologue to open the show, so he borrowed from Jack Paar. Really in truth, we'd have to also give credit to Arthur Godfrey, who went on the air and just talked about what he did the day before or what was on his mind.

McCARTY: Joey Bishop was important in Regis Philbin's career and yours as well. What was he like?

KRESKIN: Joey Bishop was a good person who is not often brought up much in the late night talk show genre. He had a *Tonight Show*—like show live out of Los Angeles. He didn't get the attention that he deserved, because he was opposite the king, Johnny Carson. I did his show many times. I will never forget a performance, after which Joey thanked me for what he thought was an amazing feat of the mind, and I was bowing and acknowledging it.

Joey later told me when I got back from a cruise that I had been performing on that he wanted me to be on his show for one whole week. They told me that the expression change in my face was something to behold. Joey was part of the Rat Pack with Sinatra, Sammy Davis, Peter Lawford, Dean Martin, etc. He had with him a rather remarkable announcer, namely Regis Philbin. Yes, that was when Regis came to the attention of the rest of the country, as he had just been doing local shows on the west coast.

Joey Bishop was a natural on the air. He had been a stand-up comedian, but with a slower pace who still managed to make his performances work. I remember gaining insight into his personality when one week on the show I attempted a week ahead of time to predict what I thought would be the major stories in the *Los Angeles Times*. I delivered the package to Joey one week early. He had me on the entire week, every night showing the package which he had kept locked in his office. One day during the week I received a call asking if I would come to his office in the afternoon. I went there, not knowing what he had in mind. I never prearranged anything on the program. He and I never discussed what I would do ahead of time.

Bishop was very kind, and said if ever I wanted to move out there he would find accommodations for me and people who would make sure everything would be taken care of. I demurred, saying that I needed to keep a home base and keep my roots together. I've always maintained my home in New Jersey, although I've been to the west coast hundreds of times. But I knew there was something more. He finally got to it and said, "You know, Milton Berle's been calling me every day asking about the prediction." Oh my God, a legend in my life. "Uncle Miltie" was the king when I was a kid, watching him on TV every Tuesday night.

This was the final day when they would open the prediction that night. That afternoon, Joey asked me, "Kreskin, how accurate have you been? How close? Did you get any of your prediction correct?" And I went over to him and shook his hand and said, "Joey, I've got to keep it the way it is. You have the package, I don't, but you've got to wait until we are on the air to open it, and let's just keep it hanging." He smiled, obviously somewhat frustrated, and said, "I'll tell Milt what you said."

Oh, by the way, one week later when he opened the package, I had successfully predicted the key words and subject matter of the headline of that day's *Los Angeles Times*.

McCARTY: Let's talk about Mike Douglas of The Mike Douglas Show. *I remember watching that talk show as a kid, and I have many fond memories. You have mentioned him a number of times in this book, so I thought it was fitting we talk about him, too.*

KRESKIN: Mike is a very gentle, easygoing man who really had the general public comfortable with him. Men and women loved him in the afternoon. He wasn't nighttime fare, but his show was an hour and a half of easy viewing each day.

In my appearances on the show, the producers, including Roger Ailes, had set a format for me. In the first segment, I would simply sit down and discuss the passing scene, issues taking place around the world that I felt I might have insight into because of my work. But there was always one question they kept that they never told me ahead of time. In this instance, Mike said, "Kreskin, mind-reading acts come and go, but you seem to go on year after year after year. To what do you attribute this?"

It forced me to reflect upon myself in a way that I really never had, but my answer (in perhaps different words) remains the same today as it was then. I said, "Mike, you've got to understand. I'm a really highly competitive person. I've never seen anybody in my field. I don't get to see much entertainment, because I'm working all the time. But I'm competitive with myself. I'm always challenging my abilities to step further, if you will, one step beyond."

Michael, if I can add to that, I would probably say that I have such a zest for what I do, and I believe my audiences sense it. As I have said again and again, my career has literally been an adventure.

McCARTY: Let's talk about another Mike, Mike Huckabee.

KRESKIN: In this past couple of years, I have done four appearances with Governor Mike Huckabee on Fox Television with tremendous response and enthusiasm. He has a genuine enthusiasm and also an interest in others. Here's a man that certainly is presidential timber in the future, having already been a governor and a minister, and has a genuine charismatic quality of honesty. His crew, some of whom are students working at the studio, just revere the man.

In one case I gave him a sealed envelope during one of the shows that he was to keep in his possession until I met with him again. It predicted something that was going to happen on the show. I'm told that his curiosity was so overpowering that to ease his own temptation to peek he gave it to his wife to hold. When I came back on the show some months later, he brought four people onto the stage, each of whom put together numbers, not three or four digits, but large numbers, and they were of such size that after they were written out we had two people with calculators, as well as Mike Huckabee himself, totaling the sets of numbers, since the total was going to be in the many thousands. Understand, the numbers were created by chance. There were bowls of balls with numbers on them like you would see on a Lotto showing, and not one single number on any of the hundreds of balls was duplicated. Well, the bottom line was that when he opened the envelope that had remained in his possession, I had predicted the exact total.

McCARTY: Let's talk about Jimmy Fallon. He went from Saturday Night Live *to hosting his own talk show,* Late Night With Jimmy Fallon.

KRESKIN: When I started doing the Huckabee Show, I also found myself doing the *Jimmy Fallon Show*. Fallon attracts a different audience. He is a young man who came out of *Saturday Night Live* and other brilliant comedic appearances. He was a stand-up comedian, but now a young and very effective host of the *Late Night* franchise on NBC. He is building a career and a following that is just a joy to behold. As competitive and hard working as he is with the training from *Saturday Night Live*, which had to be intense, there doesn't seem to be an element of jealousy in his personality. He is so proud and thrilled to have his own show at that hour. It seems the last thought on his mind is to jump into David Letterman or Jay Leno's position. He's found a niche, and his audiences are clicking with him. I can tell from the four shows I've done so far in the studio, and watching him on camera, that he has truly linked with his audiences in a way that's rare. He indeed has a special gift.

As a young television personality, he is truly winning, and his show is going to build. I found myself locking a rapport with him from the moment we met. On my second appearance, I redid a test that I had done 30 years before with Johnny Carson, as I described in Chapter 3.

McCARTY: The last talk show host I think we should talk about is the late Tom Snyder. In my opinion, he was one of the best interviewers on late night television. What are your thoughts on Mr. Snyder?

KRESKIN: In 2007, we lost a fabulous radio and television broadcaster by the name of Tom Snyder. I knew him very well, having worked with him many times through the years. Most people remember him for going on the air after *The Tonight Show* with a 1-hour interview show called *Tomorrow* in the days before Conan O'Brien or Jimmy Fallon. It was so well done that it lasted from 1973 to 1982.

Tom Snyder was an inquisitive, opinionated, but learned man who could interview almost anyone. I first got to know him during the early days of my career. Back then, he was broadcasting a show out of Philadelphia on KYW. In the latter days of his show, he had up to three guests, and I often appeared with him. But in the earlier days, he had an hour-long morning show, complete with studio audience, that spotlighted a single guest, and that program was even a greater pleasure for me.

Sooner or later, Tom would have me attempt some thought-reading experiments or effects with the audience. Incidentally, one of the first times I did the show it turned out be a traumatic experience, unbeknownst to him or his staff.

The problem was my poor estimate of the travel time required on a business day from Easton, Pennsylvania to Philadelphia. I misjudged my time, and when I arrived at the station Tom Snyder had already gone on the air. I didn't know where to park, so I parked in front of the studio, jumped out of the car, and ran into the downstairs area. I discovered that Tom had already started rerunning an earlier show that I had done with him to fill in for my not arriving.

Happily, everything went well, we went on live for the hour and we were delighted with the results. I, especially, was relieved that I had not let him down. You're not going to believe this! I stayed only a few minutes after the hour, as I had work elsewhere in the Philadelphia area. Suddenly, a feeling of terror filled me. Oh yes, the "great mentalist" finally remembered where I parked. I had double-parked on a main street in Philadelphia and left the car running.

Now, over one hour later, I didn't know what to expect. I bolted out the door, and stood, surprised, to see my car still there, still running, doors unlocked. It hadn't been towed. It hadn't been ticketed. When I jumped in the car and drove away, I was filled with one hell of a feeling of relief. Sometimes even I marvel at my own luck.

McCARTY: You were incredibly lucky there. Please go on. What was your relationship with Tom Snyder?

KRESKIN: Tom Snyder and I had built a bond of trust. He often brought me on the air to discuss unexplained phenomena or strange theories of the mind. Sometimes we would pursue a topic for as long as half an hour, just the two of us.

McCARTY: Late night shows have changed over the years. What are your thoughts?

KRESKIN: Of course, the stage has changed in recent years, and there are new performers, including the Scottish host, Craig Ferguson. Although I had met him at a book signing, I've never worked with him, but I find him absolutely refreshing. I did work with the giants Jay Leno and David Letterman, and, yes, Conan O'Brien, who has his own series on a cable station. I never really got to work with Conan except the time when I got a call suddenly out of nowhere while in a restaurant in New York with the request that I do his show the next day. I got confused. I said, "I don't believe the show is in New York now. Isn't he on the road?" He sure was on the road, he was in California.

They said they'd fly me out there for this one appearance. Jim Carrey was going to be on the show and had requested that I be on as well. I did not have a booking for the next day, so I was able to get on a plane and fly out there. It was tight scheduling, but I got to the studio on time and walked out onto the stage.

Carrey was bringing out characters that he had used in his early days as a stand-up comedian. I was the last one to walk on. It turns out that one of Carrey's favorite routines growing up was imitating me in a comic way. I really wish I could have spent time with Jim and Conan after the show, but I had to literally run outside as soon as the show ended and take a flight back to the east coast because the next day I was flying to another area.

The setting today for late night shows has changed considerably. There are no longer just one or two shows. Now there are five or six shows, if not more. It is becoming more of a challenge for the hosts to build a strong following as the audiences have become splintered. Back in the times of Carson, Steve Allen, and Jack Paar, we watched the entire show without interrupting its continuity. In the case of Paar, there could be three nights in a row where the guests were boring and not that interesting, but then suddenly one night Paar would come on, get into an argument with a guest, or rant about something written about him or verbally attack the top gossip columnists Dorothy Kilgallen or Walter Winchell. The next day people at work would be standing around the water cooler saying, "Did you see what happened on Paar's show last night?"

In the earlier days there was a tremendous flavor of spontaneity that carried itself into the viewing audience. A lot of that has disappeared from the business. One of the great mistakes I see in shows deals with the movement from one guest to the next. One wonders if the director came straight out of television school. The earlier ones learned the business by working hard behind the scenes or may have been in theater. That being the case, one of the lessons they would have learned is that if something is working on the stage you move with it.

The opportunities don't seem to exist so much today in broadcasting where individuals can encompass and become involved in all areas of television production. That is why so much of television today seems to be lacking something. Oh yes, we have nighttime television shows that are successful, but sometimes uncomfortably so. A guest is on a talk/variety show and he's a hit. He's kept for a period of 8 minutes or so, and then set aside with the next guest coming on. It's almost as if some of the directors have lost the showmanship of early television. If only they had the opportunity of studying the giants of early broadcasting, from Dave Garroway to Merv Griffin, yes, to Mike Douglas and Johnny Carson, Jack Paar, and, of course, Arthur Godfrey. Many of these people came out of live entertainment, stage, theater, and in-person appearances. As a result, they were so well tuned to their audiences that if the guests were exciting the audience, it would be nothing for Jack Paar to keep guests like Cliff Arquette as Charley Weaver on for the rest of the show. Some of the guests that were scheduled to appear on the show had to be dropped. He would apologize and bring them back another time. Jonathan Winters would steal the entire *Jack Paar Show.* Taking it out of control—yes—but great entertainment. Merv Griffin had the same fault.

Fault? No, they knew from their theater background that if something is working, something is running right, keep it going. Steve Allen was a genius at this. I'm afraid that the background and opportunities which were experienced by those television people in the past are just not that accessible to people in broadcasting today, and it shows. Many of these shows are great, but in some respects, a spark and certain kind of excitement have gone out of them.

McCARTY: Before we end this chapter, let's talk about radio. It is almost impossible not to talk about Howard Stern when it comes to radio. You once said to me in one of your interviews that "I think Howard Stern is the best satirist—and I am talking about true, classical satire—since Oscar Wilde and Mark Twain."

KRESKIN: Regarding Howard Stern, I've done a number of his shows. Some were television and some radio. Howard has been a big fan and great supporter of mine. He has pronounced that he felt strongly my work was legitimate and that I can truly tune into people's minds.

One show that I did with him was an absolute classic. It was a séance for which I needed volunteers, and he got us some. They were people off the street. Some were real characters. Some may have spent more time living on the streets than in homes, others were just curious. The set was decorated for Halloween. The volunteers sat at eight or nine tables with four chairs to a table.

It was not a gimmick. There was no sleight of hand. There was not a single stooge in that room. As the volunteers sat resting their hands on the tables, it became uncanny. Stern said it was one of the most dramatic things to happen on any of his shows. The tables started to move. The people were holding the tables down with their hands joined flat on the top, insisting they were not moving anything. The tables started to rattle, and people had to stand, so the crew could pull away chairs as the tables started to move along the set and at times banging into other tables.

In fact, one table kept falling on the floor. And a dramatic moment happened as the listeners and the viewers saw and heard tables in a sense coming to life. I said to the group, pointing to each table, I want one person to take one hand off the table. Understand there were eight hands joined around the table. When I told them to lift that hand, the tables came to a "dead," if I may use that term, stillness. And it was not gradual, it was an instantaneous stop. But when they put their hands back on the tables and joined in a circle, so it was a continuous circle, the tables started shifting and moving in a circle.

The movement was caused by the unconscious vibrations created by the unconscious minds of the people, an energetic force that created this response. I could have taken it to the point of addressing one table by saying if the answer to the question I ask is YES, the table will rock twice, NO it will rock once. I could have asked a question about a deceased figure known to someone in the room, and the table would have responded.

I do not want it to appear that I'm advocating spirit communication, but getting a table to respond by the way it vibrates to a yes or no question is dramatic. A century ago, this was common, in private homes, especially for the elite, as they sat around a table and the table started to move. It was called table tilting. And questions were asked. It is from this that we get the term *table talk*.

One of my most dramatic examples of this was a demonstration that was held years ago in Washington, D.C., at a building called the Octagon House. The room where the séance was being held had a legend that decades earlier a woman had come into view at the top of a railing and thrown herself over it, committing suicide. When the séance began it was now past midnight, and the "spirit" of the experience was generating an awful lot of excitement. The tables in the room were moving, especially when I pointed upstairs to the second floor and told the people to look.

Then there was screaming and panic. Some started to run for the doors. They had seen a woman appear who proceeded to throw herself over the railing, crashing down to the first floor. There, of course, was no such person. Some kept insisting it was a ghost. I had created this reaction just as I had with the *500 Hats of Bartholomew Cubbins*. I had created a mass hallucination in the minds of the participants.

McCARTY: You mentioned Barry Farber earlier in our discussion of John Scarne. Can you talk more about Barry Farber? I really don't know that much about him.

KRESKIN: Amongst the pioneers of late night radio talk shows are Barry Farber and Barry Gray. One of Farber's remarkable talents is not only his vast command of the English language, but the fact that he speaks 16 languages fluently and over a dozen casually. He is a tremendous personality, and I did scores of shows with him.

Before Farber, there was a gentleman by the name of Barry Gray. He had a radio show which ran a couple of hours a night around 11 or midnight, originally coming from a restaurant in New York where celebrities went to eat after shows. I first became aware of him on a local TV station. He did about 15 minutes of news, more commentary and opinions, than news, and I became alerted to him one night when he came on the air with sunglasses on.

It turns out he had two black eyes. He had criticized some gangsters in town, and they got out of a car one night and just gave him a beating. I did many shows with him. He was the first to talk at night and at length, eloquently, about all kinds of subjects. He was highly opinionated, but he was also very well read. We had intellectual discussions on the air, which the listeners seemed to gravitate to.

With all these figures in radio and television, I cannot overlook a man who has played such a special role in my life as Joey Reynolds.

McCARTY: Joey Reynolds was a very popular radio DJ and talk show host. You have been on his show numerous times. I believe you even talked about my book Liquid Diet: A Vampire Satire *on that show. Thanks for the plug. Let's talk about Joey Reynolds, who has been a staple for late night radio.*

KRESKIN: For 14 years, Joey Reynolds was showcased on the WOR Radio network, with a popular talk station in New York that was syndicated around the country. His radio show ran from 1:00 to 5:00 in the morning, and for a while from midnight to 5:00 A.M., the same hours that Long John Nebel pioneered in radio years ago.

Reynolds has been one of the most popular personalities in the business, with a background of earlier having one of the most successful rock music shows in radio history, plus working on gigantic sci-fi movies, etc. He is frank to say that he has lost a couple of fortunes in his life and his family, thanks to drinking and drugs. He never avoided mentioning the downfalls he had experienced in the business and the incredible opportunities that he came across to enable him to spring back as he did.

Can you imagine five nights a week for 5 hours a night with intriguing subject matter? It was largely brought in and scheduled by his coordinator, Myra Chanin, who is one of the best broadcast booking experts I have ever known. She had booked a variety of guests when the Virginia Tech shootings took place a few years ago, and within hours an expert on serial killers appeared on the show. Within 8 days of that tragedy I did almost 16 hours of discussions about the mind of the kind of killer that would attack innocent people.

On Reynolds' show one of my favorite nights was the Jewish hour. Often, I was the token non-Jew on the show. Joey would interview and talk with a number of really top Jewish comedians who sounded like they just came out of the Catskills. The variety of guests ranged from intriguing writers to political people, opinionated news people, you name it. I have not heard such a diversity of show content for a long time in broadcasting.

The key to Joey Reynolds is that he has the ability to communicate with anybody, and I mean anybody. He makes them sound interesting, because he finds interesting content within people. One of his great gifts, which I marveled at while doing his show (since I did some 320 hours with him through the years), was his ability to go on the air and have a particular thought on his mind—it could deal with buses in New York, it could deal with the food that you find generally in restaurants, it could deal with an incident that happened in Moscow, or perhaps a peculiar statement made by some celebrity or politician. And there he would be on the air, not talking to any of us, but for the first 10 to 15 minutes of his program, expanding on that thought. It was a remarkable feat of literary creativity. That's a part of the success of Joey Reynolds.

FINAL CHAPTER 10 THOUGHTS BY KRESKIN

KRESKIN: I can't overlook the early days of broadcasting and my early experiences with some of the pioneers. I only got to work with

Arthur Godfrey a couple of times, although he was one of the two most influential people in my life, along with Bishop Fulton J. Sheen. Both left a deep impact on my life. Their ability to communicate, in the case of Godfrey in a very natural, homespun way, and Bishop Sheen in an eloquent way, left riveting impressions in my early life. I consider it a wonderful blessing that I had these two men to see and hear on television and radio and to get to know Bishop Sheen personally. One of his last letters before he passed away was to me, talking about the God-given gift that I had and how I was able to carry it to my style of show business. I will always cherish the remarks from this giant in the religious and public communications field.

11 | Up in the Air: Kreskin's Sky Adventures

THE HISTORY OF AVIATION STRETCHES THOUSANDS OF YEARS IF YOU COUNT Deadalus and Icarus, and mankind has only being flying airplanes for a little over a century. Orville and Wilbur Wright are the American aviation pioneers who first made sustained flights in a heavier-than-air vehicle. They changed life as we know it; travel would never be the same after December 17, 1903. The Wright brothers not only created a powered airplane, but were the first to invent aircraft controls that made fixed-wing power flight possible. The first commercial airline service, the Russian Sikorsky Ilya Muromets, made its maiden flight on December 10, 1913, almost a decade after the Wright brothers. What is the future of airline flights? Who knows? Maybe space shuttle trips to go to casinos on the moon.

Since Kreskin has traveled millions of miles in his career and spends so much time in the air, it seemed appropriate to do a chapter about his flights of fancy on his many travels in the United States and around the world.

McCARTY: Kreskin, have you flown more than a million miles?

KRESKIN: As far as my flying and the miles I've put in, it's become something of a record. As of 3 years ago last March, with the combined aid of a few airline industry people, we've figured that I have so far in my career flown a little over 3 million miles! Plus, with my heavy schedule, I have had to fly almost every week.

McCARTY: Kreskin, that is incredible. That is like taking a trip from the earth to the moon 12 times.

KRESKIN: (Laughs heartily out loud.)

McCARTY: Let's talk about something very topical about flying these days: the body scans and pat downs and overcrowding of the flights. What are your thoughts?

KRESKIN: I believe that this is becoming an increasingly important issue, and I would like to address it. As a further example of how intense my flight schedule can become, in the latter part of September 2010 and for approximately 6 to 7 weeks I flew approximately 68,000 miles.

Here is an example of how I maintain the intensity of this travel. I was appearing at a theater in Las Vegas for 6 nights. When I finished Saturday night, instead of going to my hotel room, I would return to the dressing room, where I had a change of clothes; pick up a small travel bag; and leave for the airport. During the travel to the Las Vegas airport, a slice of pizza would be given to me in the car. It was my only meal, because flying at midnight did not really give us the opportunity of eating on the plane. Wherever I was flying to, in one case to Canada and then back to my home office in New Jersey, I would be returning Tuesday to continue my run. I would arrive in Vegas on Tuesday, literally go to bed and sleep for a few hours before starting the week's schedule, and go on from there. Between getting up Saturday morning and going to bed when I returned to Vegas, I averaged in those 2 to 3 days no more than a total of 6 to 8 hours sleep. I never had more than that during the 6- to 7-week period. I don't advise anyone to follow this pursuit, but somehow I have managed.

So, with that in mind, I think I have something of significance to say about the security in air travel. I have recently been telling audiences that in spite of the issues arising from the war on terrorism, it is probably the safest time to fly (although it is also the most frustrating time to fly and, yes, the most expensive). Let me restate that: Notwithstanding all the terrorism incidents, I believe this is the safest time to fly in modern history. The record of successful flights is extraordinary with very, very few accidents that take place.

As far as scanning, we're going to have to follow more realistically in the footsteps of Israel and other countries. It is ludicrous that the airline business is putting everyone who travels through this ridiculous rigmarole. We are handicapped by the pressure of lobbyists and other groups arguing that profiling is just another name for prejudice. The truth of the matter is some social profiling will have to take place, since the chances at this time of babies and Catholic nuns carrying explosives are rather minimal. They haven't had a record of doing so in the past, if I can use that as an example.

What is really a serious concern—and, by the way, before we, the public, become too outraged on the techniques used—we need to protect ourselves, because it will only take one tragic incident and hundreds of people could die in a plane explosion. The Western world is going to have to think about what inevitably will be future situations where explosives could be hidden in the orifices of individuals' bodies. Then, what will be the technique to search out? People need to think about this realistically.

McCARTY: On a related topic, you must have seen a lot of changes in air travel over the years. Is it better or worse these days? How has the airline food been over the years?

KRESKIN: Everything you can imagine has happened or nearly happened to me while flying, and I've seen the deterioration of airline travel to the level that now exists in the United States. I've said so many times, if you want to go on a diet, take an airline flight. First of all, if you buy the food, it's expensive, and secondly, if you eat the food, you're courageous or using the food as a cathartic. It is horrendous. But it is the price we pay for lower fares.

One of my favorite airlines now delivers not a mud pie, but a plastic-wrapped piece that within the breaded outside either contains vegetables or something similar. If you buy it for the three or four dollars, and I don't remember which since it's been so long since I've touched it, when it's put in front of you, you have to wait because it's hot. The entire piece has been heated and is now served to you that way, so it's difficult to unwrap the plastic around it. I wonder what fool would do such a thing, because common sense will tell you when heating something that hot some of the plastic will tend to melt.

McCARTY: When you go to airports, there is a lot of downtime between flights. What kinds of things do you do in those downtimes?

KRESKIN: It is true that now more than ever before there is more downtime than anyone would care to think about. There are also fewer direct flights, and the direct flights that remain are becoming more costly. Many airlines do not want passengers to know that they are preparing for even fewer direct flights and more connecting flights because it is more economical for them. I have learned from day one to take advantage of idle time. In fact, I use idle time to create, reexamine in my own mind, and work out details for future projects. I always carry a pad or a portfolio with me and am invariably adding or writing details. I just never think in terms of there being any downtime.

McCARTY: What are some of your favorite places you have flown?

KRESKIN: I can think of favorite places I've flown to through the years—Spain, Italy, New Zealand, Japan, Wales, Netherlands, and each year thousands of miles through Canada. I have many favorite places to travel to. In the United States, I can't pick just one or two. I love traveling here, as well as touring Canada, which, indeed, is my second home, because my television series *The Amazing World of Kreskin* originated there for most of its 5½ years.

I am reminded of Bob Hope, who said to me, "Kreskin, we're not at war." He saw my schedule and, like today, I am only often home 4 days a month. Of course, he was reflecting on his travel schedule during the Second World War. He reminded me that we can't allow ourselves to become frustrated, because to be in show business one has to be a gypsy and go where the action is.

I have great warmth for New Zealand, as well as for England. I have such a reverence for the British people who survived under the most trying conditions during the Second World War. I love Holland. Like New Zealand, if you ask someone how to walk somewhere, they don't tell you, they literally walk you there. But it's really impossible for me to limit myself to a handful of places, because it is the people who have made my travels all over the world special.

McCARTY: In the movie Up in the Air, *George Clooney's character Ryan Bingham spends most of his time in the air, too. Could you relate?*

KRESKIN: When the movie *Up in the Air* with George Clooney came out, I got scores of calls from people all over the country telling me I must see the movie; "It's about you." I realized this was not the *Buck Howard* movie, this was not even a *Dinner for Schmucks* movie, but I finally took it upon myself to see the motion picture. Well done! Quite entertaining, but boy did it hit home, since in the movie Ryan Bingham spends much of his time in the air living out of a suitcase. It's not that I feel like that sometimes, but that's basically the life of a successful performer who's on the road. I wonder at times (not too often, however) how my road manager can keep up with me. Especially when I know that Bob Hope had two or three road managers so that they could keep up the pace that he had.

McCARTY: One of the downsides of flying is the possibility of an airplane disaster. Have you had any real close calls?

KRESKIN: I want to relate to you, Michael, one of the most terrifying close calls of my entire life. It goes with an incident that found its way into a ludicrous article that appeared in the *National Enquirer* on April 19, 2010. I think it's time now that the truth comes out, because the article suggested that I was cheap in not paying this pilot for the trip.

In November of 2009, I was touring Canada, one of my favorite places in the world. I was appearing in a really remote area. One day after a show a gentleman volunteered to fly me to my next destination, rather than taking the car on such a long trip. Regular commercial flights were not available from that area to the next city in which I would be working. I said I was delighted and asked if he was a professional pilot. As it turns out, he was a very successful businessman who owned his own plane.

I boarded the plane with him. It was a two-seater. We proceeded to take off. In the interim, I did not realize or reflect upon the fact that two other pilots had refused to fly me. It turned out the weather was becoming increasingly bad, and it got worse and worse. As time progressed, even the visibility of the ground diminished unless we were fairly low. The fog became heavy, and soon we were flying through pea soup. Bear in mind, with zero visibility we were flying over a mountain range, something I will never allow to happen again as long as I live, that is, in a single-engine plane. The air currents over a mountain range are extraordinarily irregular, and it is not worth the chance, especially in bad weather and in a small plane. At one point we hit an air pocket and we dropped so fast my head hit the ceiling of the plane. Thank goodness I suffered neither a concussion nor a broken neck. Oh no, you will never see me doing such a thing again. The plane dropped again. We missed the mountain. But somehow, and God knows how, we eventually dropped into an area that looked like a remote airport.

When this field was ever used I don't know, because there were no human beings there. When we landed, the front of the plane touched first, seriously damaging the propeller. Thanks to a cell phone the pilot had we were able to get help, and since it was freezing cold we needed help as soon as possible.

Aside from the propeller damage, there was a flat tire. I was brought to my hotel, and surprisingly enough did a full-evening concert that night. Needless to say I did not continue any flying with said pilot, and, if you tried to convince me to return by his plane or any other plane, I would have opted not to. So I traveled by car to another location and then took a 15½-hour train ride. It took me 2 days to get over flashbacks of that dangerous drop.

When you look at the picture in the *National Enquirer* article about the incident, you see a much more seriously damaged plane, and the accusation was that I refused to help the pilot with the expenses of repairs. You're damn right I refused, because the pictures he sent to the *Enquirer* were not the pictures taken when I landed. If you look at the one picture showing me and the plane, you will find out the commentary truly is distorted. I am shown kneeling before a plane that has hardly any damage. Kneeling, because I am thankful we landed without crashing. It is suggested in the article that I am kneeling in prayer before the flight. At the right you see the plane being repaired, because this delightful pilot decided to fly back the next day. I talked to a couple of pilots the next day, and they wondered why he chose to go through the same bad weather, for his flight back was a much greater disaster. At one point his plane tilted and spun three times in the air before it landed. So the photograph of the plane with all the damage, and it was a costly affair, was taken after the ill-fated flight back, the one I refused.

I've spoken to many pilots and people who travel, and they've said to me, "Kreskin, don't ever again fly over a mountain in a single- or twin-engine small plane, because the air currents are too strong and irregular and can wreak havoc."

Oh, there's one more factor to the story. A couple of days before leaving on my trip, I recounted to those in my office, and my secretary must've heard me say this a half a dozen times, that somehow, and I don't quite know why, this trip would prove to be a near disaster.

McCARTY: Have you had other memorable incidents?

KRESKIN: A few years ago when I was headlining at a nightclub in Reno, Nevada, I had to make an appearance on *The Tonight Show*. Flying me in and flying me back was no great stretch, since it wasn't that great a distance. I returned the same night. Or should I say, I started to return. As we sat in the plane it became clear to me that the flight was taking much longer than it had going from Reno to Los Angeles. After approximately an hour went by, I took notice of the stewardesses (as they were called then). There was clearly stress on their faces. They weren't manifesting it very strongly, but I could read in their expressions.

I finally called over a stewardess and asked her what was wrong, and she said, "Kreskin, they can't get the landing gear down and we're delaying the flight hoping we can get it down before we run out of gas." As this ensued, it was clear in their facial expressions that the supply of fuel was diminishing. I started to hear a noisy by-play in the rear of the plane, the coach area. I didn't pay too much attention, not realizing it was passengers becoming stirred and filled with fear. I got up to go to the bathroom, and for some reason, God knows what, decided to go to the rear to the plane instead of the front. I went quietly without attracting any attention. When I came out of the bathroom, I came forward, sat down, and at that point an announcement was made that the airport was being prepared for an emergency landing. As we were approaching for a landing, I heard some noise—somehow the gears were unlocking and the wheels were brought down. We landed quite safely. I was the first passenger to leave the plane. Meanwhile, the stewardesses were thanking the passengers for their cooperation.

When I finally walked down the steps, three pilots and one of the stewardesses were down there like they were waiting for me. I thanked them for handling the flight safely, and one of them said, "Kreskin, we want to thank you." I asked, "What do you mean?" He said, "When you got up to go to the bathroom and walked through the coach section, the passengers saw you and recognized you. You came back so casually to the front. The general tone amongst the passengers was, hell, if anything really was going to happen, Kreskin would have never boarded the flight." And they said, "In your own way, you calmed them."

McCARTY: Would you like to share a final incident?

KRESKIN: On December 2, 2010, I spent a few minutes in the banquet hall where I was scheduled to present an evening performance after a dinner celebration of the John Vince Foods company, a company known throughout Canada. The audience was to consist of approximately 300 people. My Canadian road manager at that time, Glenn, was talking to the sound people before the program to make sure the level was proper and comfortable. For some reason, we started to talk about traveling, since he impressed upon them the thousands of miles I was putting in and that I had taken off from Las Vegas to come and present this program. The story takes on a scenario that almost seems like fiction.

One of the representatives from the Montecassino hotel, where I was staying and in which the banquet was being held, happened to be standing nearby. My road manager proceeded to reveal something to me that he held back from telling me about when it took place, and the gentleman overheard the conversation. He had been aware of the near plane crash I had experienced in Canada months before, which you read about earlier in this chapter.

Earlier in the same year, Glenn was driving me back to the airport in Toronto after a concert. The drive lasted 4½ hours and was exhausting. We arrived at the airport at around 3 A.M., and I admonished him to go home and get some rest even though he wanted to keep me company in this lonely airport in the middle of the night. I should have told him to stay, because at 6 A.M. my flight was cancelled.

I took an incredibly lengthy, draining number of flights back to Newark because of the cancelled flight. The full picture that Glenn never told me was the reason for the cancellation. The reason the flight never made it was because when it took off from Buffalo it crashed.

What made this all the more bizarre is the gentleman who was helping to set up the room for the banquet affair interrupted us and said he overheard the conversation of the incident that happened months before. He wanted us to know that he had seen the actual plane crash with his own eyes.

The chances of individuals not knowing each other, coming together, and having some contact with a tragedy...talk about a fascinating phenomenon of synchronicity!

12 | What About Psychics?

I want to make one important fact crystal clear right from the start of this significant chapter. Kreskin clearly states he is not a psychic. He has no supernatural powers whatsoever. Psychics, mediums, occultists, and fortune-tellers have been popular in many cultures throughout history, particularly in hard times, and are worthy of discussion, so here we go.

When I used to do stand-up comedy many moons ago, I did this bit: "The Amazing Kreskin has the most amazing answering machine. I called his house the other day and his message said, 'Hello Michael McCarty, thank you for calling.'"

McCARTY: What is your opinion of phone psychics?

KRESKIN: I found the Psychic Network to be fascinating. With all the psychics on it, they weren't able to foresee they were going out of business (laughs). I am not against all psychics. I think some psychics are seriously dedicated. For the life of me, I find it difficult to find how a person sitting on a telephone miles away listening to a total stranger is really going to give them any insight into their future.

At the same time, if you really want to get controversial, it seems to me there are psychologists on the radio giving advice to people when they can't see their reactions. Who is the more ethical? The phone psychics and the radio psychologists are both using the same medium. Some people are very skillful at role-playing over the telephone.

McCARTY: Let's start out with Jeane Dixon. She was one of the most famous psychics because of her predictions in the past and her clout with celebrities.

KRESKIN: Certainly, one of the most legendary psychics in the last century was Jeane Dixon. She was a soothsayer to a number of private celebrities and politicians, but her living was made largely from doing prediction columns for some major newspapers, including the *Chicago Tribune.*

Parenthetically, one finds it interesting how many public people have psychics and/or astrologists to advise them. It's perhaps not hard to understand amongst show people where the uncertainty of the field, the precariousness of making decisions, and a desire to have some semblance of stability regarding the future could make many an actor, actress, or show person attempt to seek the advice of psychics.

It was astrologer prophet Jeane Dixon who for a number of years was held by people in the U.S. as the tops. Very often her column predictions would find themselves into other news pieces. Her most famous prediction that was reiterated many times in years after was that of the assassination of President John F. Kennedy. As I look over the newspapers of that time, what really was stated in a 1956 article in *Parade Magazine* was "a blue-eyed Democratic president elected in 1960 would die in office!"

One thing needs to be realized. Preceding that period, all presidents elected in years divisible by 20 had died in office since President Millard Fillmore. There is a problem in her prediction that a Democratic president elected in 1960 would die in office. The problem is that in 1960 Jeane Dixon predicted publicly that Richard M. Nixon would be elected.

Talk about her major predictions: She stated that World War III would begin in 1958, there would be a cure for cancer in 1967, and there would be peace on earth by the year 2000. By picking specific years she created much hope in the minds of some of her readers.

It should be realized that she headquartered in Washington, D.C., and many of her predictions dealt with politics. Unfortunately, her prediction in the middle part of the last century that Fidel Castro would be removed from office did not come about. One of the strangest commentaries that she made was in reporting to explain the difference between the assassinations of John F. Kennedy and his brother Robert. She said that her prediction about JFK was a revelation or a vision, a word from God. Statements from God cannot be challenged. Then, as hard as this is to swallow, she said that her feelings that Robert Kennedy would be murdered were obtained from some sort of telepathy. One wonders, was she reading the thoughts of Sirhan Sirhan?

It's always questionable when psychics start predicting publicly tragedies in the lives of public figures. In 1971 she publicly stated that Jane Fonda was headed for tragedy. It turned out that was the year that Fonda won the Academy Award.

McCARTY: Let's talk about Sybil Leek. Have you ever met her?

KRESKIN: One of the most intriguing characters I ever met was Sybil Leek, who had been on one of my television series shows. She claimed a rather intriguing life, and that is putting it mildly. She was English. She said she was a witch, astrologer, psychic, and an occult author. She had written dozens and dozens of books on the occult and related subjects.

By the time I knew her, she carried around a miniature deck of cards, which was really a trick deck. That is a strange accessory for a woman who surrounded herself with occultism. Of all the psychics I've met, I think she was the most interesting. I'm not saying accurate, because she doesn't seem to have any specifically dramatic predictions to take credit for.

Sybil Leek, like Jeane Dixon, authored a column. It was a popular monthly piece in *Ladies Home Journal*. One of her big predictions was that Senator Edward Kennedy would be betrayed by friends connected with drugs and alcohol during the first part of the year, the year being 1971. It's hard to figure out exactly where that figured into what really happened during that year in Kennedy's life. Her personal stories were romantically intriguing.

One can only speculate how much she embellished them, but she claims she was initiated into witchcraft while in southern France and that her initiation was to fill an opening by the death of her aunt, who had been a high priestess of a coven. She even claimed in one of my interviews that a mystical experience made her calling in life to be a spokesperson for witchcraft. Her income in the United States was really a result of her prolific writing and her client work in which she advised people as an astrologer. She even founded covens in Massachusetts, Cincinnati, and St. Louis.

Talk about wild claims. She could go on and on about the "fact" that she was recruited by the British government during the Second World War. An author who wrote about that war explained that Leek was hired to provide phony horoscopes for Germans who believed in astrology. This was not so far-fetched. There is considerable evidence that the British government studied astrological patterns. Not because they believed in astrology, but because there were so many, under Hitler, who did embrace the practice. That had given them ideas of when major actions and activities would take place.

So it makes much sense that she could be used to influence in a manner that would be favorable towards the Allies. One of her claims is that she wrote a chart which convinced Nazi Rudolf Hess to fly to England where, as we know, he was captured.

Now, let me tell you the most intriguing revelation that she gave to me. She explained that she had a pet python. In those days, there were no x-rays at airports and no reason for going through airport security. The present period of terrorism and war has, of course, necessitated and opened up a whole new industry for security people. But in those days, little thought was given, and rightfully so. She traveled with her pet python wrapped around her waist. Indeed, when she appeared on my television show, as she had done on other shows, no one knew, even when she sat in makeup, that wrapped around her waist was her pet python.

During the golden era of movies and television, it is remarkable how many actors and actresses were known to have consulted with astrologers and psychics, including people like Marlene Deitrich, Zsa Zsa Gabor, Jackie Gleason, Robert Cummings, Faye

Dunaway, Susan Hayward, Steve McQueen, Peter Lawford, Lana
Turner, Joan Fontaine, Dick Pile, and Arlene Dahl. It was extremely
popular throughout society.

*McCARTY: Let's talk about a historic figure from the 1940s, Eric Jan
Hanussen, who I think is one of the most intriguing psychics in history. He couldn't be ignored here because of his connection with Hitler. I've heard about the movie about him, but never saw it. Have you
seen it?*

KRESKIN: Hanussen is indeed a historical figure that cannot be ignored, and while I have spoken and written about him before, it is an
opportune time to reflect upon him. He was a highly successful hypnotist and clairvoyant in the period before the outbreak of the Second
World War, the 1920s through the early 1930s. While he used ruthless
techniques to gain information on the people who attended his shows
or who came to his private consultations, there is no doubt that he had
some phenomenally special gifts, and, as a hypnotist, there is no doubt
that he was outstanding.

Hanussen became privy to the private intrigues of many important
people in Germany, and with Hitler's ascendency that would include
members of the Nazi party. Hanussen started performing for and socializing with them. Further, he was not only attracting members of
the Nazi party for private sessions but also lending them considerable
amounts of money. Indeed, a number of key people in Hitler's admin-
istration were indebted financially to Hanussen.

In the 1920s and early 1930s, we saw the rotogravure of European
newspapers becoming more popular. They were the center sections
on Sundays, which often had colored pictures. A woman came to Hanussen and wanted to do a picture layout for the Sunday section in
one of the major Berlin newspapers. Hanussen was glad to pose the
way he did on stage. Many pictures were taken. The article, however,
never appeared, and Hanussen was bitterly disappointed. It turns out
the woman who did the photography was the legendary movie director and photographer Leni Riefenstahl. It was she that put together the
spectacular film on Hitler and the Third Reich *Triumph of the Will.* In it

she made him look almost like a saint and a hero and the movement inspirational. For that reason she was condemned, for it was clear that in the film she was able to poison the audience's minds with her editing. There is considerable suspicion that Hitler studied the actions captured in the photographs of Hanussen.

There is no doubt that Hitler was interested in Hanussen. Indeed, if you see the public orations and talks of Hitler, there's an interesting phenomena involved. Hitler took on some of the same demeanor, attitude, gesture, and motions of Hanussen. It was almost as if he had studied Hanussen. It has been said by a number of people, including the late psychologist George H. Estabrooks, that Hitler was one of the outstanding hypnotists, evil and terrible as he was, of the 20th century. In many respects, Hanussen became a model for Hitler. At the same time, Hanussen as clairvoyant began suggesting in his public appearances and newspaper columns the coming of a savior for Germany. The figure he described was very closely akin to Adolf Hitler. There is no question that it was Hitler that Hanussen was preparing the German public for.

There was a Polish production of a movie that was up for a "Best Foreign Movie of the Year" Academy Award some years ago called *Hanussen*. It is a brilliant, well-filmed, well-acted movie. The problem is that Hanussen is portrayed as a powerful performer who is fighting Nazism and finds his doom because of his combating the evils of Hitler's vast power. The true story is just the opposite. Hanussen was helping to build the Third Reich and was gaining incredible power within the Third Reich.

Many of Hitler's key people were beginning to resent him, because of the power he held over them since they were indebted to him for money he had lent to them. Eventually Hitler began feeling uncomfortable. Could Hanussen take over? He certainly had a remarkable hypnotic force about him. Consequently, in April of 1933 he was picked up by a handful of Hitler's henchmen, driven out into the wilderness, and shot dead.

McCARTY: I also think Arthur Ford is a very interesting figure, too, from the early 20th century. What is your opinion on him?

KRESKIN: In my opinion, Arthur Ford was one of the most magnetic and fascinating spirit mediums out of the first half of the 20th century. While I personally have never seen evidence of or a demonstration where a person has been able to communicate with the dead, Ford's activities have been most impressive.

Some considered Rev. Ford to be the greatest medium of the century. He had his problems. He was a drug addict and an alcoholic, and there is great suggestion that he was fraudulent. He was pastor of the first spiritual church in New York and a founder of Spiritual Frontiers Fellowship and President of the National Association of Spiritualists. Many people were in awe of him and literally worshipped him.

Early in his life, he developed as a medium and gave public performances where he tried to contact deceased spirits of relations of people in the audience. He had an "assistant," Fletcher, who claimed to be a French Canadian killed in World War I, and this person acted as his liaison in the spirit world while Ford was apparently in a trance. No one ever saw Fletcher, because obviously he was dead, if in fact he had ever existed. Ford gave sittings to royalty and lectures and public demonstrations in much of the Western world. Arthur Conan Doyle, the creator of Sherlock Holmes, praised him, but Doyle was not the best judge of mediumistic fraud over legitimacy. At any rate, he became a household name.

McCARTY: Did you ever meet Arthur Ford?

KRESKIN: I never met Ford, but it was interesting how I came to confront him.

One of his biggest bids to fame was Harry Houdini communication. Houdini was exposing mediums the last years of his life and getting tremendous publicity. Many of the mediums deserved to be exposed, but in many cases what the public has not been told is that Houdini framed the mediums.

As my friend, Walter B. Gibson, one of the greatest authorities of magic, who knew Houdini intimately, said that Houdini, the great escape artist, was often as dishonest as the mediums he exposed. At any rate, mediums were constantly predicting Houdini's death because he savaged them, and as a result of this he made an agreement with his wife Bess. He gave her a 10-word code, which she was to keep secret. He knew that when he died mediums would come out of the rafters and claim to have spoken to him.

Houdini instructed Bess to simply say, "Give me the correct 10 words." Ask the spirit for those words. At least in this way, she would know that some kind of paranormal phenomena was taking place. Only Bess had the code. Houdini died in 1926, on of all days, Halloween night. A few years later, Rev. Ford, who befriended Bess, had a séance that hit the headlines. During the sitting, he claimed to have communicated with Houdini's spirit and came up with 10 words that were, indeed, the Houdini code.

The next day, Walter Winchell, the extremely popular and powerful New York columnist, wrote the story that the Houdini code was finally revealed, and it was Rev. Ford who accomplished it. Years later things got kind of blurred. Bess denied or made some quasi-statements as to whether it had happened the way he had said. But it's a much more complicated story. Ford had befriended the Houdinis and knew that Bess had a drinking problem. There is a strong indication that a night or two before the séance, Bess and Ford had spent much time together, and that very likely in a drunken stupor Bess came out with the 10 words. Of course, that is highly controversial.

But the second great event, which indirectly brought me into the picture, took place some 40 years later in 1967 when Ford held a television séance with Bishop James A. Pike, who had been interested in spirit communication. The information Ford came up with impressed Pike immensely.

Not long after that, I brought up the Ford controversy on *The Mike Douglas Show*. Having become a regular on the show, I would have a separate segment in which I would not perform but would discuss a controversial topic on an incident that had happened. I was eager to approach the Ford dilemma. It became one of my strongest appearances on that show.

It turns out, yes, Ford in the Houdini séance did come up with the 10 words. There's only one problem. The year that the séance was held was some 3 years after Houdini's death. In the interim, Bess had written a book. It was ghosted by a very fine writer and was titled *Houdini.* On the show I held up the book and turned to a certain page. Lo and behold, there for everyone to see were the 10 words, which Bess simply disclosed in the biography. The problem for Ford is that the book came out at least a year before the séance. So it no longer was a question if Rev. Ford communicated with Houdini, the question was did Rev. Ford happen to read the book before he held the séance?

I have it on good authority from a person who was friends with Ford that Ford was looking at *The Mike Douglas Show* that day and became quite shaken when I came forth with the information. He never attempted to contradict it or explain it away, he just simply let it be forgotten.

After his death his credibility was destroyed. The literary executor of his estate, coming into possession of Ford's papers, found that Ford had cheated. It had been his custom to clip obituaries, look up school directories or records, or *Who's Who*, and keep elaborate notebooks with entries on various people that he used as reference for his spirit messages. He had such a vast amount of inside dope that what he was producing at séances was information he had studied and memorized.

McCARTY: The English occultist Aleister Crowley is a creepy figure. He was the subject of the song "Mr. Crowley" by Ozzy Osbourne. What are your thoughts on him?

KRESKIN: I want to make some brief remarks about Aleister Crowley, a fascinating character who today is largely forgotten. But up until a few years before his death in 1947 he was an extremely controversial British occultist described as "The Great Beast" or "the wickedest man in the world." He obviously had an impact on an element of the public. His father was a wealthy brewer and his mother was a religious fanatic who is said to have believed that her son was the Beast of 666, the Anti-Christ.

One thing seems to suggest strongly that as a child he was thoroughly pampered but was a cold individual towards those around him. At one point, he was initiated into a secret society in England, the Hermetic Order of the Golden Dawn. Members claimed to use real magic

in their ceremonies to supposedly reach higher levels of consciousness. Amongst other things, they attempted to teach astral projection
telepathy and psychokinesis.

In Cairo in the early 1900s he began to write *The Book of the
Law*, supposedly under some strange guidance, and he was preaching
a new way of leading one's life. One of the precepts of it was "do as
you please." It is thought that it influenced the hippies of the 1960s
and 1970s. He wrote hundreds of books in which he advocated the use
of drugs, which were illegal at that time, and sexual freedom. In the
mid-teens he went to the United States and then returned to the United
Kingdom where he preached Satanism and magical sexual techniques.

He was hated by the English press and moved to Italy. While there
he was falsely accused of blackmail, murder, and some kind of ritual
sacrifice with his daughter. She died of influenza, but obviously some
staggering claims were causing antagonism. Mussolini threw him out
of Italy.

Although he had inherited money from his mother, eventually
he became a heroin addict and ended up completely broke. He later
boasted and claimed he was the reincarnation of some god. Incredibly enough, with the widespread attention he had received people
debated whether he was a fraud, deranged, mentally ill, a real psychic,
a prophet, a saint, a god, etc. When he died he was no longer enamored
by the public. Only 15 people attended his funeral in 1947.

*McCARTY: One of my favorite psychics is Rasputin, the mad monk
from Russia. I've heard you speak of him before.*

KRESKIN: I have often spoken about Rasputin throughout the years.
Of course he has become a legendary figure. I don't know how many
movies have been based on his life and activities. This Russian character came out of complete poverty and probably hadn't taken a bath
for years. It is remarkable how he found his way into the hearts of
the Russian dynasty. Tsarina Alexandra had a son who suffered from
hemophilia, a bleeding disease, where a mere scrape or cut could become fatal. The doctors at that time had no clue as to how to treat such
an affliction.

The story's been told many times and interpreted in many ways, but somehow Rasputin, notwithstanding his distasteful hygiene, had a personality that intrigued people. He was brought into the family quarters where the youngster lay in pain. In his own way, Rasputin was able to ease the pain, so when he left the youngster was passively calm, showing no signs of discomfort. In the eyes of the Tsarina, Rasputin was a god or a healer. Certainly we have to credit him for his unusually strong hypnotic gift, for there is no question his personality and persona exercised successfully what could be described as hypnotic influence to the point that he was able to take the youngster's mind away from his pain so he eventually ignored it. The family, and especially the Tsarina, became enamored with Rasputin.

Rasputin became the bell of the ball in society. His harem of women was often 30 or 40. Certainly, his sexual ability was in itself remarkable. His behavior at bars and restaurants was often distasteful, abusive, and at times disgusting, but he was the healer, the man whom the royalty of Russia was absolutely enchanted with. As movies have shown, eventually jealousy started building among those socially elite and political people around the Tsarina.

Many people were envious and resentful of his influence, and in some respect his influence was too great. In spite of what he was able to do for young Alexei, it did not put him in a position to make political decisions. Nonetheless, rumors spread like wildfire and slowly people outside the royalty learned more and more about him, and there developed antipathy for this man. After all, most Russians were not living anywhere near as comfortably he was.

The dramatic unfolding of the attempt to eradicate Rasputin reads like a mystery story. A couple of men who were indirectly part of Russian government lured him to a private party of a few people and gave him food that was evidently filled with strychnine or other serious poisons. To their chagrin, it just didn't affect him, considering the filth in his life that he must have been exposed to. The germs and diseases had somehow strengthened his constitution and made it possible for him to survive and just move on, in spite of the serious deadly poisons which he was being secretly given on two occasions that evening. Rasputin just went on. Without going into greater detail, another attempt was made to kill him with a gunshot. He was shot but got up and reacted very angrily towards the people. One can only guess the number of attempts to kill him that night. They finally were able to incapacitate him and throw him into an icy river, where he was found dead a day or so later.

Here is a story that becomes romanticized as it is retold. A man seemed to heal or relieve a desperately ill youngster and sometime later was almost impossible to kill. Such is the legend of Rasputin. But his activities and the anger of the Russian people about him that the Russian people expressed helped to weaken the royalty of Russia and enabled the stage to be set for the collapse of the government. In his own way, Rasputin played a major role in the disaster of Russia.

FINAL CHAPTER 12 THOUGHTS BY KRESKIN

KRESKIN: To be honest with you, it is almost impossible for anyone to prove that they communicated or talked to the dead. It's true that a medium can have an individual in a private séance to whom they explain how they are now speaking to that person's deceased loved one. They may then reveal details about the deceased person, which the sitter or witness will or will not confirm. Well, there's the dilemma. How does one prove that they've talked to the dead? For if the information is correct, someone attending has to corroborate it. Axiomatically, someone had to know that the information is true.

The dilemma is that if the sitter knows and confirms what the medium has reported to be true, wouldn't it be easier to attribute the perception if it's not done by trickery to some form of telepathy—namely that the medium was picking up the thoughts of the sitter and not talking to a deceased person? There's no question that there have been strange, haunting-like phenomena in old houses, etc., even though with all the electronic devices and claptrap no one has been able to quite analyze these. But is this spirit communication? While I'm not condemning mediums, I do have this to say: **There are scores and scores of people who have been murdered. If a person truly can talk to the dead, why doesn't the medium talk to their deceased spirit and get information on who the murderer is?**

13 | "Amazing" Predictions and *The Mentalist*

O NE OF THE THINGS THAT HAVE AMAZED PEOPLE ABOUT K RESKIN OVER THE years is that predictions he has made publicly have come true. This chapter will converse on the subject of his predictions and also about the CBS series *The Mentalist*.

Author Bruce S. Larson suggested that Kreskin should become a Mall Santa, or "Kreskin Klaus," noting "If he were Kreskin Klaus, he could tell the kids what they wanted before they spoke. Think of all the photos of baffled but smiling children."

McCARTY: As of this writing, you've been getting worldwide attention about a challenge you've taken, and that is to predict the results of the presidential election in November 2012. Can you give us more details on this?

KRESKIN: On July 25, 2011, I appeared on *The Jimmy Fallon Show* and announced that I intended to predict what I believed would be the results of the presidential election of 2012. Sitting on the set, I wrote out a note that I did not show to the cameras or to Jimmy Fallon. He placed it in an envelope, and then the envelope was placed inside a safe. I am the only person who knows the combination of that safe, and it has been agreed that anytime I appear on Jimmy's show, there will be a guard standing next to the safe.

I wanted to establish the legitimacy of this challenge. It is not simply some magician's prediction trick. So I sent a copy of that prediction in a miniature combination lock package to Robin Leach, the gentleman who in the past had a TV series called *Lifestyles of the Rich and Famous*. For one of the episodes of that series Robin had come to my home with his crew. We bonded quite well in the years following. I knew I could trust him, and therefore he is in possession of the second copy.

A third copy of the prediction was given by me to radio personalities Jessie Frees and her daughter Julie Briggs. They have had a radio show for a number of years on WMTR in the Morristown area of New Jersey, and I have appeared with them many times. (There's a story behind this. Jessie Frees went to the same high school that I attended, but she was a couple of years ahead of me, so I never saw her in school. I felt such a warmth with her success as a broadcaster and her daughter's partnership that I just feel good to give someone successful from my own school the attention they well deserve.)

The fourth copy is in the possession of the management of Patsy's Restaurant in New York City, a well-known Italian restaurant made popular years ago by Frank Sinatra. It is, in my opinion, in the most appropriate location for a political prediction—on the top shelf over the bar.

A couple of days after the election, all parties will join us on Jimmy Fallon and compare and reveal, as each confirms my prediction.

What is dramatic about the prediction is that I named not only the party that will win the presidential election, but I named who I believed would be running on the Republican ticket. It was some hell of a challenge, since there were over a dozen candidates at that time, including two women.

Now I will reveal a behind-the-scenes story that I've never talked about before now. Many months before that evening of July 25, 2011, on *The Jimmy Fallon Show*, indeed earlier in January, I had written out what I then believed would be the results of the election. Sometime later I had a very uncomfortable experience while I was in Las Vegas. Until then I had told only five people of my intention to make a presidential prediction.

It was during my closing week at a nightclub when I received a call in my hotel room. A gentleman told me that he was in the lobby and asked to meet with me. I made it clear that I didn't have time, as I was leaving the hotel to go to the nightclub where I was appearing. He said, "You have an envelope, Kreskin." The truth of the matter is that I did have an envelope, because I intended to announce to the audience that I had just finally prepared my prediction of the election. I was not going to reveal it. I intended to lodge it with some prominent guardian. At that point, *The Jimmy Fallon Show* was not in sight. This was months before. The gentleman proceeded to tell me he had an envelope with $20,000 in it and asked if I would be willing to exchange my envelope containing the prediction for the envelope of money. I told him I wasn't interested.

I received a phone call the next night again. Indeed, after I closed in Vegas, I received a call at home about a month later. The same man was in New York and was willing to come to New Jersey to meet with me. I passed on the offer. Without going into details, we do know that there are certain tabloid magazines that have obtained stories by quietly paying informants. Does anyone think if I had accepted the cash and given this person the prediction that it would not have appeared on the front pages within a week or two? I do not propose to mention the tabloid at this time. I'm not sure it's even necessary, but the bottom line is, that is history.

Oh, there is something else I need to explain. Had I given that gentleman the prediction, it would have resulted in one of the failures of my career. You see, at that time, I had predicted who I thought would be running on the Republican ticket, and a number of weeks later I changed my mind. I had initially predicted that Mike Huckabee, whom I know and have worked with on television, would be the presidential candidate. Something told me intuitively that he would withdraw, although personally I believe he is a highly qualified and dedicated public figure of the greatest integrity. My intuition was correct, he did withdraw, and by then I had made my final decision, which was delivered to Fallon and the other three guardians not to be revealed until a couple of days after the election.

McCARTY: One of the most dramatic predictions you ever made was this: You predicted the events of 9/11 on January 1, 2001, on CNN. What exactly did you say in that prediction?

KRESKIN: While I do not have a recorded copy of it, I've had it played back to me in the past year, and I have my notes on it. In essence, I was discussing a book entitled *Kreskin and Friends* in which about 60 prominent people predict the future of their field. So Regis wrote about a talk show, and Roger Ailes wrote a few pages on the future of news television (his was the most insightful and wisest of all the predictions), Seinfeld had a few words about the future of comedy, and at the end when we were discussing it the anchorperson said, "Let's look at the back of the book...Kreskin has a couple of pages of predictions." She read the first one, in which in essence I said we were at war, and it was a war of terrorism, of which the public is not really aware of at this time, and it could possibly turn to biological warfare. And at that point, when she read that, I interrupted her and in essence I said, "I don't know why I'm saying this, but in September of this year here in New York, there could be a disaster involving two airlines."

Needless to say, after 9/11 the remarks that I made have haunted me, because I can't even analyze what provoked me to make such a remark.

McCARTY: Also on CNN, on January 2, 1998, you had an incident involving a dramatic prediction which we discussed in an interview later that year. In our interview, I asked you about the lottery. Does that incident even amaze The Amazing Kreskin?

KRESKIN: In 1998, I was doing a show at the beginning of the year on CNN. They asked me about the lottery, and I said, "It's a crapshoot. It's like throwing dice. Whatever combinations come up is pure chance."

They asked, "You don't have any other comments?" I said, "There may be a set of numbers such as 2, 3, 22. I don't what the fourth number is." Then I said to myself: "What the hell did I do? This is going out on live international television. Now people are going to go out and play those numbers. That wasn't very responsible."

When the show went off the air, the production staff was excited because of what these remarks have stirred up, with phone calls from all over the world. One of the remarks was, "It's unbelievable!" To which I responded, "Well, I hope people aren't throwing their money away."

The next day, there was the WIN4 lottery in New York. I didn't know that the WIN4 are all single-digit numbers. What makes it all the more dramatic in my memory is that the WIN4 winner was 2, 3, 2, and 2!

One can skeptically say that this is playing with numbers, but I think it is significant that I gave three numbers, the third of which was 22, and if we make them separate numbers it fits exactly into what the lottery came up with.

There's a postscript to this incident which makes the whole scenario really mind-blowing! Many months later, we haven't been able to pinpoint exactly when, but I had been appearing in the Quad City area of the United States, as I have many times in the past. I was on the air with two very fine radio personalities, Greg Dwyer and Bill Michaels, on Q106 FM. At the time that I was on the air, they were discussing with me this wild incident about the WIN4 in New York. Lo and behold, not long after, I received an excited call from them, letting me know that in the Quad Cities the same four numbers came up!

McCARTY: Was there a prediction involving a major election that took place in Canada?

KRESKIN: One of the most well-covered incidents of my career involved a prediction I made about Prime Minister Martin being re-elected to the office of prime minister in Canada in 2006. Michael, I not only predicted his election but also the exact number of seats his party would carry. My predictions had been kept in a safe on a national evening news show on the CTV network for 1 month. Every night it was pointed out to the viewers that there sat "The Kreskin Safe."

The evening before the election, I flew out to Canada to attend the national morning show *Canada AM* the next morning. When the results were read the morning after the election, my predictions proved to be exactly right.

During the live national television broadcast while the results were being shown to be correct, I suddenly interrupted and made what I considered to be a stupid remark. I made a crazy statement, which in essence said that "if this government ever collapses, it would be in 14 months, and that Martin would never be again re-elected."

Michael, many months later, when I came home from a tour there were some 80 phone messages on my answering machine. It turns out the government had collapsed. The prime minister had lost a lack of confidence vote. What unsettled me was that regarding my prediction of the collapse I was only off by 5 days.

McCARTY: Kreskin, do you have an explanation for all of this?

KRESKIN: I must tell you now that I do not understand these kinds of predictions. I suppose if I wanted to be extraordinarily skeptical I could say they are just coincidences. I have talked to behaviorists and psychiatrists whom I've known through the years and who have shown tremendous interest in my work, and they really have not been able to offer any concrete explanation. I don't know what it is within me, because these predictions have come literally out of nowhere, almost exploding within me, with no pre-plan of any kind. I feel there has to be some cognitive process within me that has put together various indications or facts and come to a conclusion that a certain action will take place. What unnerves me at times is that these are usually blurted without the slightest reflection before I make the statements.

To tell you the truth, I continue to be perplexed. A partial explanation may be one suggested by Harold Hansen, PhD. Dr. Hansen was a clinical psychologist who played an important role early in my career. He had seen me work in my late teens and twenties and offered me a room in his suite to be my own office. I worked with some of the patients he would turn over to me during the periods when I was not traveling. There were occasions when I saw about 30 of his patients in 1 week. He felt that my use of hypnotic suggestion, etc., could be supportive to his therapy. How many people in this day and age would have this kind of apprenticeship opportunity that I was able to enjoy? I can hear the echo of the late Dr. Hansen's voice when he said to me on many occasions that it may be best that I am not consciously aware of all the processes that result in much of my abilities.

McCARTY: Let's talk about the TV series The Mentalist, *obviously, because you were a mentalist long before the show. Let's talk about some real-life occurrences about being a mentalist.*

KRESKIN: In the past couple of years, there's been a very successful television series broadcast by CBS called *The Mentalist*. The star of the show, Simon Baker, who is Australian born, is brilliant in his role. His Australian accent is completely missing when he does his 1-hour series. Talk about a fine actor.

Of course, I am constantly asked if this is based on Yours Truly, and I've answered that it really isn't, because the character that Simon Baker plays was a fake psychic in the past and deceived his clients, etc. In the story itself, I would describe him as a modern-day Sherlock Holmes, because by observing details in the room or what someone is wearing, like Holmes would with someone's boots, he is able to deduce various facts about the person, which some may misinterpret as psychic abilities. Well, that's the story I've always told, but there is a behind-the-scenes story which has never been made public.

Yes, in some respects the character is based on my work. Let me introduce to you John Kleiman from Indianapolis. He has been involved professionally in law enforcement his entire life. Indeed, it was with his strong urging and impetus that we as a team put together a program that has been dubbed ICOPS, which stands for Intuitive Cops Observational Preparedness Seminars. Yes, it is a mouthful, but it has become an opportunity for law enforcement officials of all levels to learn more about the human thought process and gain insight into human behavioral actions. In seminars, I have sought to illustrate and to some degree train law enforcement individuals on how to enhance their skills in investigating crimes. No, they're not being taught to read people's minds. I have warned them and shown them that we see and hear more than we think we do, and that the memory is not always as accurate as one would believe. There's such a gigantic amount of stimuli and information that pours in; it's often difficult to sift through all of this. The pressures are even greater when investigating a crime. My aim has been to train and condition investigators on how to better tap into their own selves after they've been attempting to tap into the behavior of others. That is the key.

Of course, the Sherlock Holmes-like character that is so brilliantly played by Simon Baker may very well have something of me as a model in the initial development of the character. I have been involved in scores of crime cases through the years, some of which have received headlines in such intriguing areas as Reno, Nevada.

A year and a half before the series ever appeared on television, Daysun Perkins, Director of Development, CBS Television Distribution, was contacted by John Kleiman, who at that time had showed interest in my crime work that had evolved through the years. It is an area that I have really avoided publicizing to any great extent, as I don't consider it a part of my performances. Yet I do consider it an important part of my career, and under certain conditions I have been able to aid law enforcement. I've been involved in some 84 cases, but my participation is not always successful. In about a third of them I have been able to unearth meaningful material. As it turns out, without telling Mr. Kleiman what they really had in mind, CBS was evidently interested in pursuing work that I did in crime investigation. It should be noted that communications between Mr. Daysun and John Kleiman began early in July of 2007, shortly after they viewed a Persons of Interest (POI) project video that was sent them dealing with my work. Communications continued even up to December 10, 2008, by which time the CBS series had already hit the airways. Of course by then writer Seymour Heller had been hired to craft the successful series.

Just before the series began, John Kleiman received a statement from Daysun saying, "Unfortunately, because of our current development activity in other genres for the upcoming season, we're going to have to pass on the project at this time." Can we say that they passed but somehow the missile in sight did a strange curve, so that the word "passed" took on new meaning!

McCARTY: David Letterman specifically mentioned you and The Mentalist *on his show. Would you care to explain?*

KRESKIN: There is a refreshing footnote to this scenario. On January 12, 2010, much to my surprise, David Letterman announced my 75th birthday in a special climactic segment of his *CBS Late Night Show*. The quote at the close of that segment was printed across the screen and announced, to wit, "Kreskin, you should sue those jerks at CBS who ripped you off to create *The Mentalist*."

McCARTY: Regarding your involvement in crime investigation, isn't there an incident which took place a few of years ago in Terre Haute, Indiana?

KRESKIN: The background is that on May 24, 2002, a young college man by the name of Scott Javins disappeared soon after he had called his parents from a location not far from their home letting them know he was coming home soon. All traces of him and his car disappeared, and no clue of any kind had been uncovered in the ensuing 5 years. In a desperate cry for help, a group brought me in on May 14, 2007, with the hope of raising interest in a case that had gone cold. Without any significant clues, the police could not continue an investigation for years and years.

In television and radio interviews, as well as in a part of my concert, I alluded to the case with the hope that somebody out there, hearing or seeing me, may have reawakened within themselves some memories that were significant. Within a day or so after the performance, a gentleman came forward who contacted one of my representatives in Indiana and then the police. He was convinced that he had heard in the past somewhere remarks that he felt were now credible as to where the car was. Evidently, this sudden realization took place at some point while he was attending my performance.

It was almost as if my presence and appearance had reawakened this memory. The police had taken this information but were not eager to move with it, since the informant had no further evidence to back up his statements. The place that he described in a river reservoir area was never really thoroughly searched in spite of his personal, absolute conviction. Then, almost a half a year later, at the very place reported to the police, an elderly fisherman with some friends saw an item dropped in the water, perhaps a motor off some boat or what have you. He dove under water to locate it and came upon three cars. He became suspicious of one of them because he found a shirt when he reached into the car. When the police had their experts remove the car from the water, there was the body of Scott Javins, murdered.

WTHI Television News in Terre Haute reminded their viewers that I had created national interest in the story. Needless to say, Scott's parents have frequently expressed a bitterness that the police had not listened sooner.

One of the thousands of unexpected incidents that I experienced as I traveled the world came upon me some years ago after an appearance at, I believe, a university in Montgomery, Alabama. It was later in the evening, probably around midnight. My road manager had gone to his hotel room, and I was in mine making some notes and memos that I wanted to reflect upon in the days to come. I received a phone call from a gentleman who said that he represented the governor of Alabama, George Wallace, who would like to meet me. I was kind of taken aback and declined, and said something to the effect that I'd really like to think about this and perhaps I could call him back. As I recall, that was pretty much the way the conversation went, but when I hung up I realized I never took his telephone number, nor did I take his name.

Within about 3 or 4 minutes, the gentleman called again and said Governor Wallace would really appreciate it if you could meet with him. He would send a car; it's not that far, etc. I agreed. I went downstairs and within 4 or 5 minutes a sleek black car pulled up and two gentlemen got out to greet me. When we arrived at our destination, we came to a door which was partially opened, and one of the gentleman said, "Governor Wallace, this is Kreskin."

I can vividly remember that the room was not brightly lit. It was a soft setting. My escorts both left and closed the door. I realized in retrospect that they must have been waiting right outside the door. The Governor pulled back from the desk and found his way around to the front in a wheelchair. He had been shot four times while in another state campaigning and was confined to the wheelchair. We really only spoke for a few minutes, but I do remember him bringing up Johnny

Carson, but more clearly I remember him talking about something I had done on *The Mike Douglas Show*. There I had caused top athletes, basketball stars, to find it impossible to throw a basketball into the hoop; they kept missing. I had, through suggestion, conditioned them so their muscles wouldn't coordinate. When he finished speaking, it was obvious that he knew my concern.

The bottom line is that Governor George Wallace was interested in the possibility of my healing him, namely making him walk again. It was a difficult request to respond to, but I clearly said, "Mr. Governor, it is really not within my abilities to achieve such. If I felt there was an outside chance, rest assured that I would begin the efforts now." He shrugged his shoulders, and I walked closer to him to shake his hand and said, "I wish my answer could have been otherwise."

He didn't say anything, but nodded his head in resignation and said, "Thank you for coming, Kreskin." The only thing I said after that was, "Goodbye, Mr. Governor." When I left and my two escorts took me back, no conversation ensued. Here a man who had been one of the severest segregationists known all over the world was carrying with him a curse for the rest of his life, which he was not able to fully handle.

FINAL CHAPTER 13 THOUGHTS BY KRESKIN

KRESKIN: I have spent much of my life proclaiming that hypnosis and the hypnotic trance do not exist. There is no deep or light hypnosis, there's no hypnosis at all. The key is the fact that anything that seemingly is done with a person in a hypnotic trance can be done without inducing a special condition or state, so the trance is a façade. The subjects are not faking but are being made to believe they're in a something-special state. If a person's imagination or attention is crafted skillfully enough, they can respond to irrational ideas or be almost irresistible to suggestions. Suggestion is a much wider force than narrowing it down to the mumbo jumbo of "You're going into a deep, deep, deep trance."

In 1986, a trial took place unlike any other in the history of the behavioral sciences since I had been offering $50,000 to anyone who could prove the existence of a hypnotic trance and that phenomena done with the trance could not be done without the so-called trance. A hypnotist who was formerly a Catholic nun and then became a healer, a psychic, and finally a hypnotist said she could prove the existence of a trance. Scientists were ready to sit in on any claims to my offer and see what could be proved. No, instead, she, with a psychiatrist "expert," took me to trial in front of a jury. To say this was a mockery was putting it mildly. Needless to say, she did not win the money. On a technical point, the judge threw the case out of the courtroom but also admonished the hypnotist and her "partner" for wasting my time and that of the courtroom, and the people of the jury, and the cost to me. There is one lesson to be learned by all of this, and I can warn those of you who live in the United States. In England and other parts of the world, when you are tried and the party suing you does not win, the other side must pay your expenses. This is only justice. This is not the case in the United States. This frivolous, outrageous lawsuit against me, even though I did not lose the case, cost me $112,000 in legal expenses. To me it was important to see it through because this was a position I had taken throughout my career.

A few years ago in Canada, an incident took place during my performance which will be permanently imprinted in my mind. I had a group of subjects on stage at a dinner theater, and I was demonstrating the power of suggestion, which is a feature of the second part of my programs. This favorite test of mine is done while the people are clearly wide awake and the audience realizes they're conscious, not faking. I tell them that they are going to learn and be stunned at the experiences that they're going to have. I will go up to one or two subjects and without even speaking gesture over one of their hands without ever touching them. It is fascinating to the audience and to the rest of the subjects on stage, and even more so to the subject, that their arm starts to rise slowly, being lifted out of their lap.

In most cases they'll point out that they're not doing it deliberately, that something seems to be pulling. Somehow I've transmitted a suggestion to them and unconsciously caused their muscles to respond, and to them it seems like their arm is floating. I'll usually do this to three or four other people before I change my mind and gesture to someone and ask them to try to lift their hand. They find they can't lift it. I've reversed the suggestion and paralyzed one of their arms. But as one particular woman's hand rose, a commotion took place in the audience. Her husband and others with her pointed out to me that she had lost the use of that arm years ago in a woman's prison. She had been attacked by prisoners when one of the inmates who liked her tried to protect her by throwing her to the floor, and the impact left her arm and hand useless.

After the program, I saw her again, and within seconds without my saying anything, just gesturing, her arm started to rise in the air. What obviously must have been the case was that the physical healing had taken place but somehow the shock and the trauma had left her with an impact of paralysis that was now more emotional or mental than physical.

Way back in my teens I was performing in Bethlehem, Pennsylvania. I had subjects on stage, and at one point I told them when they opened their eyes they would find they were looking out the window of a train and watching the environment go by. Because the train had just started to move it was time that they should be waving goodbye. A similar commotion took place, and it turns out a young lady in her teens who had lost the use of her right hand and arm was now waving it in the air.

Unfortunately, on the other side of the coin is Governor George Wallace.

14 | Show Me Your Money!

I<small>F YOU EVER SAW ONE OF</small> K<small>RESKIN'S SHOWS OR THE</small> 2009 <small>MOVIE</small> *T<small>HE</small> G<small>REAT</small> Buck Howard*, the grand finale to the world famous mentalist's show is this: Kreskin randomly selects people to go on stage, than he goes backstage. The group decides where they want to hide Kreskin's paycheck for that show. After they hide the check, they bring Kreskin back to the stage. Walking around the auditorium with one of the people who hid the check, Kreskin will find where the check was hidden. If he doesn't find the check, he forfeits his pay for that show.

It is always a very dramatic way to end the show.

I've seen Kreskin do this several times over the years and it still amazes me. The most interesting time I witnessed it was when he was performing at Circa 21 in Rock Island. Someone had hidden the check behind the stage light in front of the orchestra pit.

McCARTY: How did you develop the idea of hiding your paycheck and finding it?

KRESKIN: When I was in third grade one memorable day, it was raining outside and our teacher, Miss Curtis, decided that since we couldn't go out to play she would teach us a game. She had a fellow student, Jane Hamilton, leave the room. While she was out of the room, we hid a beanbag somewhere in the classroom. It was put in someone's desk.

She then called Jane back in the room and explained that as she walked around, the classmates would say, "you're getting warmer," "you're getting colder," or when she was getting very close to where it was hidden, "you're getting hot." I was disappointed that I never got to play the game during that class period, but I was obsessed with the theme of the search. When I arrived home, my brother Joe, who is 3 years younger, met me, and since my mother was shopping, we decided to walk over to my grandparents' home. They were from Sicily, and my grandfather, with his friend, built his two-story house with his own hands. They lived upstairs, renting the downstairs, which people often did to make ends meet. While I waited outside, I had my brother hide a penny somewhere in the rooms where they lived. He then called me, and I walked upstairs into an old-fashioned kitchen that had a long, potbelly stove. My grandmother was sitting behind a large table, wondering, I'm sure, what was going on. I meandered through the kitchen, walked into my uncle's bedroom, he was at work, and I climbed up on a chair, and I found myself reaching behind a curtain rod, and there was the penny!

It dawned on me that I never told my brother to talk to me and to tell me whether I was hot or cold. We had no verbal communication at all. Of course, I have to say, with my Italian grandmother seeing this scenario, I wonder if she thought I had the evil eye. This whole incident spread through the family and friends, and I had to attempt to demonstrate this wherever I visited. Sometimes it was successful, sometimes it wasn't. It reached the point where I had people hide not a quarter, but a dollar bill, which gave me a little bit of profit when I found it.

By the time I was 11 or 12, I was getting paid for shows, big money, $5 an hour, but I was not doing this test as part of my program. When I entered high school, ninth grade, I did a fundraiser for the school, and it ran over 2 hours. This was the beginning of my full-evening concerts. By my late teens, I began to take a chance on a few occasions of having my check hidden for the evening show. While I did not do it all the time, the check would amount anywhere from $50 to $100 dollars. Word-of-mouth sparked tremendous interest to the point that in booking appearances I was asked if I would consider it in my program.

If you read the full-color comic printed in the middle of this book, which is titled, "How Kreskin Become Amazing," by Joe St.Pierre, an incredible comic artist, you will see a comic about this true story from my childhood.

McCARTY: How many times, Kreskin, have you failed to find your paycheck and had to forfeit?

KRESKIN: Have I failed? Yes, you bet I have. I've failed exactly nine times. On one occasion, for the Medical Association of the College of Surgeons here in Atlantic City years ago, I was performing in a large banquet hall. It was tremendously crowded with doctors. In fact, extra chairs were put up so that the doctors who were attending and did not have regular seating could also join. I kept walking up to one doctor, having her get up and turn the chair over, and there was no check.

I must have done this six or seven times. I finally gave up, and the president of the College of Surgeons said they would pay me anyway. I said no. I cannot accept the money. I have to keep the integrity of what I do. The reason they wanted to pay me is that I was within an inch of the check. While I was outside being guarded, so I didn't know where the check was being hidden, they had moved all the tables and furniture away from the area where she was sitting, rolled up the carpet and put the check on the floor underneath it, rolled the carpet back down, and refurnished the area. The doctor was literally sitting in a chair over the check. At one point, I was standing and my foot was literally over the check. So they felt I should get paid, but since I did not have it in my hands, I forfeited it and donated it to Seton Hall University in my name; Seton Hall is my alma mater.

McCARTY: You had some times you expected there was fraud going on. Can you explain?

KRESKIN: A very serious incident in my life, one that was heartbreaking, was based in Connecticut. I was performing at a high school for a fundraiser. It was an unusual fundraiser. It wasn't for the school. It was for a psychology professor and one or two other teachers who were raising funds to take a handful of kids to Colorado to go skiing.

When I look back upon this, what an indulgence—there was ski-ing in New England! It was my second year at that school. Sam Losa-gio, my road manager at that time, was with me when we were invited to a cocktail party before the show. In my life I've only attended eight or nine cocktail parties. I despise them, because no one pays attention to what's going on or hears what people are saying to each other. In the past 20 years, I would decline such a thing before a show.

We were at a private home, and the professors were there. I was preoccupied. Sam saw me when I walked into the kitchen where I was alone and asked if something was wrong. And I said, "Yes, there's something wrong." He asked, "What do you mean? These people had you here last year." I said, "I can't put my finger on it, but the mental impulses I have are telling me there's something wrong." The night of the show it was a full house. A mother of a friend of mine, Barbara Hamilton, who lived in New Jersey and booked me at my first college appearance, St. Lawrence University, was in the audience, as she lived in Connecticut at the time, and saw the scenario unfold.

The show itself was going extremely smooth. When it came to the check test, as usual I left the theater while it was hidden, and when I returned I found myself going in circles in turmoil. I just could not figure out where it was. I would go to the rear door of the theater, stop there, and come back and couldn't figure out what was going on. At one point, I turned to a math teacher who was my subject and said something that I've rarely said in my life, and that was "Are you really thinking about where it's hidden?" I caught him so off-guard, and he said, "No, we had agreed to think of the wrong place." The audience started booing and hissing. Indeed, my friend's mother said she and others were furious. I gave up. I could have and should have and had the right to make an issue and bring in a committee of honest thinkers. I gave up and forfeited the check.

A few days later I was in New York State, and I got a call from an Associated Press reporter, the story had gotten around so far. He asked me what actually happened. I told him the committee had qui-etly agreed to think of the wrong place.

To protect himself from dishonest activities involving his escapes, Harry Houdini had three or four of his assistants on stage make sure that the people they brought on stage did not sabotage the event. I, as a thought reader, have no such protection. All I could say is that someone's not thinking it, and I could be called a liar. Incidentally, for a week or so I was told that the psychology teacher disappeared. He was not to be found. I'm not sure if it was embarrassment. But I understand that night the school received hundreds of calls and complaints.

A similar thing happened in Texas at one of the major universities. I came into a gymnasium and got confused and finally found an envelope. It may have been in a baby carriage or some kind of carriage, I'm not sure, but as I was holding it walking on stage someone in the audience shouted out and said, "You better make sure it's the right envelope." And I stopped and froze.

Ah, yes, something was very wrong. I later found out the committee had a half a dozen or so envelopes and mixed them up so that even they did not know which was the correct envelope. They then hid all the envelopes throughout the place. It would have been impossible to perceive, because no one knew where it was. I should have made an issue and had it done legitimately, but I simply threw my fee away.

Later that night I was invited to the home of the dean of the university. It was a rather uncomfortable meeting, because the phone kept ringing, and the dean kept leaving the room. I found out later they were getting hundreds of calls complaining about what was done to me. A month or so later I received scores of pages accompanied by a letter of apology from the student body. That apology is one of the priceless pieces I own, because it carried the signatures of hundreds of students.

The bottom line is that in the nine failures of my seeking my check, four of them were because of fraud. The incident in Connecticut was significant to me, because even before the program I could sense from the people that I was socializing with that something truly was amiss. In the case of the other failures, it was strictly my own fault. That is, my not thinking far enough by expanding on the impulses I was receiving. In the end, I was blocking off something that I should have sensed. A perfect example was looking under the chair under the doctor, not interpreting the impulses as I should have that it was under the chair, but further under, meaning under the rug.

A similar case of that nature happened in New Zealand, and the next morning a press conference was held in front of the theater, which was broadcast nationally. The money was turned over to a crippled children's hospital, and when I went back to New Zealand a couple of years later I found out that the wing of the hospital had been named after me. The reason for the national coverage of my lack of success was that I lost my fee—$51,000.

There is a postscript to that story, one that I did not tell for years, even when I went back to New Zealand. While the press conference was being held live with scores of reporters and photographers, someone who had worked in the theater the night before came over, nudged me, and said, "Kreskin, I think you should have this." I looked kind of surprised, because I was in the middle of a press conference. He had an envelope in his hand saying "I think you should have this." The envelope had been given to him by someone who was not a reporter but was attending the press conference. He had been to the show the night before. I opened the envelope and read it, with millions watching on television, but I only read the letter to myself and quietly folded it and put it away. It turns out it was a gentleman who was on the check committee. It was the gentleman I picked to concentrate in his mind on the location as I proceeded to attempt to find it.

In the letter he said, in a confessional-like way, "Mr. Kreskin, I've watched you on television through the years, and I didn't quite believe what you did, and when it came to your searching for the check that you asked me to concentrate upon, I deliberately thought of the wrong place to see what would happen." I could have made a spectacle of that gentleman at that time. In retrospect, I wish I had. But it was my first tour there and I decided to not cause any problems, instead I simply put the letter away so nobody knew.

McCARTY: Were there times that it seemed that you weren't going to find the check, then at the last minute you ended up finding it?

KRESKIN: One of the most dramatic times took place in Rochester, New York. It was at a beautiful old theater that had special booths in a balcony where people sat the way they would at the opera. There had been a blizzard that day. I remember seeing news bulletins from my hotel room advising people not to travel, and I wondered who would come to the show, but the theater was packed. People walked through the storm to get to the event.

When it came to the check test, I had an interesting committee, a couple of university students, other nonstudents from the audience who hid the check. It was a public show.

While searching, I ended up in the balcony. Leaning over the balcony, I saw there was nowhere else to go but down. It was a one-story drop, with the audience looking up at me. I couldn't figure out why I was reaching over the railing, but it turns out there were heavy metal rods extending from this particular booth supporting lights that were clamped on and aimed at the stage.

I became convinced that the check was at the end of one of the rods. With sheer stupidity I stretched out to reach for it. My body tilted over the railing and I was slowly falling out of the balcony, legs and all. Incredibly enough as this happened, a man in the booth reached under my tuxedo, grabbed my belt, and I swung in midair. Had he not done this, I could have easily broken my neck. The audience was screaming. He pulled me back into the balcony booth, and I was carried backstage.

An ambulance was called, and some doctors from a nearby hospital came. It turns out I had wrenched my back and was in agonizing pain as I lay on the floor. They wanted to get me to the emergency ward. We talked for about 20 minutes. I refused to go and said, "I have to go back on stage." I will not tell you what their opinion was of such an asinine decision. Finally, I insisted. There were no crutches, but there was a large broom, and I took the broom and put the brush under one arm and used it as a crutch and walked out on stage to finish the second half of my program, which lasted about 45 to 50 minutes. The audience went into pandemonium cheering. Even though I was backstage about 25 minutes, nobody had left, and the show, thank God, was a tremendous success.

Oh, by the way, yes, the check was where I was trying to reach. It was at the end wrapped around some corner of metal piping, well hidden. It was an illegitimate hiding, because the understanding was that every committee member should, like myself, be able to have access to it. The fellow that put it out there was a gymnast in college and thought it was a wise thing to do to somehow scamper over the ledge and, precariously balancing, hide the check there. Wow!

McCARTY: What were some of the strangest places you've found your paycheck?

KRESKIN: One of the most unnerving locations in my life was at a university in the Midwest. When I returned year after year, audiences became more ingenious and diabolical. Having appearing at Rutgers some 18 times through the years, they became very ingenious, but in this Midwestern state I came back into the gymnasium filled with a few thousand students and parents and I came upon a man dressed in a suit. As I started to lead him towards the front where they had built a platform for my staging, I said the word "gun." I thought this is silly, he's obviously not a policeman, and he's dressed in a suit.

When we got in front of the audience, I had the urge to unbutton his jacket, and it turns out he was a plainclothes man wearing a shoulder holster. I think back to this scenario, and I can't imagine when not working professionally would I ever do such a thing. I reached under his jacket and took his gun out of the holster. You could hear silence in the audience. I turned the barrel of the gun towards me and looked down the barrel. They had taken tweezers and stuck the check down the barrel of the gun.

My program has finally taken on an x-rated quality, if I can say that, because not long ago in December 2010 I left my weeks headlining in Las Vegas for one night to appear at a special private performance in Toronto, Canada, for some 300 people. The audience was part of a national food company, John Vince Foods. It was a wonderful audience.

The check test was the special event of the night. I came back into this large banquet hall and proceeded to walk through the hall as a committee member concentrated. I came upon a lovely woman. She seemed rather conservative in her expression, and I asked her to stand. I must have stood in front of her for minutes, walking around her, and I couldn't bring myself to enact what I wanted to do. The audience was silent. Finally, I said, "I'm not going to hand you the check. It is on you, ma'am, and if I may point to it, I believe I am a half-inch from the check." I raised my finger, pointed to her bosom and her left breast, and I said, "You're going to have to hand it to me." She reached not into her bra, but closer to her body than that, reached under, and there was the check wrapped into a tiny square. Pandemonium broke out in the audience, and she smiled generously. Her conservative look was to throw me off, because she didn't want me to intrude upon her. Well, I guess that's the closest I'm going to come to an x-rated program!

McCARTY: If you gave a ballpark figure, how many times do you think you've found your paycheck? Hundreds? Thousands?

KRESKIN: I estimate that I have found my check over 6,000 times, so the 9 failures are rare. Although, I must admit that I came close to another failure a couple of years ago in Ottawa, Canada. While the check was being hidden, I was taken into a trailer and guarded by professional guards, as well as a couple of members of the audience. The window shades were down in the trailer, and it was soundproofed for all intents and purposes. My show was an outdoor event in a stadium, and the check was hidden amongst thousands of people. When I came out of the trailer, once again seeing my audience in the darkened bleachers, I found myself walking off the well-lit stage into darkness. I came to a bleacher wall and kept looking up overhead. I reached my hand forward. There was a simple crack in the wood, and I felt a tiny corner of paper with my finger. There was the check, which had been carefully shoved into the crack of wood.

FINAL CHAPTER 14 THOUGHTS BY KRESKIN

KRESKIN: The check test has become a signature for me and written about all over the world. Even I never dreamt that in 2009 there would be a Tom Hanks' movie, *The Great Buck Howard*, in which my alter ego John Malkovich would have it as the basic theme and its climax.

Even in the Tom Hanks' movie *The Great Buck Howard*, the *suggestion* of electronic devices signaling Buck Howard is used. Although at the end it becomes rather strongly suggested that such was never the case. One thing is true—a number of performers are using the device of electronic communication to fake what I do on stage.

In fact, if people watch tapes of such shows, they can see clues as to how the performer is being signaled with a piece of electronic equipment. Not in his ears, but worn on his body, where a vibration or stimulant triggered off by electricity could simply signal that the performer is in the right position or has touched the right object, perhaps one out of a dozen of boxes. It could be 1,000 boxes or it could be 20 million, for the boxes are then rearranged all over the set and the performer claiming to pick up impulses of some kind walks around and finally decides to open one box, which contains the hidden reservoir of money. The problem is that not only do the viewers see the stage while this is being done, but so does the studio audience, as well as perhaps people in the dressing room area. For wherever the assistant to the fake psychic is located, he has only to press the button or device that he's carrying on his person that will electronically signal the performer when he happens to place his hand on the correct box.

Let's take this a step further, when a performer can pretend to read the body language or expression of a host and have the host write down and conceal from him a number, let's say between 1 and 100. When the performer buries his head in some melodramatic way, he also suggests that the host show the number to the audience. Why would this be done? Why would an entire audience need to know the number? Well, as the performer looks into the eyes of the host of the show he will start naming segments of numbers, 1–10, 10–20, 20–30, and then by the eyes pick the correct set of numbers. When he has that, he simply has to count. Let's say the group was in the thirties, he would simply call out 30, 31, 32, 33, and then tell the guest by his eyes that he got the correct number and named it. In actuality, it has nothing to do with the person's eyes, etc., but to a confederate who is signaling him electronically, for just as the audience was shown the number, the secret assistant was there to observe it as well.

15 | **Our Final Thoughts**

FINAL THOUGHTS: MICHAEL MCCARTY

When I started co-writing this book with Kreskin, being that it is a one-on-one with The Amazing Kreskin, I thought he might open up about his life.

Boy, was I ever amazed. Kreskin was candid and intimate about life, and for this I would like to thank him, for sharing this with the readers. Since this is so much a personal book about Kreskin, I thought I'd like to close with the following anecdote.

On August 15, 2010, at a private luncheon arranged by The Amazing Kreskin, Kreskin announced what he considered the most dramatic statement of his entire career. To explain the bizarre sequence of events, Kreskin needs to start by referring to the release of the Tom Hanks' movie, *The Great Buck Howard*, in March of 2009. The movie was based on Kreskin, having been written by Sean McGinley, who was his road manager for a few years in the 1990s. From opening night on, he was experiencing media frenzy.

The morning after the opening, Kreskin had an appointment with his doctor regarding an earlier checkup. It was at this meeting he was told that he had prostate cancer. While treatment was urged as soon as possible, Kreskin, understandably, was excitedly beset with all the media built around the new movie. He had been expected to participate in it; this along with his regularly scheduled live concert appearances. To further complicate the matter, he was expected to open in Las Vegas within a month or so. The run was planned to last at least 3 or 4 months, although originally some 8 months were being considered.

Kreskin, to the dismay of the medical team, decided to fulfill the media appearances and show engagements. In retrospect, he has felt that this was an unwise decision. He did not use the best judgment. Ironically, the Vegas agreement fell through, but in spite of that Kreskin had before him one-night stands in different areas of Canada and the United States, plus, an extensive tour of Canada.

He felt that he had to fulfill this multitude of appearances, and this brought him into the late fall. Now Kreskin had Halloween promotions and appearances, and the holidays were around the corner, when medical staffs would be downsized. He completed the year, which amounted to 303 appearances.

In actuality, it was literally 1 year later that the decision was made to initiate treatment—1 year later! At this point, a medical team of three top specialists plus their support people presented Kreskin with a decision to make. It was decided that instead of chemotherapy the treatment would be radiation therapy. After a 12-month delay, he had to make a decision, and the decision was to go through what he was confronted with, a therapy that would probably cover 44 treatments. They extended from mid-March 2010 to the end of May, some 2½ months later. During this time, Kreskin did not lessen his work schedule, except for his not being able to travel outside the east coast during the specific days of the treatment. He worked within the states that could be accessible by driving in the latter part of the day and night. A remarkable fact is that he managed to keep this so confidential that not one single person of his staff or his range of friends and family had the foggiest idea of his illness or treatment. The 44th treatment day was at the end of May.

On July 29, 2010, a meeting was arranged with Kreskin's personal physician, Dr. Aherne, at which time Kreskin was given the verdict... "Kreskin, you are completely cured!"

FINAL THOUGHTS: THE AMAZING KRESKIN

Subsequent to my conversations with Michael McCarty, there arose some stories that I find significant on the important issue of hypnosis.

Stuck in a "Trance"

In June 2012, an intriguing story came out of Montreal, Quebec, Canada about an event that took place at a private girls' school. It was reported that during a hypnotism demonstration in a classroom, as many as 13 of the students did not come out of the trance. The hypnotist, Maxime Nadeau, who was 20 years old, had to contact his mentor, Richard Whitbread, for backup. When Whitbread came over an hour later, he told the press regarding the subjects, "Their eyes were open but there was nobody home." Apparently a few hours after the demonstration the subjects were brought out of the trance. The school's principal, Daniel Leveille, stated at a news conference attended by parents and students, "There were fortunately no bad effects."

In interviews by press and broadcasters in various parts of the world, I was asked how I would have handled the situation. Years ago, these incidents happened more frequently, and I would be called in because some half-baked amateur hypnotist had such a dilemma. It is much rarer today because the public has become too sophisticated and suspicious of what the real nature of the behavior is.

I would have walked into the classroom, told the audience of a few dozen people watching the demonstration to "Get their carcasses out of the room, we're all going to go get something to eat. I'm going to talk to you about what this hypnotic business is really all about. We'll close the door and leave the subjects in there. If you need me, I'll be back tomorrow, but don't worry about them. I'll come back tomorrow. I want to get a good night's sleep."

I would admonish them to give me their word that they would not open the door for at least 12 hours. I will tell you now that as we got up to leave the room and left the "sleeping subjects," within minutes their eyes would start to open and they would have suddenly "come to" feeling "relieved," etc. The key would be that they would be aware there was no one there to help them linger or malinger with the trance or to give them the attention that they had been receiving.

The real clue to the story was the remark that Whitbread told the CBC inadvertently, namely, that "Nadeau's good looks may have played a role in the trance." You're damn right; he was only 20 years old and those kids were 13 or 14 years old. They were no more in a trance than the man in the moon. Whether they were relaxed, standing, dancing, weightlifting, or just sitting there, they were conscious of everything that was going on and they were having a hell of a good time, especially since he was the male person guiding their life for some minutes. They had a chance to have their own quasi-romantic experience with, of all people, a hypnotist.

Whitbread, Nadeau's teacher, also entered the science fiction area when he stated that after hypnotism shows people who attend "feel trance-like effects hours after the event." I don't know where he got this information. I've traveled the world and haven't had people lingering with trance-like effects after shows unless they've been drinking, having a sexual interlude with the person they came to the show with, or perhaps they're aliens from another planet.

Of the thousands of emails I've received about this event, some questioned whether I was concerned about people of this age being hypnotized and suffering any deleterious effects. The answer is very simple. Unless the hypnotist suggests the person jump out the window, do a tightrope-walking act, or a sword-swallowing act, etc., the whole hypnotic experience is one I wouldn't have the slightest concern about, no matter what their age. In fact, I would have to smile to myself, because there was no damage at all. Since the subjects were not in the hypnotic trance, how could harm be created?

That's right. There is absolutely no evidence of a hypnotic trance. For many years I have publicly stated that nobody is under a special state, condition, etc. when they are apparently hypnotized. They are simply responding to the power of suggestion, which has been arranged and contrived in such a way that it gives a mystical sleeplike setting. In reality, sleep, trance, or special conditions have nothing to do with it. I've shown all over the world in public demonstrations that by pure suggestion I can duplicate everything associated with people who are supposed to be in a trance. Let me repeat what I've said in radio, television, and newspaper interviews around the world: This burlesque is a dramatic presentation of a ludicrous, ridiculous, and inanely preposterous science fiction scenario often created by half-baked "hypnotists" who'd be better off giving courses in Voodoo, alien abduction, and superman space jumps.

To the question asked me, could the children be harmed, I have to be very honest. My answer is yes, but the harm would be created by parents or other adults who would suggest to the students that there may be some deleterious effects that have taken place. This would be planting negative seeds. So if the child comes down with a bad headache, has a stomachache, has a backache, feels depressed, they can start blaming it on this half-baked pseudo-fake experience of a hypnotic trance. Parents and intelligent adults would never have such a concern if the students had gone to a rock concert or some exciting sports-like experience. Now prepare yourself for a shock. Nobody showed much concern, even parents, when teenagers fainted and swooned at Frank Sinatra concerts or other performers who had captured young bobby-soxers. The phenomena they were reacting to were exactly the same as the purported "hypnotic trance." It is simply a contagious response for an idea, in one case taking place in the setting of a swooning crooner, in the other of a hypnotist. Yes, the parents and adults would have been blamed if some deleterious "feelings" were experienced.

Sybil

Years ago there was a movie based on a book called *The Three Faces of Eve*. With Academy Award-winning acting, the theme was based on the true story of a patient who under "hypnosis" apparently revealed that she had multiple personalities. The story doesn't end there.

Not too many years later, a bigger case of multiple personalities came forward. Using the pseudonym Sybil, the story was written by a journalist, along with the psychiatrist Dr. Cornelia Wilbur, who treated Sybil, and it revealed that the patient had 16 different personalities! Under various drugs and with the use of "hypnosis," memories were elicited of child abuse and so forth. Once the book appeared about the treatment of Sybil, multiple personalities became the new popular disturbance that was discussed on television and radio talk shows. Dr. Hansen, whom I refer to earlier in my book, would often say to me, "Kreskin, I don't buy this crap." And by the way, he was not a show business person or a public figure, but a fine clinical psychologist. He said this was a lot of B.S. Into the picture came a person considered by some (not me) to be an outstanding expert on "hypnosis." It was psychiatrist Dr. Herbert Spiegel, who after a while began to use Sybil in his demonstrations of hypnosis before classes at Columbia University's College of Surgeons. He was more interested in producing age regression, where this supposedly deeply hypnotized subject was able to regress and experience early periods of her life. Dr. Wilbur and Dr. Spiegel became estranged as time went by, because Spiegel didn't buy the multiple personality theory. After hearing remarks from the patient, he began to suspect that Wilbur was creating these personalities to write a book.

I'm not going to go through all the double-talk of various levels of hypnosis. "Experts" had defined hypnotic levels from 6 to 50 different stages. I had a confrontation with Dr. Herbert Spiegel on *The Larry King Show*. A group of "medical experts" on hypnosis were discussing it, and I was brought in later on the second half of the program. I demonstrated something with one of the members of the staff which was very dramatic, and Dr. Herbert Spiegel, in his commentary about what he saw, implied that he wouldn't want to really do that with hypnosis. There was only one problem—the person I did the test with was never "hypnotized." Dr. Spiegel apparently didn't hear me say this before I even began the demonstration.

Oh, by the way, Sybil, whose real name was Shirley Mason, became a money-making subject for the psychiatrist who treated her and the journalist who wrote the book about her. In fact, the three of them formed a company called Sybil, Inc., which has an interesting aftermath. The story and the treatments started to smell to me, not only when I met the psychiatrist after a performance that I did before a professional group of medical people, but, and hear this, when I learned that the psychiatrist and her partner, the journalist, drove a considerable distance to meet with my manager in Pennsylvania. They had some ideas of how to make big money with Sybil. When my manager explained this to me, I said, "this doesn't seem legitimate," and he responded in agreement that the meeting just didn't sound right.

Now understand that Sybil had a lot of experience being "hypnotized" by Dr. Wilbur. She then had a theatrical experience by being put on display in front of an audience where she would be age regressed under so-called deep hypnosis by Dr. Spiegel.

A book by Debbie Nathan, *Sybil Exposed*, was published in 2011 which unfolds the entire story, showing that it was fraudulent. There were no multiple personalities. Sybil admitted that she, with the encouragement and persuasion of her psychiatrist, had crafted an absolutely false story. I hate to say this, but I knew that long before the book ever appeared.

Concluding Remarks

In my concluding remarks, I'm going to leave you, my dear reader, with much to reflect upon and information that may prepare you for a dramatic scenario that's certain to come about in the not too distant future—a year, maybe a bit longer.

"Hypnosis" has been used for years to create some of the most atrocious, fabricated lies or distortions or idiotic themes, especially in the area of psychiatry and psychology. It is based not on a trance whereby memories are uncovered—it's based on suggestion. The fools in these stories, those most deluded, are those who are enraptured with the "romance" of "hypnosis" rather than scientific realism. Thanks to hypnosis, the diagnosis of multiple personalities became for many years one of the great fabricated rackets of clinical psychotherapy.

So, I have a warning when in the months to come you learn that an attempt is being made to vindicate the killer of Bobby Kennedy, one Sirhan Sirhan, of any responsibility. Bear in mind the mud and the distortion that is being used to put this together. Are you ready? We're being told that he was "hypnotized." In fact, recently an "authority" on hypnosis from a university spent many hours with Sirhan Sirhan and decided he was the victim of hypno-programming and memory implantation! We are told that an Associate Clinical Professor in Psychology went to see Sirhan Sirhan in person and got him to recall under hypnosis the shooting for the first time. Can you believe that after almost four decades he remembered it for the first time? Excuse me for a moment, my dear reader, this is just too much to swallow. We are told that through hypnotic techniques and mental programming he was made to believe that he was at a gun range shooting at circular targets, not Bobby Kennedy. It is said that the authority is "one of the world's foremost experts on hypnotic programming," whatever that is!

Oh, by the way, years ago, soon after Sirhan Sirhan was indicted, when a case for his defense was being prepared, a great "hypnosis" expert was brought in to see him and proceeded to state on television and even in a film "documentary" that a very deeply hypnotized subject can be made to commit antisocial actions, activities that would be against his will. He also said that Sirhan Sirhan had been hypnotized many, many times, as he went into a trance so easily. That psychiatrist was none other than the late Dr. Herbert Spiegel!

Unbelievably, there is a movement to suggest that Sirhan Sirhan was programmed a la *The Manchurian Candidate*. You may remember that old movie which starred Frank Sinatra and Angela Lansbury, amongst others. The story is based on the writings of Andrew Salter, a popular New York society psychologist hypnotist in the 1940s and 1950s who defined hypnosis as a kind of condition reflex response to words or ideas. Actor Khigh Dheigh opens the movie in Communist China doing a demonstration on the stage with "hypnotized" subjects. He obviously is sinister. He is not there to entertain, but he is establishing the fabric of the story that these people are being brainwashed during this hypnosis demonstration. Actor Laurence Harvey is programmed by the hypnotist, so that when he comes back to the U.S., whenever Angela Lansbury shows him the Queen of Diamonds, he is to immediately follow whatever he is told to do. Frank Sinatra, working for the government, investigates and slowly breaks down the case of this man who is going to be programmed to assassinate the president of the United States.

You can understand the gravity of my public statement for so many years, namely that there is no hypnotic trance and that it is pure suggestion. My conviction is so strong that I've continued through the decades to offer a substantial amount of money for proof of a trance that is capable of producing phenomena that cannot be done without this so-called special state. Incidentally, I was told by two associates of a comment made by one of the most famous medical authorities on hypnosis, Dr. Milton H. Erickson, who said, "Don't touch Kreskin now. We don't need the controversy." Since that time in the 1980s, not one single medical or stage hypnotist has dared to challenge me.

Let me leave you with a few thoughts. Can you conceive that Sirhan Sirhan had amnesia all these many years and that he was programmed by a hypnotist to enact what took place on that horrendous night in history, and somehow the amnesia was broken through by a re-induction of hypnosis?

Remember what I'm about to say; if a person under a so-called deep hypnotic trance is given a posthypnotic suggestion that they will forget something or some action that they enacted, think about this— they need to remember what to forget!

"It's a wise hypnotist who knows who is hypnotizing whom."

~~The End~~
To Be Continued...

About the Author of the Foreword

Roger Ailes
Chairman and CEO, Fox News
Chairman, Fox Television Stations

Roger Ailes serves as the Chairman and CEO of Fox News as well as the Chairman of Fox Television Stations. In this position, Ailes oversees all national operations for Fox News and serves as a senior advisor to Rupert Murdoch, Chairman and CEO of the News Corporation Limited. He also has oversight of Fox's 27 broadcast television stations and Twentieth Television's syndication group. Recognized by *U.S. News and World Report* as one of America's Best Leaders in 2005, Ailes was also awarded The Media Institute's Freedom of Speech Award, as well as the Radio and Television News Directors Association First Amendment Leadership Award.

Since joining Fox News in February 1996, Ailes created Fox's first weekly public affairs show, *Fox News Sunday*, which has one of the youngest median ages amongst the Sunday talk shows and is now available nationwide. Ailes also oversaw the successful creation and launch of *Fox News Channel* (FNC), Fox's 24-hour cable news channel, the fastest growing news network in the country, which currently reaches more than 90 million homes. In January 2002, FNC passed CNN in ratings in all day parts and became the number one news channel in America. On October 15, 2007, Ailes launched the Fox Business Network, a new 24-hour financial news channel.

Prior to Fox, Ailes was President of CNBC, NBC's business news and talk network, beginning in September 1993. Under his leadership, CNBC established itself as the leading source for business news and became the fastest growing major cable network in America. During his tenure at the network, ratings more than tripled and profits increased from $9 million to over $100 million. Ailes also oversaw CNBC's 1995 worldwide expansion to Europe and Asia.

In addition, Ailes was President of America's Talking (A-T), an information talk channel, which later became MSNBC. Between A-T and CNBC, he was responsible for more live programming than any other television executive in America—31½ hours daily. He also created the CNBC "Talk-All-Stars" concept, attracting such notable stars as Tim Russert, Geraldo Rivera, Chris Matthews, Dee Dee Myers, and Gerry Spence, which dramatically increased CNBC's primetime ratings.

Ailes' television roots are deep and well established. In 1965, at age 25, Ailes rose from prop boy to executive producer of *The Mike Douglas Show*. Under his supervision, the show was nominated for two Emmy awards and won its first Emmy in 1967, becoming the most-watched syndicated talk show in America.

Over the years, Ailes also produced several television specials, including: the Emmy Award-winning and nationally syndicated *Television and the Presidency*, featuring historian Theodore H. White; *Television: Our Life and Times*, a nationally syndicated 2-hour retrospective of television entertainment programs; a nationally syndicated documentary on the legendary Italian film director Federico Fellini; and an hour-long wildlife special, *The Last Frontier*, with Robert F. Kennedy, Jr.

In 1981, Ailes served as Executive Producer of the NBC program *Tomorrow: Coast to Coast*. Additionally, in 1991, after the Gulf War, Ailes was Co-Executive Producer of *An All-Star Salute to Our Troops*, a 2-hour entertainment special, which aired on the CBS Television Network.

For more than two decades, Ailes has worked as a top consultant and/or executive producer for several major television projects, including work for Twentieth Century Fox and Paramount Television. From 1970–1992, he owned Ailes Communications, Inc., a diversified communications consulting company whose clients included three U.S. Presidents, several senators and governors, as well as *Fortune* 500 CEOs. In 1992, Ailes retired completely from political and corporate consulting to return full-time to television. In 1987, Ailes authored a critically acclaimed communications book, *You Are the Message* (Doubleday), recognized as "one of the year's best" by *Wall Street Journal.*

Ailes recently completed a 3-year term as a board member of the National Hemophilia Foundation, a member of the Director's Guild of America, and a Trustee of the National Trust for Historic Gettysburg. He is a native of Warren, Ohio, and a graduate of Ohio University, which awarded him an Honorary Doctorate in Communications in 1990. In 1999, Ailes was awarded the Silver Circle Award by the National Academy of Television Arts and Sciences. In 2001, 2002, 2006, and 2007, respectively, *Television Week* (formerly *Electronic Media*) named Ailes the Most Powerful Person in TV News. He was also named *Broadcasting & Cable*'s first-ever Television Journalist of the Year in 2003 and *Advertising Age*'s TV Marketer of the Year in 2002. In December 2007, Ailes was awarded an Honorary Doctorate of Laws from Pepperdine University. In October 2008, he was inducted into the *Broadcasting & Cable* Hall of Fame, and received the Navy SEAL Patriot Award.

About the Artist of the Book Cover and "How Kreskin Became Amazing!"

Joe St.Pierre

JOE ST.PIERRE HAS BEEN DRAWING COMICS SINCE HE CAN REMEMBER. SOME of his first tools were a stack of loose-leaf paper and a colored pencil that was red on one end and blue on the other.

Upon graduating from the School of Visual Arts in New York City, Joe began his professional career as an illustrator, writer, and designer for the comic book industry. Joe has illustrated some of the most recognizable superhero properties in history, including *The Amazing Spider-Man*, *The Fantastic Four*, *Wolverine*, *The X-Men*, *Batman*, *Superman*, *The Green Lantern*, and *The Transformers*.

Joe has since expanded his creative range to include commercial illustration and intellectual property design with a graphic-novel approach. Pop Art Properties provides intellectual property development in all phases of production, from inception to publication. Clients have included MTV, the Discovery Channel, Nickelodeon, Warner Bros, the Cartoon Network, *The New York Times*, and Toshiba.

His publishing company, Astronaut Ink, was formed to highlight his own creator-owned properties Megahurtz®, Bold Blood, and the New Zodiax.

It seems naturally fitting, and long overdue, that The Amazing
Kreskin would become a larger than life, graphic-novel character, and
Joe is happy to make that happen!

Websites
www.shannonassociates.com
www.popartproperties.com
www.astronautink.com

Other Major Books by The Amazing Kreskin

The Amazing World of Kreskin
Kreskin's Mind Power Book
Kreskin's Fun Way to Mind Expansion
How to Be a Fake Kreskin
The Amazing Kreskin's Future with the Stars
Secrets of The Amazing Kreskin
The Power Within
Commanding the Inner You
Mental Power Is Real
Kreskin Confidential

For more information, please visit: www.AmazingKreskin.com.

Other Books by Michael McCarty

NONFICTION

Masters of Imagination
Modern Mythmakers
Esoteria-Land
Giants of the Genre
More Giants of the Genre

FICTION

Liquid Diet: A Vampire Satire
Monster Behind the Wheel (with Mark McLaughlin)
Dark Duets
Attack of the Two-Headed Poetry Monster (with Mark McLaughlin)
Out of Time (with Connie Wilson)
Fallen Angel (with Amy Grech)
A Little Help from My Fiends
A Hell of a Job
Partners in Slime (with Mark McLaughlin)
Lost Girl of the Lake (with Joe McKinney)
Rusty the Robot's Holiday Adventures (with Sherry Decker)
All Things Dark and Hideous (with Mark McLaughlin)
Professor LaGungo's Classroom of Horrors (with Mark McLaughlin)
Laughing in the Dark
Little Creatures

Index